From
CENTRAL
PARK
to SINAI

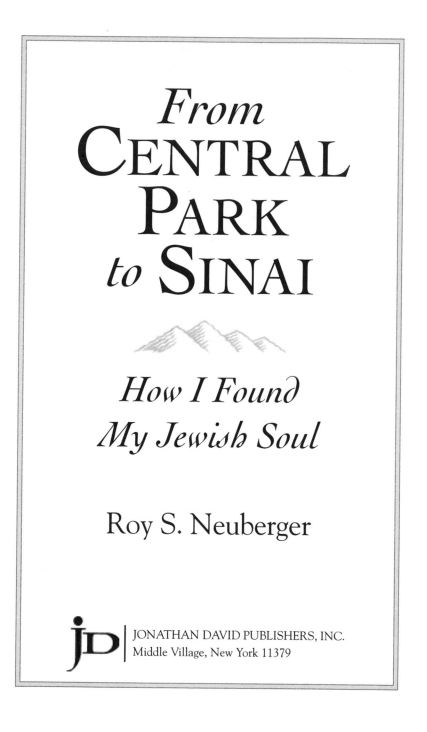

From CENTRAL PARK *to* SINAI

How I Found My Jewish Soul

Roy S. Neuberger

JD | JONATHAN DAVID PUBLISHERS, INC.
Middle Village, New York 11379

FROM CENTRAL PARK TO SINAI
How I Found My Jewish Soul

Jonathan David Publishers, Inc.
68-22 Eliot Avenue
Middle Village, NY 11379

www.jdbooks.com

2 4 6 8 10 9 7 5 3 1

Library of Congress Cataloging-in-Publication Data

Neuberger, Roy S. (Roy Salant), 1942–
    From Central Park to Sinai ; how I found my Jewish soul / Roy S.
Neuberger
        p. cm.
    Includes bibliographical references.
    ISBN 0-8246-0431-8
        1. Neuberger, Roy S. (Roy Salant), 1942– 2. Jews—New York
        (State)—Biography. 3. Jews—Return to Orthodox Judaism.
        4. New York (State)—Biography. I. Title.
    F130. J5 N48 2000
    296. 7'15'092—dc21   00-031452
    [B]   CIP

Book Design by John Reinhardt Book Design

Printed in the United States of America

I dedicate this book to

"Hamalach Ha-Goayl osi mi-kol ra," *the angel who kept me from evil.* I am sure that very early in my life G-d sent an angel who would not let me rest until I had found His Torah.

My father and mother, Roy R. and Marie S. Neuberger, who never failed to help and support me in every way. Their lofty souls and profound integrity inspired me to pursue truth.

My wife, Leah, with whom I have been privileged to share these high adventures. Together we have traveled the road, with all its twists, bumps, and potholes. G-d brought us together before we understood that He exists. I am thankful that He enabled Maurice and Ruth Villency to raise such a daughter. May our family always sanctify His name.

Rebbetzin Esther Jungreis, a gift from Heaven to this lost generation. She saved our lives and countless others. May she see the day when the world returns to G-d and His Torah in unity and glory.

Acknowledgments

I have been blessed with a wonderful family and friends. How can I acknowledge all the help I have been given in writing and producing this book? I would have to start at the beginning of my life.

I want to thank the many great rabbis and countless friends who gave me their blessings. I do not take any blessing lightly.

From those very close to me I received constant help and encouragement in every phase of this book.

I was actually not going to mention my wife, Leah, here. I felt it would be doing her an injustice. It would be like thanking myself, because this journey is ours, not mine alone. It goes without saying that she read every word of the manuscript and made countless suggestions. But then I thought better of it; one has an obligation to express gratitude for everything in life. We shared the production of this work as we have shared our life together. It is hard for me to find words of sufficient gratitude to G-d for having given me the privilege of sharing my life with this magnificent *ayshes chayil*.*

---

* The phrase *ayshes chayil* is commonly translated "woman of valor," from the phrase in Chapter 31 of the Book of Proverbs.

I want to thank all our precious children for their heart-felt support and many vital suggestions as well as constructive criticism: Shlomo and Sarah Lancry, Osher and Yaffa Jungreis, Avi and Miriam Hess, Ari Neuberger, and Yaki and Nechami Slatus. Their goodness and holiness and constant brightness of spirit serve as a constant source of inspiration to Leah and me.

My brother, Jimmy, read the manuscript very carefully and made numerous subtle and pertinent observations on a wide range of topics. The book has been greatly enhanced by his suggestions.

Many members of the Jungreis family helped me. Slove Wolff read the entire manuscript many times and provided much valuable guidance. Rabbi Shlomo Gertzulin provided advice from his vast storehouse of practical counsel. Rabbi Yisroel and Rivki Jungreis and Rebbetzin Goldie Jungreis made many important suggestions. Rabbis Jacob Jungreis and Yonason Binyomin Jungreis provided fascinating and otherwise unknown details of Jungreis family history.

Rabbi Yechiel Perr, *rosh yeshiva* of the Yeshiva of Far Rockaway, provided extremely important assistance to me, for which I am very grateful.

I am proud to thank my dedicated literary agent and friend, Erwin Cherovsky, who has guided me through the waters of the publishing industry with great dedication and skill. His love for this book and his appreciation of its purpose gave me strength and constant encouragement from our first meeting. Erwin's talented daughter Kim, a close friend, has been a source of unceasing encouragement, help, and blessing.

The process of choosing a publisher for this book was filled with twists and turns, and it is not until now, after having worked with Jonathan David Publishers for several months, that I appreciate my good fortune in finding them. My relationship with David Kolatch is a continuous pleasure; I feel as if I am working with my brother. I would like to express gratitude to Rabbi Alfred J. Kolatch and the entire Kolatch family, Marvin Sekler, Fiorella deLima, and the Jonathan David staff, all of whom could not have been more helpful. I also want to thank my editor, Deborah Fogel, and Mike Stromberg, who did such a magnificent job on the jacket.

In addition, I want to express my appreciation to the following people who assisted me with countless aspects of this book. Without their goodwill and dedicated help, I am sure I could not have achieved whatever success has been possible: Rabbi Yaakov Bender, Rabbi Aaron Brafman, Abish Brodt, Mr. & Mrs. Alfred Connable, Rabbi Meir Eichler, Dr. and Mrs. Leonard Feiner, Rabbi Binyomin Forst, Carole Fromer, Nathan Gold, Robert Gordon, Rabbi Moshe Grossman, Richie Grossman, Heshy Grunberger, Henry Hirsch, Mr. and Mrs. Aharon Hirshman, Rabbi Yaakov Horowitz, Barbara Janov, Dr. Yosi Jeret, Rabbi Yehoshua Kalish, Rabbi Yechezkel Kaminsky, Ken Kiron, Rabbi and Mrs. Tzvi Krakauer, Milly Marmur, Rabbi Mordechai Merenstein, Steven Mero, Rabbi and Mrs. Zalman Mindell, Henry Neuberger, Dr. and Mrs. Stanley Newhouse, Shaya Ostrov, Paul Packer, Phil Pilevsky, Stephen Pollan, Esq., Shmuel Prager, Esq., Mr. & Mrs. Joe Russak, Sasha Salama, Dovid Schulman, Dr. David Smolanoff, Mr. and Mrs. Michael Snaid, Michael Sukin, Mr. and Mrs. Meir Weissman, Ann Crane Zakay.

I want to express appreciation to Mesorah Publications, Ltd., publishers of the ArtScroll Series, for allowing me to use their translations of texts. I have also followed the general style of transliteration into English used in ArtScroll publications.

I would also like to acknowledge the help I received from the book *Frumspeak, The First Dictionary of Yeshivish*. This small volume was of great assistance, especially for a newcomer like me, in understanding the language used in the *yeshiva* world. I happen to have a special attachment to this book because my own beloved son-in-law, Rabbi Yaakov Slatus, assisted the author in writing it.

▲▲▲

I am sure I have forgotten to thank some people, and I ask their forgiveness. The omission is not through lack of gratitude, but only because of an oversight.

Please do not attribute the shortcomings in this book to those who blessed me and helped me. They may have suggested corrections or improvements that I did not follow or understand. The shortcomings are mine.

ROY S. NEUBERGER

Contents

Foreword

by Rebbetzin Esther Jungreis

IN THE EARLY YEARS of our Hineni organization, I was lecturing at a hotel in the Catskills when I was approached by one of the guests. "Rebbetzin, you must go to Newburgh, New York. There is a congregation there that is in turmoil, and I really believe that your speaking there could make a significant difference."

As a young girl, my father taught me never to ignore such messages. "You never know whom you could reach, whom you could touch."

And so it was that one Sunday I came to that small upstate community over the protestation of my friend Barbara, executive director of Hineni. "It's a long drive. It's a waste of your time. You won't have more than a dozen people. You can't run every time someone tells you to go somewhere!"

Surprisingly, the synagogue was packed. There wasn't a seat to be had. I spoke from my heart about the meaning of our Judaism, our history, our faith, and our covenant. The response was electric and inspiring. Little did I realize, however, that the impact of that evening would reach far beyond the synagogue, that it would affect my life as well, for it was there that I met Roy and Linda Neuberger, who soon became major forces in our Hineni organization.

A few days after my program, I received a sensitive and moving letter from Roy. The message of our faith had entered his soul and he wanted to know more—but how? He had no clue where he should start. Roy wrote that he was prepared to travel and do whatever was necessary so that he might participate in our Hineni Torah classes.

In those days I was teaching in Brooklyn, and despite the sincerity of his letter, I doubted very much that he would make a weekly trek from Newburgh to Flatbush, where my classes were held. It was simply not realistic. To complicate matters further, it was the height of the energy crisis, and people had to wait in line for hours to buy gasoline. The likelihood of Roy and Linda making such a trip on a regular basis seemed to be very slim, so while I gave him all the information, I never really expected him to show up. But incredibly, he and Linda came. Week after week they were there, and on each occasion I became more and more impressed with their devotion and commitment.

Roy was one of those people who was determined to give back to the world. He could have had an easy life. His father is the founder of the prestigious Wall Street firm Neuberger Berman, but he was constantly searching for ways to reach out and help. A graduate of the finest universities, he had done volunteer work for multiple causes, but in his letter he wrote that none of these endeavors had ever fully satisfied him. His soul yearned for something more, but he couldn't quite identify it. Once he discovered Torah, however, he knew that he had come home, that his long journey had finally reached its destination. He embraced the teaching wholeheartedly, and the observance of *mitzvos* became his way of life. Seldom have I seen someone give himself so totally and with such love and devotion as Roy did. Week after week he came to study, and every lesson was absorbed and applied.

When I announced that during the spring of that year I would be leading a Hineni group to Israel, Roy and Linda made immediate plans to join us. That trip culminated in a total metamorphosis. Roy and Linda made a momentous decision: to relocate to a community where they could fulfill their family's spiritual needs. This meant not only a change of location, but a change of career for Roy as well. No matter—once he discovered Torah, Roy would not allow anything to deter him. With enthusiasm and zeal, he and Linda went house-hunting in my neighborhood and established their home just a few blocks away from me. Instantaneously, they became pillars of our Jewish community. Their home became a true replica of the tent of our father Abraham, open day and night to guests in need of lodging, support, warmth, and love.

Having Roy and Linda living so close was a great source of blessing to me. In my outreach work I come across many young people who need guidance and loving care. Roy and Linda have always been there to help fulfill that need. Over the years, I have brought back countless people from cults and dysfunctional families. Roy and Linda opened their hearts and homes to them. These young people lived with them for months and even years, until such time as they married and established homes of their own.

Soon, Roy and Linda became Hineni Shabbos chairpersons, and everyone knew that they could always count on having a beautiful Shabbos and yom tov in their home. My father of blessed memory, Rav Avraham ha-Levi Jungreis, zt"l, gave Roy the Hebrew name Yisroel and Linda the name Leah. My father looked upon them as dear, loving children. The name Yisroel was most appropriate for Roy, for we discovered that, on his mother's side, he was a descendant of Rav Yisroel Salanter, the founder of the *mussar* movement. Roy's impeccable ethics and moral excellence were not only inherited from his highly respected father but also from his renowned ancestor.

Many years have passed since that evening in Newburgh, New York, and I can only marvel at the Divine Providence that guides our lives. Today, I am proud to say that Yisroel and Leah's beautiful daughter Yaffa is my precious daughter-in-law, continuing our family's tradition together with my son, Rabbi Osher Jungreis. Their home is always open. Their Shabbos table is always surrounded by guests, and every day they bring more people back to Torah and *mitzvos*.

Since Yisroel became part of our Hineni family, he has affected countless lives. I have no doubt that this book will do the same and will bring people to greater commitment and love of our faith.

BEFORE THE BEGINNING

Over a quarter century ago, when Leah and I decided to change our life, we entered a new world. We had grown up for thirty years as "Americans," not Jews. I didn't know what *challah* was. I didn't even know what Yom Kippur was.

I was thirty-one years old the first time I ever saw *tallis* and *tefillin*. We were flying to Israel with Rebbetzin Esther Jungreis and a small group from her Hineni organization. On the eleven-hour flight from New York, if you leave late at night, the men get up for morning prayers at about 4:00 A.M. New York time. I had been asleep. I awoke suddenly and saw men with little boxes on their heads. Had we landed on Mars?

Maybe I was dreaming.

Maybe I was waking up in another world.

Actually, I *was* waking up in another world!

When we decided to become religious, in the summer of 1974, we had to jump into a life that was so new we had no conception of what to do.

How did we know it was right?

For one thing, I was sure I had tried everything else in the world, both secular and religious. Nothing else had worked. Nothing.

In addition, our souls had that feeling of "chemistry" you get when you know you have finally found what you have been searching for. Rebbetzin Jungreis was speaking about the very questions that had been rattling around in my brain since I had first started thinking. No one else had even understood what I was talking about, let alone answered the questions. Here she was, speaking about these things before I had even asked her.

I had always felt there could be greatness in a human being, a nobility of character that could bring healing into the world. I aspired to it, but I felt unable to achieve it.

Here was this *rebbetzin* (What *is* a *rebbetzin*, anyway?) coming to tell us that we are descended from patriarchs, kings, and prophets—great people who spoke to G-d. We could receive their legacy and continue their work.

Starting a new life. Was this just wishful thinking? We knew it wasn't. After decades of rejecting various answers, we weren't afraid to start something completely new or reject it if it didn't work. But for the first time we started to feel that our inner emptiness was being replaced by the presence of G-d.

Inviting G-d into our life changed the entire nature of our existence. It's not that life suddenly became a paradise. The troubles didn't end, but for the first time *we were not controlled by them*. We were not slaves. We had help. We were *not alone*.

When we asked G-d to help us, the Help was there.

▲▲▲

You will read in the pages ahead how we were brought into the world of Torah by Rebbetzin Esther Jungreis. When we wanted to jump into that world, we moved to her community. The Rebbetzin's father and husband, *may their memories be for a blessing*, were our mentors. We became even closer when our daughter Yaffa married Rabbi and Rebbetzin Jungreis's son, Rabbi Osher Anshul Jungreis.

Countless thoughts, ideas, concepts, and stories in this book come from Rebbetzin Jungreis. The book is filled with phrases we have learned from her. Leah and I have heard her speak publicly and privately for literally thousands of hours over more than a quarter-century, and we have always come away uplifted with concrete Torah wisdom to elevate our lives. My head is filled with her beautiful Torah thoughts, which are reflected in every sentence in this book.

The Rebbetzin brings Torah to us in a way that makes it real in our lives. It's not arcane or academic; it applies to the constant process of confronting life that all of us go through every second of our lives. We have learned through the Rebbetzin that the Torah is *"lo bashamayim hi . . .* not in Heaven,"* but close to us, a guide that G-d has given us to navigate the waters of this world successfully.

The Rebbetzin never tires of telling us that the Torah is a *shulchan aruch*, a set table. There is food for every diet and it is all kosher.

You don't have to approach Torah my way. In fact, if you want to be successful, you must approach Torah YOUR way, using the particular gifts and abilities G-d gave you.

---

* Deuteronomy 30:12

As it says in the Book of Proverbs, "*Chanoch la-naar al pi darko* . . . Train the child according to his way."*

Or, in another classic Rebbetzin phrase, "G-d made the world in technicolor." The world is an orchestra: some people play the first violin, some the second violin. Some play the flute; some play the drums. And there is one Conductor. All have an important part to play, although each role is different. If we each play our part correctly, the harmony is beautiful.

My experiences may be helpful to you in finding your way. That is why I am writing this book. I want you to feel the book is for *you* and not just for me. I want you to feel it is expressing ideas that you recognize. Down deep, all of us really want to come closer to G-d.

▲▲▲

A word about words.

As I got more and more into the Jewish way of life, I became more comfortable with Yiddish terms like *shul* for "synagogue," or Hebrew usage, like "Yitzchok" for "Isaac." I like using Hebrew or Yiddish or "yeshivish" terms because I think they impart some of the flavor of Jewish life. When you find them in the book, they will generally be italicized. I try to explain them either in parentheses right after I use them and/or in the Glossary at the back of the book. Many can be understood just from the context. I don't want anyone to be intimidated by them. But I also don't want to overuse them so that you find it hard to read. I have tried to employ a happy medium: just enough to give the flavor that only such words can give, but not

---

* Proverbs 22:6

enough to mar the smooth flow of the narrative. I hope I
have succeeded.

Throughout this book I use the Jewish convention of
hyphenating the word "G-d" or using the word "Hashem,"
which means "the Name," as a substitute for the actual
name of G-d.

The idea behind this is that words are holy. The very
name of G-d must be treated with great respect. It would
not be appropriate, for example, if a book or a page containing the name of G-d would be thrown away, dropped
on the floor, or brought into an unclean place like a lava-
tory. To prevent such a situation from arising, we do not
use the actual name of G-d, but rather we imply it by ab-
breviating it or substituting for it.

In a Torah scroll, prayer book, or other *sefer* (holy book)
various names for G-d are spelled out, and such a book is
treated with great respect. Even when it is too worn out to
be used anymore, a *sefer* is buried in accordance with Jewish law.

When Rebbetzin Jungreis's *zayda* (grandfather), Rabbi
Tzvi Hirsch ha-Cohen, was in his last few moments in this
world, he asked to be helped out of bed so that he could
bid a personal farewell to each of his *seforim*. He kissed
each book "goodbye." They were his close friends and the
bearers of G-d's holiness.

▲▲▲

Throughout the book I use the Ashkenazic rather than
Sefardic pronunciation when transliterating Hebrew words.
The difference would be apparent in the Hebrew word for
"covenant," for example. The Ashkenazic pronunciation
would be *bris*; the Sefardic would be *brit*. The Sefardic pro-

nunciation is more common in Israel. The Ashkenazic is associated with eastern Europe. My background is eastern European, and the Jungreis family, who "raised us" as Jews, are Hungarian, so I use the Ashkenazic pronunciation. I have tried to be as clear and consistent as possible in the transliteration of Hebrew and Yiddish words.

▲▲▲

Every story in this book is based on firsthand experience. I saw and heard everything, unless specifically noted. In recounting incidents where I was not actually present, I have taken the liberty of presenting conversations as I imagine they would have occurred.

Many of the names in the text have been changed for various reasons, but primarily to protect the privacy of the individuals involved.

CHAPTER ONE

IN THE
BEGINNING

I n november 1942 the holy Jews of Europe were being martyred. Hitler, *may his memory be erased,** was striding east and west, trying to crush the light of G-d. A little girl in Szeged, Hungary, was still relatively safe, but in a short time she would be forced from her home and deported to Bergen-Belsen.

In Lenox Hill Hospital a baby was born to prosperous parents ensconced in the assimilated German-Jewish world of Upper Manhattan. He was circumcised by the doctors like almost every baby boy, but never given a *bris*. He was named Roy Salant Neuberger.

A normal observer would say that these two lives could

---

* This expression does not mean that we should forget the Holocaust and those who caused it. We are enjoined, in fact, to remember. But in the end of time, when all evil is gone from the world, that tyrant's name will indeed be erased and he will not even be a memory. This expression refers to that time and is, in effect, a prayer that it will come about soon. A similar idea is implied by the custom of making noise when Haman's name is mentioned on Purim.

never cross. A normal observer would say the little girl would never survive. But what does a "normal observer" know? *"Many designs are in a man's heart, but the counsel of G-d, only it will prevail."**

▲▲▲

In our world, the world of Szeged was unknown. Of course, everyone knew there was a war. The Japanese had attacked Pearl Harbor and our boys were in Europe. The double-decker buses on Fifth Avenue were painted red, white, and blue and bore war slogans. But people did not feel as if *their family* was being attacked. Life went on.

Actually, if you note carefully the name I was given, you will see that there was a little more connection to the world of eastern European Jewish life than met the eye. At the time we ourselves did not notice it, but it was there, beneath the surface. That middle name, Salant. Where did that come from?

Ah, that's a good question.

Salant is a town in Lithuania. It's still there, but today it's called Salantai. Somehow, this little town produced geniuses of Torah learning and moral greatness. If you go to Jerusalem today you will find a Salant Street. My mother's father, Aaron B. Salant, was born in Salant, and, although he strove mightily from the time he reached these shores to live as an American, he could not completely escape his roots.

My grandfather once told me, "We are descendants of the great Rabbi Yisroel Salanter."

---

* Proverbs 19:21

He gave me an English biography of Yisroel Salanter that I have to this day.

Yisroel Salanter was a moral lighthouse, a beacon still shining, whose influence is a mighty force in the world. My name bore his legacy. My mother bequeathed to me a moral approach to life, a concern for *doing the right thing*, that was to lead me eventually to the path of Torah. She never took that path, but she led me to it.

(Yisroel Salanter's family name was Lipkin, not Salant, but if my grandfather told me we are his descendants, I do not doubt it. I was not interested when he told me, so I didn't ask him to explain the exact lineage. By the time I *was* interested, it was too late; my grandfather was gone. Usually, if you miss an opportunity in life, it does not return. I am as of this moment still unable to trace this branch of the family tree.)

My grandfather was not a religious man. As immigrants in about 1880, his family must have thrown its Jewishness overboard as they sailed to America. Perhaps his father literally threw his *tefillin* into the ocean. I hate to think so, but it could have happened. By the time I knew my grandfather, some sixty years later, there was no trace of Europe upon him except an Old World aura of culture and sophistication. He had become a successful New York businessman and a scholar of Latin and Greek as well as a student and teacher of economics. Both of his sons became distinguished economists. The fact that my mother majored in economics, unusual for a woman in those days, led directly to her job at the Wall Street firm of Halle and Steiglitz, where she and my father met in 1930.

▲▲▲

I went to the Ethical Culture Midtown School in Manhattan until sixth grade. When we were young, Dad, Jimmy, and I were all driven to work or school in my grandfather's black, very tasteful limousine. (My sister, being older, was already in high school.) In those days stretch limousines were unknown, and Grandpa wouldn't have owned one if they had existed. (To the end of her life mother would not set foot in one. In fact, she insisted on using her senior citizen's card and taking the bus until well into her eighties. We all were very much against pretense and flaunting privilege. This was part of our family's outlook; we didn't want wealth to spoil us.) Grandpa's chauffeur, Vincent, wore a very proper black, shiny-brimmed hat. Jimmy and I sat in the folding seats facing backwards toward Grandpa and Dad.

Grandma Salant had an incredible sweet tooth, which I inherited. She used to love her "schneckens," sweet rolls coated with honey and nuts. She regularly had lunch with her friends at Schrafft's restaurants. When I was a kid, there was a Schrafft's every few blocks in the nice neighborhoods. They all had little square, polished wooden tables with doilies under the plates. Schrafft's was famous for cakes and ice cream. Maybe that's why Grandma liked them so much. I remember her as a warm, dignified, really Victorian lady who took care of my grandfather in every possible way. He had time to read, study, think, teach, and play marbles and tiddly winks with his grandchildren. (Does anyone today know what "tiddly winks" is? It's too innocent for this generation.) I am sure he never boiled water or made a bed in his life.

I was a senior in high school when my grandmother died. My grandfather was still alive.

I remember that my grandfather said, "It wasn't supposed to happen this way."

I would not be surprised if they had actually discussed it, and my grandmother had *assured* him that he would pass away first. Well, it didn't work out that way. He lived on for several years, but his world had been shattered. Future events—including the death of his youngest child in a car accident—shattered it even more.

I think my grandfather died somewhat broken. Life had not gone as his logical mind had planned it. But he did not regard these tragedies as signals to reassess his view of the world. He did not return to the Torah of his ancestors.

▲▲▲

My father also has an interesting genealogy.

My father's English name is identical to mine except for the middle initial, and those middle initials tell something about us. Mine is S for "Salant," and that reveals my connection with the world of Rabbi Yisroel Salanter. My father's middle initial is R for "Rothschild," but he always maintained that he had nothing to do with the illustrious Jewish family of bankers.

I suspected otherwise, not least because of his genius for business. My suspicions were confirmed when an obituary for Baron Philippe de Rothschild appeared in *The New York Times* on January 27, 1988. The Baron's picture appeared in the wine column that day, and the resemblance goes beyond similarity. The two faces, the baron's and my father's, are identical. My father's mother, whose name was Belle Rothschild, must have been from the same stock as Baron Philippe.

Back to 1942.

During the war, my father, who was too old to be drafted, spent several nights a week after work near Delancey Street, on the Lower East Side, where he was a captain in the City Patrol Corps. To this day we have his leather holster and his white officer's helmet with the letters "CPC" against an orange shield. The job of his unit was to guard the Williamsburg Bridge against German saboteurs. The Germans had other things to do, thank G-d. At midnight, when their tour ended, these men would congregate at Ratner's, which was then open all night, for some good hot coffee and probably cheesecake or blintzes. Isn't it ironic that almost sixty years later I sometimes go with my father, who is now in his late nineties, to that same Ratner's for a good kosher meal. You can still get the world's best cheesecake and blintzes there.*

But in 1942 I didn't know about Ratner's or German saboteurs.

You may believe that babies don't have thoughts. Perhaps that's true, but pretty soon we start to know things. We have lots of information in our souls and built-in memories that go a long way back. Pretty soon we start to open our eyes and look at our new world.

My earliest memory is of being alone in my crib. It was night. We were living at 22 East 88th Street in Manhattan. My parents were having a dinner party and I could hear the chatter somewhere off in the distance. My room door was open a crack. It had to be; I couldn't stand the

---

* I regret to say that this citadel of kosher New York history has now closed forever. The onion rolls, black bread, thick soups poured from a little pot into your bowl, the blintzes, the latkes, the creamed spinach, the cheesecake, the great coffee . . . and those patented Ratner's waiters . . . who could reinvent it all? Such is life.

dark. I was afraid. And then, a gust of wind banged the door shut. DARKNESS! I let out a cry.

That was my childhood. Wonderful parents. The best of everything. But fear of darkness. I kept wondering, even as a small child: how could I have "everything" and feel so alone, so frightened, so lost?

I was afraid of the dark. What actually was I afraid of? What was so frightening about the dark?

People don't like to be alone with their thoughts. We can't live without a radio or television. Why? Does it make beautiful sounds? No, but *it keeps us from thinking*.

What are we so afraid of?

There were three of us children in this little world. I shared it with my older sister, Ann, and my younger brother, Jimmy. We got along well, except for justifiable fights like when Jimmy crashed my electric trains. I mean, it is obvious that I had to bang his head against the kitchen wall when he did that. What did he expect?

The fact is that we fought very little, and to this day all the children get along, even though our present lifestyles differ greatly. It is a tribute to our parents. It was somehow understood in our family that one just doesn't fight with one's siblings. All of us got the feeling that we were supposed to act like a family.

By the way, unless you got the wrong impression, don't think I was such a saint. I remember being kind of a trouble-maker as a kid. My ancient memory includes such things as being invited to a birthday party and standing up underneath a folding table. Naturally, everything on the table landed on the floor. I imagine that did not endear me to certain people at the time.

There was also a famous incident that took place during

a family visit to friends at Williams College in Williams-town, Massachusetts. Our host was a famous professor of economics, and I must have committed a great sin. I don't remember what it was, but I do remember the result: our hostess locked me up in a room for several hours while everybody went out and had a good time. That was un-pleasant.

When I was in third grade, Mrs. Eakright, who was oth-erwise rather fond of me, must have been provoked at my behavior one day. I had to stay in school when everyone else went to Central Park for recess, and I was supposed to write on the blackboard "I will be a good boy" one hun-dred times. What I wrote was, "I will be a good boy one hundred times." I wrote it once. Mrs. Eakright and I used to laugh about that for years after I graduated. At least she laughed then!

You can imagine, I must have been a handful. If you ask my wife, she will tell you I still am.

▲▲▲

My favorite day of the year was December 25.

Without realizing it, I was looking for G-d. I didn't know where to find Him, and this life we were living was all I knew about. We celebrated these holidays in all their de-tails because we were in America and our Jewishness meant nothing to us. Do you see what happens when there is a vacuum? It must be filled, and if you don't fill it with To-rah, it will fill itself with something else. We filled it with something that seemed "normal."

What do I mean by filling life with Torah? Well, that takes us far into the future of this story, but the point is this, and I suppose we might as well talk about it right here. The concept of religion presupposes that there is something real, an entity—G-d—Who has an independent existence outside of us. He is real, He exists, He created the world and everything in it and He runs it, now and forever. He has a set of rules for all his creatures to follow. All his creatures—*except one species*—have no choice but to follow His rules.

Guess which species that is.

Excellent! You guessed it. It's "ours truly"!

We humans are given rules, but we are also given free will to decide whether or not to follow them. The rules are called Torah. There are rules that apply to all men and women. There are rules that apply only to all Jews. There are rules that apply only to certain Jews (such as *Kohanim*, Priests). There are rules that apply only in the Land of Israel. There are many qualifications, but the point is that the Creator and Sustainer of the Universe has promulgated rules.

If a Jew deviates by one millimeter from the rules, in the course of time his deviation will become infinite. Once you are headed in a different direction, you just keep going. You tell yourself that it's normal, and you try not to think about whether it's true.

I hadn't learned about those rules when I was a kid, but when you're born you know something deep inside of you. Later on, I'll discuss the angel who teaches you the whole Torah before you're born, but in the meantime, suffice it to say that you feel there is an absolute, trustworthy truth and you try to find it. Sometimes you get so lost that you never find it. But sometimes, no matter how hard you try to get lost, you just can't run away from it.

I felt that Torah deep within me, but I had no idea what

it was. I tried to run away from it, because everything I was brought up with taught me it was evil, archaic, phony slavery. It took thirty years before I found out it was exactly the opposite of all those things. But in the meantime, I tried like crazy to make our non-Jewish lifestyle work.

Believe me, I tried to make it work. I tried for thirty years until there was no strength left in me to try any more. I *wanted* it to work. I didn't *want* to be a Jew. I wanted to be anything *but* a Jew. But I couldn't. As a kid, in the home of my parents, I accepted our way of life and did not connect it with my fear, my malaise. But as an adult who needed Truth in order to survive, it could not measure up.

▲▲▲

We always had cooks and maids in our home. They were usually Irish, with names like Bridie O'Malley and Peggy Dunne. I remember, in the 1950s, these girls listening to "Make Believe Ballroom" on the radio. I can still hear the theme song in my mind.

Isn't it amazing how these things never leave you? It just shows how important it is to be under the right influences, because impressions stick in our brain. We see this in people who are senile. They retain memories better from seventy years ago than from five minutes ago. If we hear, touch, smell, or look at something, the impression never leaves us.

I heard an amazing story recently* about a woman who was intentionally kept partially awake during brain surgery. The surgeon apparently touched a part of her brain that stimulated memories, and she began to sing Italian

---

* This story was told to me by Rabbi Moshe Grossman.

opera during the surgery, with a perfect accent and recall of the music. Later, during her recuperation, the surgeon asked her about her career as an opera singer. She told him she not only knew no opera, but she knew not one word of Italian. Upon reflection she remembered that, *decades earlier*, her elementary school teacher had taken the class to an opera. She had retained a totally detailed memory of the entire production, words and music, without being aware of it.

We must be so careful what we absorb. Even an idle glance is with us forever.

"Make Believe Ballroom," with its popular songs and weekly ratings, represented a threat to me at the time, because I felt it indicated the beginning of a breakdown in popular culture, in which social life and private matters were coming too much into public view. I think I was right, but of course I thought at the time, *"You are crazy."* Little did I know what was yet to come: rock 'n' roll, Elvis Presley, and the Beatles were still unheard of. Even Elvis might faint at what passes for music today.

The classic Irish domestic employee was Anna Ferriter. Anna came to New York in the late 1920s to work for my grandparents in their Park Avenue apartment, inheriting the job of her older sister, who probably had just gotten married. Anna used to tell us that in those days before air conditioning, on a hot summer night, the cooks and maids would take a blanket and sleep on the grass in Central Park. Can you imagine? No one worried then about the things that happen today. Clearly, it was a more innocent era, although rumblings of the future were certainly audible. Hitler, *may his memory be erased*, was at that time just amassing power.

In Radin, a small *yeshiva* town in Poland, the holy Chofetz Chaim* told listeners what was going to happen, but the rest of the world did not want to know.

Anna was with our extended family for more than fifty years. No one could make a better strawberry shortcake or a more fiery political speech (usually at breakfast to an audience of one: my father). Her political views were as red as her cheeks. With all her Irish passion, she loved us and became a family fixture. Years later, my wife Linda (Anna called her "Lindy"), my brother Jimmy, and I visited her sister's well-known inn in Ballyferriter, on the wild west coast of Ireland. At that time the Bishop of Dublin was taking his annual vacation there. In the lobby bathroom we found towels with my mother's monogram. Can you imagine? How did they get there? Mother would always give her slightly used, elegant towels to Anna.

That was mother: nothing went to waste.

Dad was usually too busy to tell stories, but if we could get him into the mood, he would sit on the bed at night and tell us about the family that lived in the giant shoe on the roof of the Brown Shoe Factory. He invented a language called "spalakoochie" that had about five words in it. This was half a century ago. It's incredible how everything is tucked away in the brain.

I was a cute little boy, with hair so curly that the policeman at the entrance to the Great Circle in Central Park would say, "Good morning, curly head," every day as I passed by. There again, it seems a more innocent time.

---

* Considered by many the greatest rabbi and holiest *tzaddik* of recent history. Yisroel Meir ha-Kohayn Kagan lived in Poland and died in 1933 at the age of ninety-five. Much of his lifelong work was dedicated to eradicating the sin of *loshon hara* (slander and gossip).

Can you imagine a policeman saying that today? Can you imagine a policeman who stands in one place every day?

One day, I rode off around the circle on my tricycle and all of a sudden I was lost. I must have been crying, because somehow I wound up inside a police car, tricycle and all. We cruised slowly around the circle until I spotted my nurse. She must have been surprised to see me emerge from the police car.

I didn't like having nurses, but it was part of the territory. Mother was busy with civic affairs and I had to accept it, as I did when Mother and Dad went out for the evening. That I didn't like at all. I wanted them home all the time and felt abandoned when they went out. I protested, but it didn't help.

Why was I so lonely? What was missing?

▲▲▲

I was sent to the Ethical Culture Schools along with Ann and Jimmy. Mother and her two brothers had also attended Ethical, and Mother later became chairman of the board of governors. My father became president of the Ethical Culture Society, the "religious" organization that officially sponsored the schools. We were the quintessential Ethical family.

What is the Ethical Culture Society? For me, it was best described by Professor Henry Marsden* of the University of Michigan. When I first attended college in Ann Arbor, Professor Marsden was my Honors adviser. He was a professor in the History Department, a devout Midwestern Catholic. It is unbelievable how this man, whose back-

---

* Not his real name.

ground could hardly have been more different from mine, hit the bull's-eye when it came to pegging my roots.

We were reviewing my transcript in September 1961.

"Oh," Professor Marsden remarked, "the Ethical Culture Society. *That's for the Jews who are too embarrassed for Reform.*"

Do you understand this? The non-Jewish world knows exactly how true to Torah we Jews are at any given moment.* Professor Marsden knew exactly how Jewish I was.

The Ethical Culture Society, founded by a German Jew named Felix Adler, was part of the rebellion against Torah life that swept across nineteenth-century Jewish Europe and resulted in the assimilation that led to the holocausts of the First and Second World Wars.

If you think I attribute the destruction of the European Jewish community to the plague of assimilation, you are correct.

*"Beware lest your heart be seduced and you turn astray . . . Then the wrath of G-d will blaze against you."***

It is said that Felix Adler once heard my ancestor, Yisroel Salanter, speak in Europe.*** Too bad he didn't listen harder. Later, he came to America and created an organization whose basic purpose was to extract the ethics from the Torah and teach it to all men and women.

---

* When Jacob returns from the house of Laban, his father-in-law, he tells Esau, "I remained true to G-d's commandments while I lived in the house of Laban." Does Esau (who represents the nations of the world) care if we Jews are true to the Torah? The answer is "yes!" If we are loyal to the Torah, the nations know they are powerless to harm us. If not, G-d forbid. . . .

** Deuteronomy 11:16-17, part of the prayer *Shema Yisroel*

*** From *Israel Salanter, Religious-Ethical Thinker*, Bloch Publishing Company, N.Y., 1953, page 189, note 20.

▲▲▲

Who needs G-d, anyway? G-d is so inconvenient. Those European Jews, saddled with outlandish, medieval commandments, are living in the past. They even dress like people from another era. They keep aloof from their gentile neighbors and won't even drink their wine, let alone marry their children. I am embarrassed to be associated with such people. I want to join the modern nations of the world. Of course, I want to live by moral and ethical principles, but so do all good men. "The place where men meet to seek the highest is holy ground." That will be our motto. There is no difference between the Jew and the rest of the world. We will spring out of this medieval ghetto.

I was raised on this philosophy and taught that "all religions are great," which of course means "no religion is great." You must extract the good from each. All men are the same, and for that matter all countries are the same. Israel is the same as Afghanistan, and Jerusalem is the same as Oshkosh. You can use your logic to live the right way. G-d is irrelevant. After all, this is the twentieth century.

"Beware lest your heart be seduced and you turn astray. . . Then the wrath of G-d will blaze against you."

The wrath of G-d. Why did I never have a moment's peace? Why was I afraid every minute? Why did I feel so lost? According to "logic," everything should have been great.

I told Mother—I must have been about eight—that I thought something was wrong with me. I had a feeling I should study religion. I wanted to go to Sunday School.

They sent me to—where else?—the Ethical Culture Society Sunday School. I learned about Greek and Roman mythology, Catholicism, Protestantism, Buddhism,

Hinduism, and every other "ism" they could think of. They even threw in a little Jewish stuff. You know . . . equal time. I was taught "humanist" philosophy by Jewish teachers. "Ethics" sounded so comforting, so logical.

I once read a story about a man who was unwittingly fed small doses of poison for years until he became demented. He had no idea he was being poisoned. This is how so many of us were raised. We didn't know it, but we became sicker and sicker.

I started to ask my mother questions. I started to worry about myself.

I remember sitting in the great Ethical Society meeting room on 64th Street on Founder's Day, the most solemn occasion in the year. I must have been ten years old. I was afraid that I would stand up and start screaming, as if there were a separate being within me that I could not control, who would overpower the "real me," like Mr. Hyde within Dr. Jekyll.

Who could control these fearsome thoughts? I was tormented, but whom could I tell? Who could understand these "aberrations"? Everybody else was normal; they never had these crazy thoughts.

No one had introduced me to G-d.

I told my mother, "I have these terrible fears."

Poor Mother. What was she to do, go and tell Felix Adler? He was dead. We were all the living dead, marching zombies, separated by our free will from Life, from G-d.

▲▲▲

Mother sent me to the shrink.

This lady was a famous, European-trained child psychiatrist. She was a spinster, gray hair tied in a bun. I saw her several times every week for years. Her name was Dr. J. R. Glumb (pronounced "gloom"—and for good reason!). She used to take pages of notes during our sessions, writing down everything I said. Her few words were in heavily accented French. I did the talking.

This lady was considered to be very wise, the best in the business.

What agony!

I was supposed to feel all better after this. I had gotten it out of my system, right?

The fact is, it bothered me even more because I kept wondering why I didn't feel better. *I mean, I must be really sick if I go to this great psychiatrist for years and I still have the same fears!*

Do you understand? If you go to the shrink and you're not "cured," you feel desperate because you are afraid there *is* no cure and you are doomed to become a slave of the monster within you. Yes . . . Dr. "Gloom" indeed.

I told myself, *you're getting better.* But I knew the truth. I hadn't even begun to come to grips with the terrible battle raging within me. The monster was taking over, but I had to pretend that everything was fine. So I went through life in a twilight state, pretending everything was great and petrified that there were no answers at all.

At school I watched the kids flirting. They all seemed to be having a great time. How come I couldn't be like them? That inner monster wouldn't let me.

I used to confide in people I thought were wise. During the summers, I would speak every day to the head of my camp in Vermont, a non-Jewish man who was very nice and very patient. But we were a million miles apart. He didn't begin to understand what was going on inside me.

Another camp director told me, "Nothing is wrong with you. Get these crazy thoughts out of your head." Of course I believed he was correct, and I tried to whip myself into shape. It "worked" . . . for about four minutes.

I went on a summer trip around America with a traveling camp. I was among girls and boys who seemed to have such an easy time with each other. Now I see it is not proper for teenagers to socialize like that. It is part of the breakdown of morality in America. But then I thought I was just a social misfit. I couldn't stand the constant cursing (which was mild compared to today). Why did things bother me that didn't bother them? I called my parents from Durango, Colorado, to persuade them to let me come home, but they were leaving for a trip to Europe. I thought I was homesick, but when I got home the sickness didn't go away. I thought to myself: maybe there is no cure for my terrible fears.

Do you understand how frightening it is to have these thoughts raging in your head? FDR hit upon a deep concept when he said, "We have nothing to fear but fear itself."

▲▲▲

I tried many strategies to run away from my worries. I thought I could get lost in the world of folk music. I had a large collection of phonograph records (remember those things?) and a twelve-string as well as a six-string guitar. My heroes were Pete Seeger, Leadbelly, Woody Guthrie, Odetta. I would sing songs and say to myself, "This is truth. I can base my life on this."

I got involved in "social action." One weekend a large group of us from school paraded for hours in front of the

Woolworth store on Broadway and 231st Street in the Bronx, because Woolworth's allegedly discriminated against black people. I said to myself, "This is truth. I can base my life on this."

Later, at the University of Michigan, I turned out flyers and was involved in protests against the war in Vietnam.

I tried strategies that seem, in retrospect, really abnormal. For example, I would focus my eyes on objects, just staring at anything for long periods of time, as if that would enable me to control my wandering mind. It didn't work.

My friend Josh and I spent a summer hiking deep in the Wyoming wilderness. We were searching for purity far away from the noise of civilization. I tried to convince myself I could base my life on this, but I knew in my heart it wasn't real.

I wrote poetry and studied "great literature." This distracted me momentarily, but I was aware that "Mr. Hyde" lurked in the background and threatened me always. I couldn't get away from him, so nothing I did to run from him had any validity. I was running from fear, and fear was right behind me. I could not escape.

In addition, I didn't want to settle for half-truth. In my innermost heart I knew that I was on earth for one shot, and I wanted reality, not lies. I tried—don't get me wrong—but these strategies just didn't work. They didn't answer the problem, which gnawed away at my insides and left me constantly frightened and alone.

"*Achas shoalti may-ays Hashem** . . . One thing I asked of G-d," says King David, to dwell in Your house all the days of my life.

---

* Psalm 27

That's all I wanted. My soul wanted peace, to dwell se-curely in its proper home. But I couldn't admit it. No, I was the boss; I knew what I was doing; I could figure out what life was all about. To put it bluntly, *I was bigger, stron-ger, and smarter than G-d.* I knew it all.

Now I will show you the greatness of G-d, the G-d of Israel, who—through all our rebellion—remains our Fa-ther and our Sustainer. Do you see how I was living? Oblivi-ous of the Torah, completely divorced from my people and my heritage, pretending I knew what I was doing but liv-ing in Hell.

How did G-d react to my rebellion? Did G-d despise me?

Please read this carefully, my dear friends, and see the in-credible kindness and love of our Creator and Sustainer, the G-d of Abraham, Isaac, and Jacob. As I spat upon Him and disdained His Torah, He was laying out for me the path to freedom, to peace, to truth, to happiness, true happiness that would open up to me far in the future. I didn't know it at the time, but G-d was taking me by the hand. All my troubles and fears were like shepherds' rods, prodding me, pushing me, hitting me if necessary, nudging me in the right direction. The rods hurt because I resisted, but they were all from the Hand of G-d.

▲▲▲

I was in tenth grade.

I want you, my dear friends, to appreciate the greatness of Am Yisroel, the Jewish people, whose sons and daughters grow up in purity and whose children are privileged to study Torah instead of being exposed to these fiery trials from which it is almost impossible to emerge unscathed. Now there are shootings at public schools in America. Do we understand what we have created? When American children go to school, what are they learning? Are they learning to live effectively in a world created by G-d or are they sinking into a quagmire of moral corruption? I escaped from this fiery furnace, but only by a hair's breadth and through the extraordinary mercies of G-d. I was supersensitive, so American culture bothered me. I was the unusual case, but for most Jews the American educational system is a straight road to a life devoid of Torah values, a spider's web from which escape is almost impossible.

A girl entered in the grade below me, a freshman. Her name was Linda Villency, and she created quite a scene when she arrived.

The seniors (three years older than she was) all wanted to go out with her. She was beautiful. And she was so nice. She lit up the school. No pretensions, no *shtick*, as they say in Yiddish. Every teacher loved her, and she was smart. I mean, this was perfection.

Do you think I'm exaggerating? In case you suspect my objectivity, here's what somebody wrote in her senior yearbook: "Linda, I question that anything as nice as you will ever happen in the Fieldston School again. Gratefully, Fen Fuller." Do you think Fen Fuller was a senior with a crush on her? Oh no, Fenwick B. Fuller was the venerable chairman of the Middle School and a teacher of French!

But all this pageantry I observed from afar. *I couldn't talk to girls.* Any sophisticated, beautiful, popular girl was beyond my reach. I could only stare with jealous glances. The cool guys could do anything. I stood in the corner and watched the parade of life go by.

Observe, please, my dear friends, the all-powerful hand of G-d, working unseen in the world, saving those who call out to Him. Somewhere in my battered, starving soul I must have sputtered out something like a prayer, something like, "I wish there were Someone somewhere Who could help me." Just a little chink in the Ethical Culture armor, a little hint of submission, humility, a few hidden tears.

▲▲▲

I was sitting at a track meet one day, the little *nebbach* Roy Salant Neuberger, watching our great Ethical Culture team under the legendary coach Alton Smith. We were all cheering them on. Rah rah, yay yay!

I happened to glance to my immediate right.

There she was.

I, Roy S. Neuberger, the *nebbach*, was sitting next to Linda Villency!

What would I do? What could I say? I was so afraid.

Almighty G-d, Who prepares the way for us, Who opens our mouths and our hearts if we allow Him to enter, now stepped into my life in a way that was so dramatic I still cannot believe it.

My mouth opened, like the mouth of Balaam's donkey.* Was I any more than a donkey? For me, this was as great a miracle.

I spoke.

I, who could never speak to girls, especially popular girls, especially beautiful girls, I, Roy Salant Neuberger, was speaking to none other than the most beautiful, popular girl in the world. And I was not making a fool of myself.

The words were coming out NORMAL.

Are there no miracles in life? When the course of nature is altered, that is the Hand of G-d. When the Red Sea

---

* Numbers 22:28. See Glossary under "Balaam's donkey."

split, the course of nature was altered. Of course, that miracle was publicized to the ends of the earth.

When a miracle occurred at the track meet, only G-d and I knew about it. There was no way I could have spoken if G-d had not been opening and closing my mouth, moving my tongue and vocal cords. He was right there, pulling the strings.

My radar locked onto the target. Something deep inside me told me that this girl was my destiny. By the way, Linda was also Jewish, although her last name sounded Italian.* Believe me, I wouldn't have cared at the time, but G-d cared, and His hidden hand was shaping our future. We started to go out. G-d kept pulling the strings and we were able to talk to each other. Meanwhile, the school was buzzing: *Linda Villency is going out with HIM!*

I have a letter in my files from someone a few years ahead of me at Fieldston. Here's an excerpt: "I especially remember that when the two of you started going out together, there was a large bunch of guys waiting for you to break up so they could go after Linda. I guess they are still waiting!"

Miracles!

Our first "date" was at the "JV Party."

---

* "Villency" actually was once "Vilensky," meaning "from Vilna." And where is Vilna? Amazingly enough, not far from Salantai, in Lithuania. Vilna was the home of the Gaon of Vilna, one of the greatest figures ever to emerge in the millennia of Jewish history. Linda's father told her that "Vilensky" was once "Rabinowitz," the name of a great rabbinical family in Vilna. When Linda's father's father went to Scotland to design the Russian Pavilion at the 1906 World's Fair, he stayed and changed the family name to reflect the place of his origin. Linda's father was born in Glasgow. In 1916, the young family sailed to America, narrowly and miraculously avoiding being sunk by German subs. The family settled in Binghamton, New York, where the children grew up. That's when her father's name was changed to "Maurice Villency," from "Morris Vilensky." He went on to become the founder of a well-known chain of furniture stores in the New York City area.

I was manager of the junior varsity basketball team. We had had a great season, 17 wins and 1 loss. There was a victory party at Ted Selig's house. I got up my nerve and invited Linda. She came! Although it was over forty years ago, I remember that night as if it were yesterday. It was a big, beautiful house in Riverdale. There were a lot of people around, but we found a couch over by the wall. I think she was sitting on the couch and I sat on the floor with my arm on the cushion. We spent the whole evening discussing my previous summer at University Settlement Work Camp. People from Fieldston liked to work at places like that because the kids in the regular part of the camp were poor people from the Lower East Side. It made us feel good to collect the garbage and the linens from the bunks. We felt guilty about being rich, so this assuaged the guilt. It was a real "Fieldston" thing to do, with all the ethical overtones. I must have done a good job of describing the work camp, because next summer Linda went there.

It was one of those charmed evenings. The two of us just hit it off. We were both idealists and we still are. That's why we were able to pursue our dream together.

Nothing happens by chance. If it hadn't been for that 17-1 season, many other things would not have happened. Everything in life fits in with everything else. Even little things that seem insignificant. There is a plan from above.

We had a coach on that basketball team, a charismatic undergraduate from Manhattan College, which was just down the hill from Fieldston. He had a motto: *"If you think you're green, you're growing. If you think you're ripe, you're rotten."*

I don't think he invented it, but he used it to teach our team an attitude that inspired us. I am still inspired by it.

▲▲▲

Linda and I went to a Pete Seeger concert at Carnegie Hall.

We went bicycling on Staten Island. There were still farms then, no Verrazano Bridge. We took the bikes on the ferry and it was a day in the country. We built snowmen in Central Park. We did everything together and spoke for hours on the phone every day. I began to wonder: *maybe I'm normal now. Maybe everything is OK.*

I quit Dr. Glumb. I was sixteen.

I am free. I am liberated.

I began to hope.

It was not to be.

I remember how Mother used to love to tend the flowers in the country. We have a beautiful house in northern Westchester County, overlooking the Croton Reservoir. It is called Florival Farm, the "valley of flowers." We have owned it for over fifty years. When we first started spending summers there, the area was really rural, a kind of oasis that made it seem as if the earth were peaceful. Mother would spend hours in the garden. It was the closest she got to tranquility. But she had an endless war with the Japanese beetles. Getting into the Garden of Eden isn't so easy.

Creepy things also started crawling through my Garden of Eden.

I was very possessive. Frankly, I don't know how Linda stood for it except that she also must have felt the pull of destiny. If she would so much as look at someone else, let alone go on a date, it was not just that I was jealous. I felt that the sun had exploded and the universe had collapsed. I knew we were meant for each other; the whole order of nature was built on that certainty.

In 1961 I graduated from Fieldston and began my freshman year at the University of Michigan. Linda was still in
New York.

In retrospect, it seems silly that I went to Michigan, but
no decisions were really rational then. I didn't get into Har-
vard, so I went to Michigan. Normal people from Fieldston
didn't go to college in New York; it wasn't sophisticated.
You had to go far away to show that you were independent. So I went to Michigan. And then I began to think,
"What am I doing here?" We were far away from each other,
and the phone bills were very high. I thought, like all my
fellow sophisticates at Fieldston, that college is essential,
but I didn't really know why. We all went because everybody went. You *had* to go. My mind was on Linda and our
future, and I was nervous, because it's hard to maintain a
relationship by phone.

Sometime around January of that first year I began to
detect a coolness in her voice, an uncharacteristic hesita-
tion. I kept getting this funny feeling that something was
not quite right.

Of course, you understand that I was completely calm.

I told you about the sun exploding and the universe collapsing? One day on the phone I asked her point blank:
What's going on?

Well, what was going on was that she had started to go
out with a real cool guy in her class. This guy was decent-
looking all right, but no sophistication, a real *heavy*.

I mean, how could you do it? What do you see in that guy?
Hey, she is my girl. Who does he think he is? That bum.

But could I reasonably expect her to refuse all invita-
tions when I was five hundred miles away?

You bet I did.

If I had had an atomic bomb, I would not have thought twice before dropping it on this guy. So it destroyed everything else in a 200-mile radius. I mean, *what gall to interfere with my destiny!*

I didn't handle it too well.

After I got off the phone, I wandered out onto the streets of Ann Arbor in a daze. It was a cold winter night, a real Michigan freeze. There was a crisp quarter moon in a black sky. I didn't know where I was going. I was talking to myself. I seriously considered walking in front of a car.

I got a train ticket to New York. The heck with classes; this was reality. I wasn't too calm. I think I must have been talking to myself the whole train ride. Linda's parents weren't so happy to see me. They thought she needed to "play the field" a little and were glad to have me far away in Ann Arbor. But I have a certain quality of persistence. And as I said, the radar was locked on the target, and I would not, I could not let go.

I didn't know then why she didn't tell me to get lost, but I do now. We both knew inside that we were meant for each other. There is such a thing as destiny.

There is a concept found in the Torah that explains this. Please, dear reader, concentrate on this idea.

When G-d creates a man and a woman, they are created together. A man and a woman are one being, so to speak. "*G-d created man in His image . . . male and female he created them.*"*

The commentator Rashi, quoting ancient rabbinical sources, says about this verse: "*[G-d] created [man] with two faces, one side male, and one side female. . . and afterward He divided him.*"

---

* Genesis 1:27

Those two beings, male and female, divided from one source, want to reunite. They are created to reunite. In fact, we learn from this that their destiny is to reunite. The concept of *basherte*, which means that two people are destined for each other from even before conception, comes from this source. One of our missions in life is to find our other half. G-d always gives us the opportunity to do this, but whether we recognize our *basherte* depends on whether our minds are attuned to the signals we are getting from Heaven.

There is the famous story of the middle-aged *chassid* who came to his *rebbe* and complained, "Rebbe, why haven't I found my *basherte*?"

His *rebbe* told him, "You did find her, but you rejected her because you thought her nose was too long."

We all have our *basherte*.

Linda and I sensed this, although we had never heard the word.

We agreed that she would follow me the next year to the University of Michigan. I wanted to get married right away, the summer after high school, but that was vetoed by all four parents. Getting her parents to agree to Michigan was struggle enough.

▲▲▲

My years in Michigan are a blur.

The first year my roommate was a blond guy named Ted. His background was Ukrainian. He was a good guy, but we had nothing in common and I kept wondering, *What am I doing here?* In fact, what are the other 42,000 people doing here? We all went to college because "everybody in America" is supposed to go to college.

When I read what the alumni association sends me today, I am wondering the same thing.* Here are some of the
learned topics being written about: A history professor
writes about eighth-century Japanese attitudes toward "gen-
der relations and sexual meanings." A professor with an
Arab name writes an article entitled "Genealogies of the
Secular: The Jewish Question and Dilemmas in
Postcolonial Modernity" (subliminal message: "secular"
equals "Jewish"). A professor of psychology conducts a
major study showing that "college students who experience the most racial and ethnic diversity in classrooms
and . . . on campus become better learners and more effective citizens." (I assume she also conducted the definitive
study establishing the meaning of the concepts "learning"
and "effective citizen.")

Main memory of my first year in college: missing Linda.

Main memory of my second year in college: Linda arrived!

Somehow, she convinced her parents to allow her to do
it. But you have to remember, the hallmark of our Fieldston
crowd was independence and sophistication. Basically, kids
could do whatever they wanted. With Linda in Ann Arbor, life became a lot more livable.

▲▲▲

There were walks in the "Arb," really a beautiful place.
(I hope it still is.) There was a coffee house with great
cinnamon buns and a place that served great steaks.

I bought a bike. But the check bounced because I didn't

---

* Following examples excerpted from *LSAmagazine* (College of Literature, Science and the
Arts, University of Michigan), Fall 1999, pages 30 and 34.

realize you had to know how much was in your bank account. That actually *was* a learning experience.

My most useful course—to this day—was touch-typing. I am using it NOW. It wasn't given by the university, but rather by a typing school on the second floor of a building around the corner from the cinnamon buns.

It's amazing when I think about it, but I really don't remember much that I learned. I remember the names and faces of a few professors, but I don't remember what they taught me.

The only thing I can remember from a classroom is when I made the following ridiculous suggestion. The professor was asking the class what book we should study next. I raised my hand and proposed that we should study *Alice in Wonderland*. I was serious. I mean we were sophisticated, deep students and I was sure that *Alice in Wonderland* contained the deepest secrets in the universe. Listen to this: everyone agreed!

I remember Professor Zaros, from the English department. He became our friend. He was lonely. He had no family. We used to invite him over to eat.

Professor Paparotti was hot stuff, a very popular art history professor. He lived in an apartment overlooking the Huron River. He served us Cherry Heering.

Isn't it funny? I don't remember what I learned, but I remember the food.

We used to go on Saturday mornings to the outdoor Farmer's Market. It was rustic. I can taste those Macintosh apples. Perfect tartness and crispness. Linda was always very big on fresh fruits and vegetables. (She still is.)

I remember being afraid during the Cuban Missile Crisis. We thought we really might die if Russia fired missiles at the United States. I remember a group of us huddling in the halls outside the classroom, wondering what Nikita Khrushchev would do next. All of us liberal antiwar activists had a kind of superior attitude then, in the midst of our fear, as if to say, "Hey, we told you it would come to this if you didn't get rid of all your weapons."

I remember when President Kennedy was shot. I was in a store a few blocks from our apartment when the news came over the radio. I was crying for Jackie Kennedy and Linda was angry at me. She had a right to be angry, because she herself was upset but she didn't get any comfort from me. I was too worried about Jackie.

That's how it was with us. We were both Phi Beta Kappa honors students, but we didn't learn one thing from all those courses at the university.

What were all those students doing? Besides a few scholarly types, they were mostly kids who I thought at the time would be better off on the farm learning from their parents how to be farmers or on the boat learning how to be fishermen. Maybe even learning to be polite or modest or socially responsible.

When they got into the classroom far from home, they behaved like rowdy children. The scary part is that they were too big to be children. Boys and girls got together in ways they should not have done, and this was in the days *before mixed dorms*, when the university actually tried to control things. I don't even want to think what goes on today. And all the while we hear that our colleges and universities are essential to the future of America.

▲▲▲

After my second year of college my dream came true; Linda and I got married on a beautiful summer day at Florival Farm. It was outdoors, and I guess about as perfect as you can get, with a beautiful meal in the garden, proud grandparents, parents, and friends. How come, when I look at the picture of us coming down the aisle, I see on my face an expression of abject fear? I don't know if anyone else would see it, but I see it, and I know it is true. I was petrified. I didn't think I could handle marriage. Here I was marrying the greatest girl in the world, and I knew I was going to mess it up, and I couldn't do anything about it.

Let me give you an idea of how we were thinking. Do you know what we requested for our wedding presents? Contributions to charity! We didn't need money. We didn't need material objects. We were very spiritual people.

What kind of fantasy world were we living in? How could we have believed ourselves at the time? But that's how we were, very obtuse. But when you want to believe something, you don't let logic get in the way. As Rebbetzin Jungreis puts it, some people are so open-minded that their brains fall out.

The one thing I asked from our parents for a wedding present was a car. Listen to this. What kind of car did I ask for? A Land Rover.

Today, Land Rovers are "in." Then they were practically unknown outside African safaris. But I was a tough guy. I wasn't a Jew from New York, I was a wilderness trekker who tried to get my identity from the "natural" side of life.

This car was a joke because—while it may have been great in the veldt—on U.S. highways it sounded like a garbage truck at any speed over 35 miles per hour. Not only that, it chose to break down on a perfectly good highway in the middle of the Arizona desert at about midnight! This was way before cell phones! About an hour after it broke down, the next car passed us. I didn't know whether public enemy number one was in that car, but we didn't like being all alone in the middle of the desert at midnight, so I flagged it down. About two hours later, a broken-down tow truck arrived to bring us back to civilization. We drove (in the Land Rover) to Wyoming, where our honeymoon consisted of camping out in Grand Teton National Park for the entire summer. Considering that the nighttime temperature got as low as 28 degrees Fahrenheit in June that year, it was an interesting experience. We had to order a new, winter sleeping bag from Colorado by parcel post. Until it arrived, we were somewhat chilly.

This was how we thought at the time of the wedding, and of course I was the main instigator of this ridiculous, irrational attitude. I was always the crazy one. Linda was so normal—somehow, even after decades of marriage to me, she still is!—that it's just amazing. Why did she stick with me? I know that G-d is very merciful when I think what that girl has suffered through with her nut-case of a husband!

What kind of a wedding did we have? Well, I wanted an Ethical Culture wedding like my sister's, but Linda's grandfather insisted on having a rabbi.

A rabbi? At my wedding? Too much to bear. But Linda's family was insistent, so we "compromised." The compromise was a rabbi who was as Reform as possible and promised not to use any Hebrew during the service. Such was my "allergy" to G-d. I broke out in spiritual hives at the mere whiff of Torah.

So we had no *kesubah*, the marriage contract stipulated

by Jewish law. There was no *chupah*, marriage canopy, over our heads. There were no kosher *aydim*, Torah abiding Jews who act as witnesses. Leah did not immerse herself in the pure waters of the *mikveh* before our wedding. There was nothing Jewish about our marriage.

But these are archaic, meaningless customs.

It took us eleven years to realize that we couldn't live without these archaic, meaningless customs. It took us eleven years even to realize that they existed! In the meantime we found out that marriage is not necessarily the Garden of Eden. I had expected paradise, but I soon got kicked out. *Marriage is the most difficult situation in the world if you don't live by the Torah.*

I remember being jealous of every guy at the University of Michigan who spoke to Linda. I can see her now, standing in the corridor between classes, talking to some guy. We were married, but it was going downhill and I didn't know how to stop it.

Do you think that was fun? Not too much.

G-d and the Rebbetzin saved us. It is not that married life *improved* when we adopted the Torah. Much more than that.

Married life *began* when we adopted the Torah.

As the commentators tell us,* if the presence of G-d is not in the home, there is a ravaging fire. The Hebrew word for "fire" is *aysh*. The name of G-d is spelled with the letter *yud* and the letter *hay*. If you add *yud* to *aysh* you get *ish*, "man" in Hebrew. If you add *hay* to *aysh* you get *ishah*, "woman" in Hebrew. In other words, if you add the name of G-d to the fire, you get "man and woman," and G-d

---

* Rashi on the Talmudic tractate *Sotah* 17a

controls the fire so that it gives life but does not destroy. Without the name of G-d, the fire rages uncontrollably, destroying everything in its path.

Why do you think so many homes are on fire? G-d has not been allowed to enter.

Our home was on fire. Yes, we were meant for each other. But without G-d, without the holy laws of family purity, Shabbos, *kashrus, mezuza*, prayer, all the commandments of the Torah that tell us how to live, there is no hope. All the amazing miracles we had seen were going up in smoke. We were not going to make it.

The second summer of our marriage, we got a job with the National Park Service as fire lookouts in Crater Lake National Park, Oregon. This was paradise, one of the most beautiful spots in the world, and we were literally on top of it. We lived in a cabin atop the tallest mountain in the park, some 11,000 feet above sea level. We had a view extending 150 miles in every direction, from California in the south to Mount Hood in the north. Eagles soared above. We could see the sun rise over eastern Oregon and at dusk turn toward the Pacific for the most awe-inspiring sunset. We were in perfect physical shape and could run up the two-and-one-half-mile trail, backpacks full, without stopping to catch our breath. We were paid to be the guardians of Eden.

Why were we miserable? Why couldn't we get along?

Like Adam and Eve, we messed it up.

One night, a thunderstorm passed right over our mountaintop cabin. Long before it reached us, we could literally feel it coming. Our hair stood at attention. Everything started to buzz. Otherwise, there was an eerie silence. Blue sparks flashed from the green metal shutters. We followed instructions and sat on our beds, which themselves were resting on glass insulators, the kind you see on electric poles. As lightning exploded and thunder crashed all around us, it seemed as if we were in the middle of Hell. How could you have Hell in the middle of Heaven?

We knew all about it. We had everything and nothing. We had all the pieces, but we couldn't put the puzzle together.

Our hopes were fading. Even if Linda loved me, how long could she tolerate my incapacitating worries and fears? Marriage was supposed to be the ultimate solution. Marriage was going to solve all the problems. Marriage was going to save me.

The sun was exploding, the universe collapsing.

CHAPTER TWO

WE MEET G-D

T 2:00 P.M. ON MONDAY, January 10, 1966, I awoke with a start.

Things had not been going too well lately. Our marriage seemed to be falling apart, and I began to think I myself was coming unraveled.

Through all the years I had always done well academically, but lately, in graduate school at Michigan, I couldn't concentrate. There was one course, Old English, that I just couldn't deal with. I kept getting bad marks, and I began to think I was cracking from the strain. In graduate school, if you get bad marks, you are in trouble. You're supposed to be good to be there in the first place. I was afraid I was going to be thrown out. I was afraid I was going to be thrown out of my marriage. I was afraid everything was spinning out of control.

Old English finals were scheduled for Friday at 9:30 A.M. I had stayed up very late Thursday night studying. Friday morning, from some distant place, I heard the sound of an alarm clock. I must have gone back to sleep. Sometime later, I groggily opened my eyes.

"NO!"

"It couldn't be."

9:20!

I grabbed clothes and ran out of the house. I jumped on my bike. As I weaved through the Ann Arbor traffic racing for the final, tears streamed down my face. I'm cracking, I thought. My life is coming to an end.

Sunday night I was lying on that old green couch with the stuffing coming out. I can see it now, decades later. I couldn't breathe. I didn't know where to turn. I couldn't discuss the problems because I felt so selfish just talking about myself. But the problems wouldn't go away, and I didn't know how to make them go away.

When I awoke at 2:00 A.M., I was desperate. I saw a chasm opening in front of me, a pit from which there was no escape. I looked back on my life. I was twenty-three years old and we had been married just over two and a half years. Linda and I loved each other, but there was something between us; tensions were at the snapping point.

I felt as if my life were a long corridor, with many doors on each side. I had opened each door, hundreds of doors. There was a door for "hiking in the wilderness." A door for "singing folk music." Doors for "toughness" and "coolness." There was a door for "political activism." A door to the psychiatrist's office. A door for "writing poetry." A door for "comparative religion" and a door for "The Ethical Culture Society." Each door had led *nowhere*, into a blank wall. *Was there no door that led to truth, to freedom, no door to sunshine and happiness?*

I began to cry. I was through. There was no future. I was dying. There was no place I hadn't tried, no door I hadn't opened. I was drowning. My life was ending. Can you imagine this feeling? There was nothing to live for. No hope.

I was sliding: down, down, down . . . falling through space. And then, as I fell, a thought brushed by me. A little thought, a little voice, like a feather floating by in the midst of the void, a crazy little idea.

No, it couldn't be true.

But then . . .

What else was there besides death?

All my life I had been raised as a good American boy. I went to the finest schools and met the most sophisticated people. *Nobody normal believed in G-d.* I mean, where is G-d? Maybe thirteenth-century monks believed in G-d, but that was the Dark Ages. What else did *they* have in life? *But we live in reality.* This is the twentieth century, the enlightened blossoming of world culture, the age of science and technology. We are liberated. I mean, just where is G-d? I don't see Him. I can't touch Him.

I'm supposed to believe in something I can't see?

There was one big problem.

If all that stuff were true, how come I—the sophisticated product of the culmination of all civilization—was a total failure who couldn't succeed at even the simplest things in life? I couldn't breathe. I couldn't prevent myself from getting angry and alienating those I cared about. I was a slave.

I "knew" that G-d didn't exist.

The problem was that I felt *I also didn't exist.*

Something was terribly wrong.

Suddenly, I began to turn the whole question around. Like Hagar in the desert,* my eyes opened and I saw something I had never seen before. There was one unopened

---

* Genesis 21:19

door in that long corridor. Why had I never noticed that door before? It was the door to G-d.

I had been sure that G-d did not exist. But now that my own life seemed to be falling apart, I began to wonder.

Maybe I had to turn the whole thing upside down. When I examined it, it was very logical. When I was honest about my life, I saw that *I did not exist*—my life was empty—and at that time I was sure that G-d did not exist.

But what if G-d *did* exist? Maybe then I could *also* exist. *Maybe my existence depends on G-d.*

Maybe there was a life I hadn't even dreamed about. *Maybe if G-d were really alive I could be alive.* Maybe I had been looking at things "upside down" or "backwards" or "inside out."

Why did my intelligence have to be the measuring rod of reality? Maybe I did not understand and G-d did understand. Did I have to comprehend something for it to be real? Was I the center of the universe?

Maybe there was a reality beyond my understanding.

I began to have this crazy thought. Could G-d exist? No, it's crazy. CRAZY! All my life I had been raised on "reality." *No normal person believed in G-d.*

And then I began to wonder if I had ever met any normal people.

They say there are no atheists in the foxhole. I was in a spiritual foxhole. I was fighting for my life in a "war to end all wars." My entire civilization was falling apart. I felt the coldness of death and black nothingness where chaos reigns.

When you are drowning, you grab the life preserver. You don't ask questions. I was drowning, and all of a sudden out of the sky came this life preserver. I grabbed it.

What choice did I have? *I wanted to live!*
G-d, do You exist? Could You exist?

▲ ▲ ▲

Dawn was beginning to break in Ann Arbor as a new light began to glow inside me. All of a sudden, I started to have this incredible feeling of hope, a new idea that would enable me to live.

Do you think we survive on "bread"? No, we survive on ideas. Our life emanates from our soul and our soul emanates from G-d. *"Some [trust] in chariots, some in horses . . . but we [trust] in the name of G-d."** This "crutch" that I had always rejected, the "opiate of the masses," maybe this was the missing link.

As the sun rose, I picked up a pen and began to write. A volcano of thought and emotion exploded onto my paper. I began to reassess my entire life. All of a sudden I let G-d enter my soul and the sun came up.

Can I describe to you the feeling of hope I had? For the first time in my life I felt what it is like to live without fear. I thought to myself that something good and all-powerful governs the universe and that tremendous force would take care of me, through everything, internal and external, that life would throw in my way. There was something more powerful than Mr. Hyde. There was Someone to protect me, Someone to take care of me, Someone to show me the way.

I happened to look in the mirror. I saw my face, but it was not the face I had always looked at. It was a shining face, a radiant face, mine but not the old face. It was what

---

* Psalm 20

I could be, or what I really was. Maybe I wasn't a monster, after all. Maybe I wasn't crazy.

I wrote continuously for a few days, with words ceaselessly pouring out. For the first time, I could permit myself to see the truth of my old life, the agony, the stifled cries, the constant fear. I could let myself see it because now I knew that there was another way, a path to freedom.

Every year since then I have had a personal holiday on the night of January 9/10, the anniversary of my liberation from Hell.

It's a little hard to describe what Linda went through at this time. You're going to say that this sounds like a fairy tale, but she's really a *malach*, an angel. She suffered when I got upset or paralyzed by fear, because it's not easy to live with a person who is depressed. And sometimes she even doubted that I was going to get out of my mental instability, and she wondered if our life could ever work out. But basically, she has tremendous stability and patience. She is very calm. She just tolerated, tolerated, tolerated. She had a deep ability to wait, and an intuition that somehow this crazy life would lead somewhere good. So as excited and wild as my brain was, hers was as placid as a mountain lake. This in itself demonstrates the incredible kindness of G-d, because there is probably not one other woman in the world who would have tolerated me for even five minutes.

We were beginning to make progress, but there was one big stumbling block. That ego—I just couldn't go all the way.

I wanted truth. I wanted reality. But *I couldn't equate devotion to G-d with being Jewish.* After all, what do Jews have to do with G-d? I believed that Jews were just what anti-Semites portray us to be. I was a Jewish anti-Semite. I was embarrassed by the Jews who had "stolen" the Land of Israel. I was repelled by men in black hats. I was alienated from people who study Torah. In the end I was alienated from myself.

What path did I choose? Well, the *real holy people* in the world were the ascetics. Couldn't you see it? Mahatma Gandhi and his disciple at that time, Martin Luther King, Jr. Wasn't it obvious that they were real? And so I began to investigate Eastern religion, the farther from home the better. We studied the Hindu religion with an Indian professor at Michigan. I bought esoteric books about the wanderings of the soul. I got up in the middle of the night so that I could remember my dreams, because I felt that if I knew where my soul went, I would find Truth. There were special books that described these mystical things, and I delved into them.

I won't say there is no truth in these ideas. We know that all religions and philosophies that gain currency in the world have grains of truth, and that is why they survive. Whatever truth they have is inevitably derived from our Torah, because it is universally acknowledged that G-d spoke to the world through the Jewish people. We know that the soul returns to G-d every night and is given back to us every morning. So the idea of "following" the soul on its nightly journey to G-d's realm is not without basis in reality. But this is dangerous stuff, and our Torah warns us not to look *"across the sea"** for G-d. It is a dangerous journey. That is why G-d put the Torah into *this world* for us to find it on our very doorstep. *"Lo bashamayim hi . . .* It is not in Heaven."**

---

* Deuteronomy 30:13
** Deuteronomy 30:12

"Little curly head" at Florival Farm in the 1940s.

On a pony across the street from Central Park. What thoughts are beginning to percolate beneath those curls?

Three generations of Salants and Neubergers in the mid-1950s. My father is in the center in the middle row. To the left of him are my Salant grandparents; my Aunt Edna and I are on the right. In the back row, from the left, are my Uncle Walter Salant, my mother; my sister and her husband, and my Uncle Bill. Jimmy's in the front row, center, with Salant cousins on the left and Uncle Bill's fiancée on the right. On the wall behind Uncle Walter is a valuable painting by the artist Jackson Pollack.

Linda as she looked in 1959, when we first met at Fieldston. Big things were about to happen.

On the Saddle of the Grand Teton, Jackson Hole, Wyoming, in the summer of '61. Looking for the Garden of Eden.

Our first "wedding," at Florival Farm in '63. No Hebrew allowed! (Note: Linda's gown in this photo has been retouched in accordance with the Jewish laws of modesty.)

*"For this commandment that I command you today—it is not hidden from you and it is not distant. It is not in heaven, [for you] to say, 'Who can ascend to the Heaven for us and take it for us, so that we listen to it and perform it?' Nor is it across the sea, [for you] to say, 'Who can cross to the other side of the sea for us and take it for us, so that we can listen to it and perform it?' Rather, the matter is very near to you—in your mouth and your heart—to perform it."**

Those who search "across the sea" for what G-d put at our fingertips end up drowning, unless they are so fortunate as to be thrown a life preserver before it is too late.

For years I studied Eastern religions, and then I began to wonder.

For one thing, I didn't feel any different. I still felt that I was in that long corridor with the doors leading nowhere. My soul still had no place to rest, like the dove that Noah released from the Ark.

Intellectually, I began to wonder. These ascetics had crazy lifestyles. It's one thing to read a book about all these "holy people," but do I want to live that way? *Do I want to be a Buddha?* I'm a person. I'm married. I eat. Do I want to live on a mountaintop or in a cave? If "truth" means that I should sit secluded all day in silent contemplation, if it means that I should divorce my wife . . . Is that life, or is it a cop-out?

I began to feel that everything I had experienced since January 10, 1966, had been lies, and that I wasn't any closer to G-d than I had been in the beginning. Yes, G-d must be real because He saved me then, but this path wasn't leading to Him.

So how about Western religion? Now that's closer to

* Deuteronomy 30:11–14

home. All those holy saints. Those beautiful pictures in those beautiful churches.

After college, Linda and I spent a year in Europe. I was enrolled at Balliol College, Oxford, and our "major" was traveling around Europe, eating in the best restaurants and seeing all the cathedrals and great art. Officially, I was a postgraduate student in English language and literature and Linda was an art student, but it was an excuse, because we really didn't know what we wanted to do, and so we immersed ourselves in travel.

I thought to myself, "Now I will study Catholicism and Protestantism."

Exploring these religions is the ultimate rebellion for a Jew, because they are based on the assumption that the covenant between G-d and the Children of Israel was broken by G-d because we violated it.

This is patently absurd. If G-d had wanted to break the covenant with us, then the Torah would have said so. The Torah tells all about Israel's sins. Nothing is hidden. *No book written by Jews would say all that bad stuff about Jews.* It obviously wasn't written by a Jew.*

So who wrote it? An anti-Semite?

Well, if it had been written by an anti-Semite, then how could it be so explicit regarding the eternal covenant between G-d and the Jews?

Clearly, it could only have been written by G-d, because not only does it detail with dazzling clarity the sins of the Jews, but it describes with dazzling prophetic accuracy the eternal covenant that we have seen fulfilled throughout the ensuing centuries.

---

* Some of these ideas are drawn from a tape by the late Rabbi Shmuel Yaakov Weinberg, *zt"l.*

Who knew in advance that we would rebel? Who knew in advance that we would be "scattered to the four corners of the earth"*? Who knew that we would survive as a small minority wherever we were scattered, frequently subjugated and enslaved, yet not assimilated into the host nation? Is there another such nation on earth? Is there another nation exiled from its land two thousand years ago that still survives as a distinct entity in every country to which it has been driven? Is there another nation about which it has been said that "I will return you to your land," and which has returned to its land after two thousand years?

*"It will be that when all these things come upon you—the blessing and the curse that I have presented before you—then you will take it to your heart among all the nations where Hashem, your G-d, has dispersed you and you will return unto Hashem, your G-d, and listen to His voice . . . Then Hashem, your G-d, will bring back your captivity and have mercy upon you and He will gather you in from all the peoples to which Hashem, your G-d, has scattered you . . . to the land that your forefathers possessed and you shall possess it."**

Should anyone be surprised that the Children of Israel are living in the Holy Land today? It was all written thousands of years ago. And the world knows it. Of course the nations say the covenant was annulled. If they didn't say so, then on what basis would they try to deny our deed to the Land of Israel? On what rationale would they base their persecution?

But what happened to our persecutors and conquerors? Do they survive? Is ancient Egypt still here? Ancient Babylonia? Ancient Greece? Ancient Rome? Are the Cru-

---

* Isaiah 11:12
** Deuteronomy 30:1–5.

saders still here? Where is the all-powerful Inquisition? Where are the Cossacks? The Turkish Empire? The British Empire? The Nazi Empire? They are only a memory, a page in the history book. They were the conquerors of the world in their day and we were dust under their feet. They were the warlords and we were slaves. Yet here we are. *Am Yisroel chai*, the People of Israel live! We are still here as a distinct entity, adhering to our everlasting Torah, and they are gone. Has there ever been another such people?

I think it is appropriate to quote here the eloquent words of a non-Jew, Mark Twain, written in 1897: "If the statistics are right, the Jews constitute but one percent of the human race. It suggests a nebulous dim puff of stardust lost in the blaze of the Milky Way. Properly the Jew ought hardly to be heard of; but he is heard of, has always been heard of . . . The Egyptians, the Babylonians and the Persians rose, filled the planet with sound and splendor, then faded to dream-stuff and passed away; the Greeks and the Romans followed and made a vast noise, and they are gone; other peoples have sprung up and held their torch high for a time, but it burned out, and they sit in twilight now, or have vanished. The Jew saw them all, survived them all, and is now what he always was, exhibiting no decadence, no infirmities of age, no weakening of his parts, no slowing of his energies, no dulling of his alert and aggressive mind. He is as prominent on the planet as any other people . . . He has made a marvelous fight in this world, in all the ages; and has done it with his hands tied behind him . . . All things are mortal but the Jew; all other forces pass, but he remains. What is the secret of his immortality?"*

---

* From the essay "Concerning the Jews," *Harper's* magazine, September 1899.

Look what is written.

"But despite all this, while they will be in the land of their enemies, I will not have been revolted by them nor will I have rejected them to obliterate them, <u>to annul My covenant with them</u>—for I am Hashem their G-d. <u>I will remember for them the covenant of the ancients</u>, those whom I have taken out of the land of Egypt before the eyes of the nations, to be G-d unto them—I am Hashem." *

G-d had ample opportunity to break the covenant. Yes, we sinned. Yes, He is angry. But also, yes, the Torah goes to great lengths to stress that G-d will *never* break the covenant.

From the very beginning we Children of Israel demonstrated our rebelliousness. Before the Torah was given, the brothers sold Joseph. And yet the Torah was still given.

As Moses came down from Mount Sinai, we were dancing around the Golden Calf. And yet he went back up Mount Sinai and came down with the second set of tablets. That day is commemorated as Yom Kippur. Yom Kippur is for *real people*, people who struggle, people whose path is not straight up. If we weren't real people, we wouldn't need Yom Kippur. G-d created the Torah for people who would stray and return, people whose covenant with G-d is eternal. In the end of time, we will return and then never stray again. And the covenant will always be there.

The entire basis of the Torah is the assumption that we need a way to emerge from our imperfections. So how could anyone argue that those imperfections caused G-d to abandon His covenant with us? Only someone who doesn't understand the Torah would argue that.

---

* Leviticus 26:44–45

The Torah could have concealed our sins. If the Torah had concealed our sins, then maybe one could say, "G-d didn't take the sins into account when He wrote the Book." But the Torah leaves nothing out. Sometimes it seems as if all the Torah talks about are the sins of the Children of Israel. The Torah doesn't hide the facts; it broadcasts them.

So there is no logic to the argument that the covenant has been broken. But it's easy to believe something if you turn off your brain. My brain was on "sleep" mode.

▲▲▲

I started to believe in Catholicism and Protestantism. I wasn't the churchgoing type, although the Ethical Culture Sunday School curriculum was filled with trips to Buddhist temples, Hindu shrines, and every kind of church you can imagine: Catholic, Unitarian, Greek Orthodox, you name it.

In our travels during the Oxford period we visited many European churches and cathedrals, even the Vatican, whose sub-basements are reputedly filled with the vessels of our Holy Temple looted by the Romans two thousand years ago. Even aside from the religion, our excuse was that this was great art. We stared at walls filled with these "priceless treasures of Western civilization." We wandered the streets of Florence and floated down the canals of Venice. Somehow, we thought, this was good for our souls.

In Rome, a man came up to us and said, "It's so good to see a *landsman*, a fellow Jew." *Uh-oh. How did he spot us? Don't tell me we look Jewish!*

One memorable car trip during the Oxford era ended with a visit to Linda's "French family" in the champagne country. She had lived with them as part of a summer program several years earlier. They were Catholic, but to us there were no differences between people. The whole world was gray; everyone was the same.

Linda had remained close with this family. The climax of the stay was a huge, multicourse meal, each course accompanied by the appropriate wine, ending with dessert and champagne. Nothing was declined, of course, and all the wine went down along with all the accompaniments. It was definitely delicious and definitely enormous. And I was definitely sick. That night I discovered the converse of the famous dictum, "Everything that goes up must come down." Everything that had gone down came up.

I must have slept a lot the next day, because I don't think I could have done much else. The next night we left at about 2:00 A.M. and headed for Paris. We toured the famous Les Halles, the Paris food market that operates all night. It was then still in its centuries-old home, torn down a few years later. This was the place where all the great chefs would go, while the city slept, to select fresh food for the following day. A fishmonger threw an ice-chip snowball at us. It was all very playful. We must have looked so American and so naive. We checked into our hotel at 6:00 A.M., slept for a few hours, lunched at Maxim's, and caught a plane back to England, arriving in Oxford in time for the new term.

Sounds idyllic.

In fact, we were not just physically sick from this way of life, we were spiritually sick. As we ate each meal, we thought of the next. Life was a gastronomic merry-go-round. Where does it end? What happens when the music stops?

▲▲▲

We came back from Oxford in 1967 because of a gnaw-
ing feeling that we had to find a direction to our life. I was
just not cut out to be a university professor of English.

I got a job with the Parks, Recreation, and Cultural Affairs Administration under John V. Lindsay, New York
City's young, handsome mayor. In those days there was
great hope centering on idealistic, creative government.
August Heckscher, the former editorial page editor of the
New York Herald Tribune, had been persuaded to come into
public life. He was my boss. My specialty was conservation, and I was still trying to create the Garden of Eden.

I did my part to make New York City more pleasant. I
set up areas that would be kept in a natural state and prepared guidebooks to them. I became involved in the legal
process of preserving open spaces as well as the esthetic
process of designing their use. I served on boards of semi-
public institutions like the New York Zoological Society.

Perhaps the most interesting thing I did was to write
speeches for "Augie," who as an old newspaper hand was
very careful about his words. I always loved to work with
words. But after two years I got tired of government. Politics was brutal. People did anything to get ahead, since the
basic motivation of such a life is power. There is no money
in politics, so most people spent their time trying to step
over other people.

Religion and writing were still on my mind, so Linda
and I moved up to the beautiful community of Cornwall-
on-Hudson, New York, where we thought I might be inspired to write the great book about discovering one's spiritual heritage.

I studied the classic works of Catholicism so I could get to the roots. I wanted to learn the "Bible." After a few years, I actually wrote a book titled *Why the Jews Are Wrong and the Catholics and Protestants Are Right*. One of G-d's great acts of kindness to me is that this book was never published. The fact is that, when I read it today, I see why nobody wanted to publish it. It's so confused and turbid that, besides making no sense, it's completely unreadable. But it illustrates my attitude at the time: *I was so embarrassed to be Jewish.*

Years later, Rebbetzin Jungreis told me that I must never throw this book away. I must keep it to remind myself where I had been, because there is always a danger that a person will deny the past.

It is so important to remember where we came from and Who brought us here.

After years of "believing in G-d," but rejecting the Torah, I began to get depressed.

I began to get that same empty feeling as in 1966. I was still opening doors that led nowhere, only this time the doors were labeled "Hinduism," "Buddhism," "Catholicism," and "Protestantism." And now, I told myself, there were no doors left. I had come once again to the end of the Corridor of Life, but this was *really* the end. This time I had *really* tried everything. There was nothing, absolutely nothing I hadn't experimented with. Of course, there was that Jewish stuff, but I am talking about *real* things. I knew all about that Jewish stuff. I had even written a book proving that it was completely empty. It was not even worth a second of my time.

After the book attempt bombed—*How come nobody was interested in it?*—I had to do something to justify my existence. The local paper, a small-town weekly (circulation just over 3,000) with a history going back to 1885, was for sale. With my father's help and a local partner, we bought the paper and a small print shop on the premises.

The paper was called *The Cornwall Local* and our partner was a young lawyer whose parents were my parents' friends in New York. People in town became excited about the paper, because we were energetic and adventurous. Linda also helped, and of course we discussed everything together. We tried to make the paper great: great graphics, great editorials, increased circulation and revenue, stuff like that. We began to win awards, such as for quality of layout, reporting, and photography. That doesn't mean we were making money, but the awards were better than nothing.

Linda and I became close friends with Arthur Lambert, the president of the American Weekly Newspaper Association. Arthur was a scintillating, brilliant man, a charismatic speaker and leader. Only now do I know that he came from a famous rabbinical family that had escaped from Germany before the war. Part of the family remained in England; Arthur's branch found its way to America.

Arthur owned several newspapers near Binghamton, New York, and in the autumn of 1973 he invited us to visit his plant. We jumped at the opportunity to learn from a real pro whom we greatly admired. So Linda and I drove up to see him. He showed us around and then invited us home for coffee and cake. It was time for the six o'clock news, so he flicked on the television. All of a sudden he was crying. Riveted to the screen, he was watching news reports showing Israeli general Ariel Sharon's troops having crossed the Suez Canal, surrounding the Egyptian forces.

The Yom Kippur War!

With tears rolling down his cheeks, Arthur exclaimed: "What a miracle. Last week, Israel was finished. It was all over. And now, look at this. They have the Egyptians surrounded; they are marching on Amman; they are marching on Damascus. What a miracle!"

He looked around. He stared at me. My face was blank.

"There's a war? Oh yeah, I guess I saw something in the papers. . . ."

Suddenly, Arthur started to yell.

"You call yourself a Jew?"

(Hold on. This isn't fair. I never called myself a Jew in my life!)

"What's wrong with you? Don't you have a heart? Don't you have a soul? Are you made of stone? Don't you have any feelings? How could you not care what's going on? What kind of Jew are you anyway?"

What kind of Jew are you?

Wait a minute. What's going on here? How can he say that to me?

Those words kept echoing in my brain. They didn't go away. In fact, they are still echoing in my brain. *What kind of Jew are you?*

I began to wonder. Could that be the missing link?

No, it's *impossible.*

Our daughter Susan was five, and we were about to send her to first grade at Catholic school. Her best friend was named Theresa. Many of the Jews in Cornwall sent their children to the Bishop Dunne School.

The Jewish kids sat out in the hallway during religious instruction.

What's wrong with that? That's more than fair, isn't it? I think it's very tolerant of them. I hear it's a great education.

Very personalized instruction, and those nuns are extremely dedicated. We certainly wouldn't send our children to public school.

Susan was asking us these embarrassing questions, like "Who is G-d?" Ironically, with all my religious studies, I had never really thought about that. Who, actually, is G-d? What does G-d do? What does G-d want *me* to do?

Susan was also asking slightly impertinent questions like why we never invited her to our dinner parties. Who is she to be asking such questions? Adults like to have dinner parties and kids aren't invited. Isn't it obvious why adults have dinner parties? They sit around and eat and drink and talk about . . . actually why *do* adults have dinner parties? Come to think of it, I *hate* those stupid parties. I get so nervous with these people, and there really is nothing at all to talk about.

I began to have these crazy thoughts, like "Could Judaism be real?"

It always seems that the most obvious things take the longest time to dawn on you. We look for complicated things. I had written my book, and then I began to think: "You fool. You know all about Hinduism, Buddhism, Catholicism, and Protestantism. You 'wrote the book.' You 'proved' that Judaism is all wrong. There's only one problem: *You don't know the first thing about Judaism.*"

How much of a fool could I be? This was amazing. I had written a book "proving" the emptiness of the Jewish way of life, and yet I did not have a clue as to what the Jewish way of life is. When this began to dawn on me, I could not believe my incredible arrogance and stupidity.

The words of Arthur Lambert kept ringing in my ears: "Who are you? What kind of Jew are you?"

Susan kept asking those questions about G-d.

And I felt like the hypocrite of the ages, because I had written a book taking a strong stand on a subject I knew nothing about.

It didn't make sense.

About six months after the Arthur Lambert incident, I was having lunch with my friend Bob Ushman, one of the advertisers in my newspaper. Bob and his brother, Milton, owned the local hardware store. They were active in their synagogue in nearby Newburgh. I got an idea.

"Bob, I've never been in a synagogue in my life. Would you mind taking us some time? We'd like to see what it's like."

Bob called me that evening and, reading from the synagogue newsletter, told me that a lady named Rebbetzin Esther Jungreis was coming to speak the following week. The pamphlet described her as "the Jewish Billy Graham."

"'The Jewish Billy Graham,'" he said. "That sounds a little crazy. Do you want to go?"

The rest, as they say, is history.

▲▲▲

I want to point out the incredible workings of G-d.

How is it that Rebbetzin Jungreis was scheduled to be in Bob Ushman's synagogue on that day, at the exact time when, after thirty-one years of living on this earth, I was ready to come home to G-d?

I, this endlessly restless soul, had exhausted every option, and Linda was exhausted from living with me. I had opened every door in that long corridor. I was played out. I had no more excuses. My pride and defenses were broken. There was truly no door unopened except the door to

Torah. I couldn't say that the Jews had an empty religion, because I had just realized I didn't know what the Jews believed or how they lived. Besides, I had tried everything else. The only thing left was G-d and His Torah. At that very moment, at that very microsecond, Rebbetzin Jungreis was sent into our life.

I say "sent." It didn't just happen.

The Children of Israel left Egypt at precisely the last second. One more instant and assimilation would have swallowed us up forever; we would have been lost. At the exact bottom, G-d scooped us up and we were saved.*

At precisely the moment in my life when I was willing to say, "OK G-d, I give up. I am willing to admit I am a Jew. I am willing to put a *yarmulka* on my head. I am willing to walk into a synagogue," at precisely that moment G-d sent His angel to rescue me.

I wasn't a baby. We had lived around the world and attended the finest schools. We had heard what seemed like every point of view and had sought out wise people to guide us. No one had ever opened the Torah for us until we met Rebbetzin Jungreis. Everyone else had his individual viewpoint, his axe to grind, his "agenda." We had never before met anyone who had obliterated his or her ego in order to let Truth be transmitted.

There is no such thing as coincidence in this world.

Eight years earlier, I had cried in Ann Arbor, Michigan: "G-d, if You exist, please save me." I had begun to believe in G-d, but He didn't show me the Torah. Why? I had prayed from my heart. I was sincere. Why didn't He show me the Torah right away? It wasn't fair.

* This concept is explained by Rabbi Yitzchok Luria, also known as the "Arizal."

It is so clear to me now. Of course G-d didn't open up the Torah for me then. How could He when I was embracing idols? How could G-d open the Torah for me when I was opening Hindu, Buddhist, and Catholic books? I asked Him for help and then I turned my back. Oh no, He was waiting for *me*, waiting for me to show that I was sincere. If I had really meant it, then I would have run to the Torah just the way I did when I said to Bob Ushman, "Please take me to your synagogue." G-d was waiting for my heart.

I had to drain all the poison from my system before the pure water could enter.

The instant the poison was gone, the healing came. As we walked into the synagogue on that April evening in 1974, we heard the voice of Torah and our lives changed forever.

We had no idea what was coming. We walked in there as if we were going to the movies.

▲▲▲

This is the kitchen. Oh, two kitchens. Yes, we have heard about that custom. One for meat and one for dairy. People really do that? Very interesting.

And these are the classrooms? Very nice. It would be good to have some Jewish education for our children. We don't know anything! How much is membership? That sounds like quite a bit, but maybe it's worthwhile. We're also going to check out the Reform congregation. We hear they have a fabulous Hebrew school teacher.

People were laughing and talking. Everyone knew everyone else. It was sort of sociable. I joked around with some people I knew.

Hmmm. They belong to this synagogue? I wonder about that business deal I could never clinch with him. Now if we met here every week, we could sort of talk about it. That's pretty interesting.

The speaker's here? OK, let's go. Rebbetzin who? What's her name? What's a rebbetzin anyway? Hey, she's good-looking. I don't get it. I thought she's supposed to be Orthodox.

BOOM!

The world turned upside down.

This lady started to talk. She spoke so quietly, it was almost a whisper. All of a sudden, my insides were quivering. My soul—or whatever was in there—started shaking. My eyes were wet. Why was I crying? What's going on here? What is she talking about?

"You are a Jew. You have created civilizations. You have given birth to every ideal that has shaped mankind: Justice, peace, love, the dignity of man, have all had their genesis in Your Torah. But, above all, you have been given the unique mission of proclaiming the Oneness of G-d.

"You are a Jew. You have traveled the four corners of the earth. You have become a part of every people and yet you have remained a people apart. You have known every form of oppression. Your body has been scorched by fire. You are weary. Your spirits flag; your memory fails. You have forgotten your past. You cannot even recall your father's prayer.

"But there is one prayer, one little prayer, that you do remember, a prayer that has been a beacon of faith throughout the centuries of darkness, a prayer that has brought you back to the faith of your ancestors, a prayer that speaks of your own mission in life: 'Shema Yisroel . . . Hear, O Israel, the L-rd our G-d, the L-rd is One.'"

Hey, man. What's going on here? Why is she getting to me?

The words kept marching on, like battalions of little soldiers, each one entering my ears, my heart, my mind. In all my life, some thirty years of listening to teachers, clergymen, professors, wise men, doctors, lawyers, artists, and friends, I had never heard such words before. Even Arthur Lambert's cry, while it entered my mind, did not enter my heart. But these quiet words entered my heart and made me cry.

I was sobbing. I was ashamed, but I couldn't help it. It was too much for me. Why did these words affect me so much?

Since that nursery door had slammed and plunged me into darkness, I had always been afraid. I was afraid not of the darkness in the room; I was really afraid of the darkness in my heart. I thought to myself: maybe I am in essence dark and evil. Maybe I am going to go mad and be unable to control myself. I was so scared by that thought that I ran and ran and ran. And I couldn't tell anybody because it was so horrible that I couldn't even think about it. So I was alone in the universe with my horrible fears.

As I got older, I began to think differently. I thought like this: I am not in essence dark and evil. No, I think I am good. I *want* to be good. In fact, if I am in essence dark and evil, why am I afraid of being dark and evil? I would like it. So I must be basically good inside, but my goodness is so weak that it is subservient to the dark and evil force that won't let it prevail. The good is terrified of this monster and locked in by the forces of dark and evil within me. This scenario is actually more frightening, because I am forever a prisoner of "Mr. Hyde." Who is this dark and evil monster that has me trapped? I don't know, and for most of my life up to this point my mental processes revolved around trying to figure out who this dark, powerful force is and how to get away from him.

In the background there was a picture in my mind that somehow a human being could be a great person, living a noble life in a perfect world. That's one reason I sought out the wilderness. I was looking for the Garden of Eden. I was looking for something that had not been spoiled by man. I had a mental image of a man who always used clean and beautiful language, who lived a perfect, moral life in a beautiful, pristine world. Why did I admire Gandhi and Martin Luther King, Jr.? I felt there was spiritual reality and that somehow they were in touch with it. I didn't know any other way. I wanted to be like them, but I couldn't live as they did. Anyway, they were both murdered, so somehow they didn't fit into the world.

And now we were in this room and this lady was speaking. Her words were marching into my heart. She was small, but she dominated the room. Her soul glowed on her face. It was shining. She was very quiet, but she was full of emotion. And I realized that what she was saying were the very words that I had been saying deep inside myself all my life. That vision of greatness, that noble being had found his words:

"You are a Jew. You have created civilizations. You have given birth to every ideal that has shaped mankind: Justice, peace, love, the dignity of man, have all had their genesis in Your Torah. But above all, you have been given the unique mission of proclaiming the One-ness of G-d."

It was at that moment that I realized, *for the first time in my life*, that I was not alone. There were others who shared my vision. Perhaps that noble person in my soul did not have to be trapped forever by the forces of darkness. *Per-*

haps there was a way that good could really prevail in the real world. Gandhi and King were murdered, but perhaps there was something even greater, even higher, that could never be murdered, something so strong that the forces of evil couldn't even touch it.

Do you understand what was happening? From that day in the nursery until now I had been in mortal fear and darkness. All of a sudden these quiet, little words were entering my heart. This Rebbetzin was speaking and the sun began to shine for me, a sun that I knew could never be covered by clouds or go behind the horizon. OK, it would require work to achieve it, but the idea was that it could be done and that I was not the only person in the world who thought about these things. Other people also were struggling with dark forces and had found a way to make the light prevail.

Do you know what that means? If you have hope that goodness will prevail, then you can live. You can get through anything. If you think the opposite, then you will be depressed and never get out of bed; you are dead; you are finished.

Linda and I were too moved that evening to say anything to the Rebbetzin. We were so drenched in emotion and awestruck by truth that we couldn't speak.

You might have thought that Linda wouldn't have been so moved, because she hadn't been such a restless soul in the first place. But she was also crying.

As I said earlier, everyone has to approach G-d in his or her own way. Linda's way was calm, and she allowed me to do the thrashing around. But she was just as moved as I was when we arrived at the gate to the Garden of Eden. After all, we were traveling together, two different people who have joined to create one entity. That's what marriage is, and the cliché that "opposites attract" is true almost by definition. Marriage is the union of a man and a woman. If they were the same, it wouldn't be marriage. Just as they are physically "opposites" so they are spiritually opposites, but when you put the two together, they should form that united entity. They should complete each other. We were arriving together.

I also want to clarify something else.

From what you've read up to now, you might think that in our relationship I had no redeeming qualities. I was the restless, searching soul and Linda was the calm, peaceful soul. That may be close to the truth, but there was at least one way I could help her.

There is a certain danger in being good. Good people tend to be innocent. They tend to feel that the entire world is good, because they can't even imagine anything that's not good. They can't imagine people who are not good. As a result, they are sometimes taken advantage of, victimized by their own innocence.

Linda wrote an essay in elementary school called "Journey to a Dreamland Paradise," which we always joked about. I told her that she sometimes thinks the entire world is a dreamland paradise, because it doesn't come into her head that people could be mean.

What happens in a case like that is very subtle, but innocent people can be corrupted precisely because they are so innocent. They are not looking. The train can hit you if you are looking the other way.

I had lived with conflict all my life. I had a brain that was never at rest. I saw all kinds of evil in the world and it frightened me, because I thought maybe it was inside me. I was always on the lookout for evil.

I was able to protect Linda. I was able to show her when she was in danger.

The problem with a dreamland paradise is that it's only a dream. If you really want to get back to the Garden of Eden, you've got to go past the flashing swords that were posted at the entrance when we got kicked out in the beginning of time.* As King David says, "Though I walk in the valley overshadowed by death, I will fear no evil, for You are with me."** Once you're out of the Garden and death has been introduced into the world, then you've got to go through the valley of death to get back into the garden. There's no other way. And there's no other way, in my experience, to get through that valley of death unless "You are with me," unless you are holding onto G-d very tight.

So I was able to help Linda and she was able to help me, and that, I think, is what marriage is all about.

We bought a record of the Rebbetzin's Madison Square Garden "event" of a few months earlier and then staggered away. It says in the Talmud*** that G-d lifted Mount Sinai over the heads of the Jews. We felt that night as if Mount Sinai was resting on our heads.

Sometimes you meet a person and you know that "this is it." Sometimes you hear certain words and they resonate in your soul. The Children of Israel said in the desert, "Na-aseh v-nishma . . . We will do and then we will learn."**** We said in our hearts that night, "We will do and then we will learn," because we knew it was right. It wasn't just that a lifetime of experimentation had preceded this event.

---

* Genesis 3:24
** Psalm 23
*** Talmud, tractate *Shabbos* 88a, quoted by Rashi on Exodus 19:17
**** Exodus 24:7

That was part of it. The other part is described in the Talmud: every Jew is instructed in his mother's womb by an angel, who teaches him the entire Torah.* But when he is born, he forgets everything he learned.

Why does he learn and then have to forget? Well, these are deep concepts, but one thing is clear: Torah sticks inside us forever, and when we hear it again, we recognize it. "*Hey, I know that from somewhere.*" This is the ultimate déjà vu.

If we hadn't forgotten it, then we wouldn't be able to discover it for ourselves.

But if we hadn't learned it originally, then we wouldn't know what it is when we discover it.

That is the purpose of our lives: to rediscover what the angel taught us in the womb.

When Rebbetzin Jungreis was speaking those holy words, Linda and I recognized them from the time the angel taught us in the womb. That is how we knew they were true.

▲▲▲

We listened to that Madison Square Garden record many times. That had been the "official" beginning of the Rebbetzin's Hineni organization, a "happening" in November 1973 at which thousands of unaffiliated Jewish kids were invited to join a "voyage of spiritual discovery." They came by the thousands and were turned on by Torah.

I wrote to the Rebbetzin.

"If what you say is true, then there must be a next step. Please tell us what it is."

The Rebbetzin wrote back: "You must attend Torah classes on a regular basis."

---

* Talmud, tractate *Niddah* 30b

At that time the Rebbetzin was teaching every Tuesday evening in a little room in a Sefardic synagogue on Ocean Parkway in Brooklyn. This synagogue was two hours away from our home. It was spring 1974. The Arab oil embargo was in full swing and you had to wait in line for gas, sometimes for a half-hour—that is, if you could get it at all. How could we possibly get there?

In addition, my weekly newspaper came out on Wednesdays, and I usually stayed up all night Tuesday putting it together. There was no way we could carve out a big chunk of Tuesday to go to Brooklyn.

So forget it, right?

HOW COULD WE FORGET IT?

"If I forget you . . . Jerusalem, may my right hand forget its skill."*

Oh no, this floated above Arab oil and was more important than all the newspapers in the world. This was life itself, the voice of G-d's Torah calling to us. *Not to go would be death*, and we knew it.

We realized that we had no choice but to go. Our life had to fit around it.

So we changed our schedule. I began to get up at 2:00 A.M. on Tuesdays. By 5:00 P.M. I would be finished with the paper. Then Linda would pick me up and we would use our precious allotment of gas to travel to Brooklyn.

This was so exciting. It became like our Shabbos, the holy Sabbath. Half the week we would live on the pleasure from it, and half the week we would look forward to it. It became the anchor for our lives. The healing words of Torah began to flow into our souls. The words we had

---

* Psalm 137

learned from the angel were coming back to us. They were sustaining us.

One week became two weeks, then a month, then two months. Something was happening to our lives.

G-d told the prophet, "Prophesy over these bones! Say to them, 'Oh dry bones, hear the word of Hashem!' So I prophesied as I had been commanded. There was a sound as I was prophesying. Then behold, there was a noise, and the bones drew near, each bone to its matching bone. Then . . . the spirit entered them and they came to life. They stood upon their feet. . . ."*

We stood upon our feet. We, who had been dry bones, were coming to life. Every Tuesday night, as we drove home, we were exhilarated by the new Torah we had learned. The day-to-day events, the newspaper and all our other activities, started to fade into the background as a great new reality and hope began to dawn upon us.

In the beginning, the Torah class was just words, but each week the words begged more and more to be put into action. Learning Torah was not like learning biology or history. That stayed in a notebook and possibly became the basis for a career, but it did not enter your soul. Torah begged to be translated into action.

About the third week, we brought our friends, the Presbyterian minister from Cornwall and his wife, to Hineni. We knew them socially, just the way we knew many people in Cornwall, Jew and non-Jew. They were very interested, inspired, and impressed by the Rebbetzin, but that's where it stopped. It reinforced their notion that the Jewish people were special. But for us, it did not stop. We had to find a way to translate these words into action, action that would

---

* Ezekiel 37:4–10

change our lives. As with a pregnant lady in her ninth month, something was getting ready to pop. We needed a catalyst.

▲▲▲

Late one night the phone rang at the Rebbetzin's house. It was a call from "Israel." Assuming her son Yisroel was calling from his *yeshiva* in Brooklyn, she picked up the phone. On the other end, speaking from Jerusalem, was an army officer.

The Israeli consul general, Shlomo Levine, had heard the Rebbetzin speak at Madison Square Garden. He was deeply moved and had spoken to the army commanders. They wanted the Rebbetzin to speak to the soldiers, to give them strength. At first she had said no, reasoning, "Who am I, an American, to go to Israel and speak to the soldiers?"

But they kept asking, and the phone call from Jerusalem clinched it.

In late May 1974 the Rebbetzin took a small group with her to Israel.

We had never been interested in going to Israel. I had always believed the Jews had stolen the land from the Arabs and had no right to live there.

Now everything had changed. I had heard the voice of Torah, the voice which proclaims that G-d Who created and sustains the world had given us this land as an eternal inheritance. Now we understood. We weren't embarrassed anymore. We wanted to visit our Holy Land.

Zayda, the Rebbetzin's father, used to say that the word "Israel" has a special meaning even in English. It tells you that Israel "is real." When you go to the Holy Land and you see the Western Wall, the Tomb of our Patriarchs and Matriarchs in Chevron (Hebron), the grave of Mama Rachel in Bays Lechem* (Bethlehem), the graves of our ancestors and sages, the places where Biblical events took place, you know it is all real. *Israel "is real"!*

We arranged for the staff to take over the paper. It wasn't easy. I had never taken a vacation since we bought the paper. There was a lot of grumbling. Nobody thought they could do it. But as with the original decision to attend the Rebbetzin's classes, this was clearly a matter of life and death. We *had* to go to Israel. We had to *live* the Torah, not just talk about it. The time was now, and we could not wait another minute.

Linda's mother came to stay with the children. By now, there was not only Susan but also Juliet, two years younger. It was all very complicated. What would Linda's mother do if this or that happened and we were eight thousand miles away? Good questions, and they had to be worked out. But we had to go. Nothing could stop us.

"Oh dry bones, hear the word of Hashem!"

▲▲▲

When we arrived at Kennedy Airport, we were buzzing with excitement. Zayda and Mama (the Rebbetzin's mother) were there to see us off. Mama, as always, had been hard at work. For weeks she had been making Hineni *yarmulkas* for the soldiers. All the soldiers in Israel, it seemed! Leave it to Mama! We were shlepping thousands of Hineni *yarmulkas* to Israel. The Rebbetzin handed me one. I put it in my pocket.

---

* I am using the Hebrew name here because the name Bethlehem is so well known in the Western world that it threatens to obscure the eternal Jewish identity of this town.

"Oh no . . . it goes on your head."

Am I really going to do this?

For the next two weeks I lived like a Jew.

The plane took off and we were on our way. Little did we know what was in store for us.

I dozed off. About five hours later, somewhere over the Atlantic or western Europe, the sky began to get light. I heard noises and opened my eyes. *"Hey, what are these guys doing?"* I saw men walking very determinedly toward the back of the plane. They were taking big black-and-white striped shawls out of cloth bags and putting them over their heads.

"Uh oh, what's going on?"

And then they had these little bags. Out of each bag came two little boxes. And each man was tying a box on his arm with a strap. And then he put another little box in the middle of his forehead, fastening *that* with a strap.

Where am I? Did we land on Mars?

What are these men doing?

Oh G-d, there was so much we didn't know!

For the next two weeks Linda and I had our own voyage of spiritual discovery.

We experienced the first Shabbos of our lives in Kibbutz Lavi, a religious settlement overlooking the Sea of Galilee and the city of Tiberias.

How can I describe this to you? For the first time in thirty-one years I could breathe. In all our years we had never had a moment of peace, a moment when our souls felt at rest. Life had been a nonstop treadmill. Do you think we knew why we were running every minute? We asked ourselves, but we were too busy to wait for the answer. We had been running through life so fast that we had absolutely no idea why or where we were running. Maybe we had just been running "away." But we didn't even know what we had been running away from. We had just kept running.

All of a sudden, this Friday night, as the sun sank below the Mediterranean Sea, the treadmill stopped and we got off. We breathed. We had nothing to do. The world stopped. Everything was quiet. We looked around.

"The bones drew near, each bone to its matching bone. Then . . . the spirit entered them and they came to life."

Our souls had finally found rest in this world, the peace of Shabbos, when the noise and grit is shut off for a full day and a Jew is free to spend his time with G-d and his family, reconnecting with the world of Truth.

Shabbos showed us that there is freedom from slavery.

Linda and I wandered through the beautiful grounds of Kibbutz Lavi. Spring flowers bloomed on every side. All we heard was birds singing and the holy breeze of Israel rustling the young leaves. There were no machines to mar this tranquility. Standing on the hills high above the Sea of Galilee, we could see the Golan Heights. All was peaceful. Only a few months earlier this entire area had been a major battleground in the Yom Kippur War. The words of the psalm came to mind: *Let a thousand [enemies] encamp at your side and a myriad at your right hand, but to you they shall not approach. You will merely peer with your eyes . . .** War seemed so far away on that beautiful day that brought peace to our souls. I felt that it was a sign of things to come: somehow here was a way in which we could really end all war and heal the world.

Picketing Woolworth's was not going to do it. The Peace

---

* Psalm 91, said at the end of Shabbos.

movement and the Civil Rights movement and the mimeograph machine in Tom Hayden's basement at the University of Michigan were not going to do it. Living in the wilderness and singing folk music were not going to do it. The shrink was not going to help.

Shabbos was going to do it. The Jewish people were going to bring peace to the world by coming home to Torah.

▲▲▲

The previous night, after ushering in the holy Shabbos, I strolled on the beautiful kibbutz grounds with Rabbi Jacob Jungreis, the Rebbetzin's brother.*

"I know why you came back to Torah," Rabbi Jacob told me. "Your *zayda*,** Rabbi Yisroel Salanter, had no peace in the World of Truth because his grandchild was running away from G-d. It is in the merit of your holy ancestor that you returned. He has been beseeching G-d to bring you home."

That is why, after we returned to New York and began our new life, the Rebbetzin's father gave me the Hebrew name Yisroel (Israel).

After our beautiful Shabbos at Kibbutz Lavi the next stop was Jerusalem, where the Rebbetzin had another eye-opener for us. She introduced Linda to the life-changing experience of immersion in the *mikveh*.

We had been married eleven years. We knew we were "destined" for each other, but that's not enough to make marriage work. There are so many stumbling blocks in ev-

---

* The Rebbetzin is a Jungreis by birth as well as marriage. Her late husband was a cousin with the same last name.

** The term *zayda* can also be used in the sense of "ancestor" in general. Rabbi Yisroel Salanter was not literally my *zayda*.

ery relationship, most of all marriage. When you don't walk with G-d, you stumble and you can't get up. When you walk with G-d, you're still human, so you may stumble, but He *lifts* you up.

Before a Jewish woman goes under the *chupa*, and then every month of her childbearing years, she immerses herself in the waters of the *mikveh*. This is not a bath—in fact, she must bathe *before* she enters the *mikveh*—it is a spiritual cleansing, a bath for the soul. Her soul is actually reborn, because the *mikveh* is like the waters of her mother's womb, and she emerges as a newborn person, free of sin and ready to start a new life. That is why bride and groom fast before their wedding. It is like Yom Kippur; they are cleansed of sin.

Linda and I needed to be purified from the stains we had picked up in our journey through life. We needed to know that we had pure souls and *could* walk with G-d from that point on. We needed to know that marriage could be holy and that we need not be afraid.

The *mikveh* was our first step into the sanctity of Jewish marriage.

The ladies who supervised the *mikveh* in Jerusalem were weeping as the Rebbetzin brought this young lady of thirty to the purifying waters for the first time. Now the Rebbetzin was showing us the secret of Jewish marriage, the secret of bringing G-d into our home. It all started with holy, pure water.

In Jerusalem, on the second Shabbos of our lives, I was given an honor in synagogue. Here's how it works. In the Ashkenazic tradition,* the Torah scroll is first taken out of the ark and then placed on a table where the *baal koray*,

---

* Sefardim raise the Torah *before* they read it; Ashkenazim raise it afterwards.

a person specially trained to read the Torah, reads that day's portion. Afterwards someone is given the honor of lifting the Torah and turning it in every direction while holding it open so everyone in the synagogue can see the words. Then he sits down, holding the Torah open, and another man turns the two scrolls until they close tight. He then ties the Torah closed with a *gartel*, a special belt, and places the covering, usually including a cloth mantle and a silver crown, on top. The last honor is called *galila*, and that is what I was given.

When I was asked to take this honor, I had no idea what was coming. I was shaking with nervousness. I thought, "Maybe they want me to recite a half-hour sermon in Hebrew." I was going to run for my life. Soon a friend came over and calmed me down. He stayed with me every step, and I found that it was not hard. Many new things are this way. In anticipation they look like climbing Mount Everest, or maybe *jumping off* Mount Everest! When you actually do them, you find that you had nothing to fear. In a way, the whole Torah lifestyle is like that. Before you live it, you think of it as weird and alien. When you live it, you find that you have come home to the most familiar place in the world.

We visited the holy places, the Western Wall, the graves of our Patriarchs and Matriarchs in Hebron and the grave of Mama Rachel in Bays Lechem. We were "introduced" to our ancestors, whose presence is felt in the very air of Israel. We learned how to connect our souls to G-d. We toured army bases with the Rebbetzin and observed how Jewish people all over the world are hungry and thirsty for the word of G-d.

I remember an army base high in the mountains west

of the Dead Sea. Just to get there, we had to take hidden roads through steep passes in army jeeps. The base commanded a tremendous view of Jordan to the east. It was night. The soldiers were watching the borders of the Holy Land. As we watched with them, the moon illuminating the hills across the Dead Sea was reflected in the shimmering waters below us. It was a sight we will never forget.

That night the Rebbetzin spoke to the young soldiers about war and their mission as Jews. Their faces reflected the gravity of the responsibility upon their shoulders. But the Rebbetzin told them not to be afraid. *"Some [go] with chariots, and some with horses, but we [go] in the name of Hashem, our G-d."** The soldiers, beautiful Jewish children, were crying.

Later that week, the Rebbetzin spoke at an air force base with a young Yemenite captain. He told the story of his family. When his grandfather was a young man in the 1920s, he began to hear about stirrings in the Land of Israel, then called Palestine. Incredibly, he took his family, *on foot*, with a few camels and donkeys, across the desert. The pilgrimage took months. How did they make it? They brought with them a Torah scroll and one prayer book. Each member of the family had an assigned position around the book. Thus, one person learned to read from the right side and one from the left. One could read only upside down, because his position was at the top of the book. Somehow, they got across the desert and arrived in the Promised Land.

Today, the grandson flew over the desert beyond the speed of sound. But he still read from that old Torah.

Then it was our turn to fly. After two weeks of total

---

* Psalm 20

immersion in the Ocean of Torah, we returned to America. Early on a June morning, we arrived at Kennedy Airport. There was Zayda, waiting to greet us with his reassuring smile and long white beard. We loaded our baggage in the car and waved goodbye. Zayda waved back. As his beautiful face faded into the distance, we returned to Cornwall, to our old life, and to our children, one of whom was about to be enrolled in Catholic school. We returned to everything we had left behind.

Cornwall looked strange. We had new eyes. Our former life had disappeared. In Israel, a new reality had entered our souls. We looked at each other. The decision was clear. We would leave. Immediately. There was not a moment to lose.

▲▲▲

We decided to put our home and business on the market and move to the Rebbetzin's community on Long Island. My father would later criticize me for being too anxious to sell the business, and—from a financial point of view—he was correct. But we were so anxious to start our new life that we could not abide another moment in the old one. Somehow, I told myself, everything would work out. My guts told me that G-d would help us. The main thing was that we knew we had in the Rebbetzin a trustworthy guide. We would follow the Torah that she taught us.

In the ensuing days one event followed another at blinding speed. First, we had to speak to our parents. Linda and I went to meet them at Florival Farm. It was a Sunday in June, just after our return from Israel.

They had raised us to follow the Ethical approach, just

as *they* had been raised. All four of our parents had been very tolerant of our previous "adventures," but those adventures had always been within the limits of the liberal way of life we had been brought up with. In other words, if either of us had chosen to go out with a non-Jew, no one would have objected. No one asked where we were going on a date or how long we were staying out. Before we were married, we could have gone away together and no questions would have been asked. This was the way our crowd lived. After we were married, when we studied Eastern or Western religions, the "Ethical view" accepted it as part of a sophisticated way of life. Trips to shrines in Europe were part of one's education. It was normal to spend weeks in Florence and eat at Maxim's in Paris.

But now, we were desperate for a way of life that could satisfy our souls. In the words of the prophet Amos, "Behold, days are coming . . . when I will send hunger into the land; not a hunger for bread nor a thirst for water, but to hear the words of Hashem."*

This was not going to be another European idyll. We were going to step off the merry-go-round and leave the amusement park altogether. We were going to abandon the way of life all of us had known exclusively since we were born. We intended to move to a community where we could be close to our spiritual mentor and become Torah-observant Jews.

Were we entering a cult? These were tumultuous times; many children were being victimized by charlatans. The Rebbetzin was constantly pulling Jewish children out of these deadly fires.

---

* Amos 8:11

For our parents all this was a little scary. Even though they had half-expected it after the trip to Israel, it was a lot for them to grasp. Actually, it was a lot *for us* to grasp.

I think what held things together was the fact that they really trusted our character. They felt that, while perhaps we were somewhat naïve, we were serious and responsible about life. It is a tribute to them that they were able to accept and later even to support the change in our life, even though it was so alien to them. But after all, Mother was a child of Yisroel Salanter, and every Jew who is alive today comes from ancestors who, over our two thousand years of exile, followed the Torah even at the risk of their lives. All Jews come from holy ancestors who have passed on to their descendants sparks of Torah clarity that can survive the blinding fog of assimilation. *We have all been instructed by that angel in the womb.* If we will it, we can remember that Torah and survive.

There was also something in our parents' characters that gave us the inspiration for this change, for they in their own way were people who had not been afraid to re-assess their lives.

I have always been inspired by the story of my father's early years. He was an orphan at the age of twelve and went to live with his older sister. His passion as a young man had been tennis. He was not interested in academic pursuits, and he dropped out of New York University to work for B. Altman & Co., then New York's largest and most elegant department store. He started on the loading dock and soon became a fabric buyer. He was very successful, but he had a romantic heart and wanted most of all to be an artist. With an inheritance from his father that enabled him to be somewhat independent, he left

B. Altman—despite the president's offer to double his salary —to pursue his dream in Paris.

He stayed in Paris for four years. What impresses me is not only that he made a passionate attempt to live a life that matched his talents, but that he had the courage to recognize what he was good at and what he was not good at. To be specific, he found that he simply did not have the talent to be a painter. A person of less integrity would have kept on trying and ended up being a mediocre artist. My father was not content with mediocrity, so he disciplined himself to confront his strengths and weaknesses.

The Torah world calls this a *din v'cheshbon*, a calculation of our *mitzvos* and sins, successes and failures, strengths and weaknesses. From that ongoing calculation we are supposed to refine our existence continually to an ever higher level.

Our Father Jacob blessed two of his two sons,* Yissachar and Zevulun, in accordance with their abilities. They formed a "partnership." They both knew that the Jew is placed in this world to learn and teach Torah. But Zevulun's talent lay in commerce, Yissachar's in Torah study. Zevulun acknowledged this fact by entering into a pact with his brother to support him materially. The benefit of Yissachar's learning is shared by the two brothers, both in this world and the next. But Yissachar could not have devoted his life to learning if his brother had not provided his material support in this world. Such is a true partnership.

A good marriage is based on the same concept. G-d creates each spouse with certain abilities and weaknesses. It's up to each to maximize the opportunities presented by their respective characters.

---

* Genesis 49:13-15

Rebbetzin Jungreis frequently cites examples of how a person can utilize his talents to the highest degree. Many people, for example, feel faint at the sight of blood, but there are some who don't flinch at all. Such people could become violent criminals who don't hesitate to kill. Or they could become surgeons who save lives. The choice is theirs.

Zayda gave the example of a thief. Either he could steal from others for his own use, or he could steal from himself for the benefit of others. How do you steal from yourself? You "steal" your own money that you would prefer to spend on yourself and give it to charity. You "steal" your time and give to others. If you feel depressed, you steal that *farbissener* face from yourself and put on a smile.

My father was a natural businessman. He also had a great eye for art. In Paris, he got a job selling antiques, and soon the owner of the store could retire because my father brought in so much business. Yet his abilities as a painter were meager. He decided at that moment not to give up on art, but to approach it in the way in which he could be a big success.

He decided to use his eye and business abilities to support artists who *did* have talent. In other words, he maximized his strengths and minimized his weaknesses, never giving up on his dreams. He succeeded beyond anything he could have imagined.

Isn't that amazing? It is a lesson for all of us.

In 1929, about six months before the stock market crash, Dad returned to America determined to go into Wall Street, because "that's where the money was." He went into Wall Street with an altruistic motive, and that is why, in my view, he was uniquely successful. His success was not only financial. The firm he and Robert Berman founded ten years later (my mother was also an initial partner) became a model not only of high-class money management but of tremendous integrity. That is perhaps what set it apart from other successful investment houses. Its reputation for integrity formed the foundation for its transition into a respected financial institution.

My father had the foresight and wisdom, because of his altruistic approach, to bring in talented partners, giving them enough of the business to make it worth their while. If he had been shortsighted and selfish, Neuberger Berman would have remained a two-man shop and nobody would have heard about it. My father was willing to slice the cake generously so that talented partners would be attracted to the firm. The reward for his wisdom was that most precious of assets, a good name.

*"A good name is more precious than good oil."**

Do you realize how rare this quality is? In order to see what is really beneficial, one must look beyond the desire for immediate gratification and see the results of one's actions in the future. My father realized that he lacked artistic talent but possessed business talent. He used his business talent to pursue his dream. He purchased the works of living artists and became among the first patrons to recognize the talent of many painters who later became very famous. He did not sell the art he bought, but rather donated it to museums so that others could enjoy it. He followed through on his dream. As Zayda, the Rebbetzin's father, would have put it, he "stole" from himself to give to others.

This is a tremendous lesson for every person, and I think it gave courage to Linda and me to pursue our dream of finding

---

* Ecclesiastes 7:1

our place in the world without compromising our perception of truth. Dad could not say, when we informed him and my mother of our plans, that one should not follow one's dream in life. He himself had inspired us to follow the dream.

My mother also influenced our return to Torah, but from a completely different angle. Mother was more of an analytical thinker, a quality she inherited from her father and her *zayda*, Rabbi Yisroel Salanter. She pondered hard on whether her own actions fit in with the ethical framework she knew exists in the world. She could be ruthlessly critical of herself, and I inherited that self-analytical attitude. My parents' influences—the analytical approach of my mother combined with the intuitive approach of my father—together formed the basis for the relentless drive I felt toward finding G-d.

Linda's parents were obviously also surprised by our decision.

There had always been a little more Jewish tradition in her family than in mine. We had absolutely no tradition. The Villencys had an echo.

We used to go to her relatives' house for Passover, but it meant nothing to us. It was like a family meal with matzos instead of bread. People were reading some book out loud, but nobody paid any attention to it.

In my opinion, an experience like that is worse than not having Passover at all. If you don't have it, at least you know you don't have it. But if you have something that is supposed to be Passover and it's not, then you think you know what Passover is and you reject it because it is meaningless to you.

In the same way, Linda used to stay home from elementary school on Yom Kippur. She didn't go to synagogue and she didn't refrain from any food, but she stayed home. I, on the other hand, went to school on Yom Kippur as if it were a normal day. I had no idea what it was. Of course Linda didn't either, but maybe she thought she did since she at least altered her regular program.

In any case, we had decided to go the whole way, and our parents realized that the tide carrying us along to a new life was unstoppable. They were somewhat apprehensive, yet they had raised us to live as we pleased, and now they were, in effect, reaping what they had sown. None of us had anticipated that it would turn out this way, but we were learning that life contains many surprises. Perhaps the most amazing thing is that sometimes those surprises can be pleasant.

▲▲▲

Our parents came to meet the Rebbetzin at a Torah class in Brooklyn. That itself was a big step. They were surprised by her warmth. The way I grew up, people didn't embrace each other freely. There was a touch of Victorian formality in our lives. In the world of religious Jews, it is not unusual for women to greet women warmly and men to greet men.

Later, as our parents and the Rebbetzin met on more and more occasions, a great respect developed. The Rebbetzin has always stressed the importance of the commandment to honor one's parents, demonstrating it for us by example in the way she treated her own parents. Over the years, our parents saw that our way of life was solid and stable. As our children grew, our parents saw the beautiful character traits they developed. This was the most graphic demonstration to them of the correctness of our decision and our way of life.

In addition, the Rebbetzin's husband helped so much.

His warmth charmed everyone who met him. He would always be sure to stop by when our parents were visiting our home, and they came to love him.

The Rabbi was the child of a different world, a man who at the age of seventeen had been torn from his own parents and enslaved by Hitler, never again to see his family, almost all of whom were killed in the Holocaust. He came alone to America, unable to speak the language. But despite these terrible burdens, he never complained, and his smile was so strong that it melted all obstacles and enabled him to communicate lovingly with all he met.

Of course, when our daughter Yaffa (formerly Juliet) married the Rabbi and Rebbetzin's son, Rabbi Osher Anshul, the relationship became much more than just the meeting of strangers from two different worlds. By then our parents knew that there was nothing to worry about.

▲▲▲

During that tumultuous summer of 1974, we had to make many practical arrangements, like selling a business and finding a new job, selling a house and finding another. We were hungry to jump into our new life. After all, we were not just moving physically. We weren't going to dip our toes into Torah, we were going to plunge all the way in. Our children didn't just switch schools and friends; they switched planets. Do you understand the transition from "Bishop Dunne Parochial School" to "Torah Academy for Girls"? It's mind-boggling. That perhaps is one reason we wanted to rush it, so we would not have to think too much about the chasm we were leaping over.

Amazingly enough, in just one day we located a house one block from Rabbi Jungreis's synagogue and just down the street from the Rabbi and Rebbetzin's home in our new community. Through a college friend, I was able to get a job as an editor on *The Long Island Press*, a large afternoon daily paper. It was very different from operating *The Cornwall Local*, but by then I didn't have the time to run my own business. I had to learn to be a Jew.

When we left Cornwall, the reactions of our friends were revealing. The Gentiles were almost universally supportive. They thought we were doing the most amazing thing. We were following our destiny and returning to G-d. They had only praise and blessings for us. Possibly, there was some pretense to this. Some people may have wanted that "Jewish editor" out of town. I hadn't cared about being Jewish at the time, but "they" cared. I had received threats in Cornwall over the years. They had escalated to the point that the local police chief and I once had a talk with the FBI. But whatever their motive, the non-Jews gave us generous blessings when we left.

On the other hand, the Jews, with the exception of a few like Bob Ushman, were appalled. They basically suggested that we could benefit from psychiatric help. Such is the reaction of a Jew who rebels against the heritage of his fathers to such an extent that he can regard a returning Jew only as a deviant. Had his own father been a deviant? His grandfather? His great-grandfather? If you go back far enough, we all get to our father Abraham. Well, says the modern Jew, the world has changed. It's now the twenty-first century and he wants to prove that he has no medieval prejudices. If we were normal, then he was abnormal. So most of our Jewish neighbors labeled (or should I say "libeled") us "abnormal."

But we couldn't stop to worry about what these people

said. We had to take responsibility for our lives and the lives of our children. We had found G-d. He had rescued us from the stormy sea in which we had been drowning. He had sent His emissary, Rebbetzin Esther Jungreis, in a Torah lifeboat, and we were now sailing for home, comfort, and safety, toward a life of stability, structure, and hope.

We moved to North Woodmere, Long Island, a few weeks before Rosh Hashana 1974, at the beginning of the Jewish year 5735. It was indeed a new year, a new world, a new life. Our children attended new schools, Jewish schools. Can you imagine: Susan had to learn *aleph bays*, the Hebrew alphabet, which her peers had learned as toddlers. (Years later, she graduated at the top of her class.)

We also had to learn *aleph bays*. We had to receive Hebrew names. I had to receive a *bris*. (Although I had received a medical circumcision as an infant, this is not a *bris*. I had not been officially welcomed as a child of Abraham.) Linda and I had to get *really married*. She had been to the *mikveh*. Now we had to have a *chupa*, a Jewish marriage ceremony, and I had to give her a *kesuba*, a marriage contract. Without all these fundamentals, how could we have expected marriage to work?

We had to learn to incorporate the entire Torah into our life. This is the constant challenge faced by every Jew, but usually not starting at the age of thirty-one! With G-d's help, we are still working on it, every day, every minute, every second. It is a fascinating story, with many miracles from G-d to help us along. That is the story I will endeavor to tell you, my dear reader, in the pages that lie ahead.

CHAPTER THREE

A NEW LIFE

W HEN WE MOVED to North Woodmere, we didn't know the first thing about a Jewish life except that it was right for us. We were plunging in the same way little kids jump into a swimming pool. Sometimes they forget to think about whether they know how to swim. G-d, His angels, the Rebbetzin, the Rabbi all were standing by the side of our swimming hole, teaching us to swim and ready to pull us out if we started going under.

"Susan" and "Juliet," of course, also knew nothing. Their *yeshiva* classmates, even though only in preschool or first grade, were already well versed in Hebrew letters, holidays, and many other facets of Jewish life that these bright children had absorbed from their families and teachers since birth. Many of their parents were rabbis and teachers.

But Hashem was infinitely kind to us. We had been rescued not a second too soon.

Susan was five when we moved. You say that is young? Just a little girl, right?

We learned that personality is formed very young. By now, she has done a remarkable job and is a mother in her own right, but she struggled in those early years. She was pulled out of a whole world of friends and had to reorient and reeducate herself in an instant. For an adult who makes the decision, it is one thing, but Susan was not an adult at the time. Even her name was changed. Overnight her world was turned upside down. (Or should I say, "right side up"?)

For Juliet it was a little easier. She was three. Those two years made a difference. But every good thing in life is a struggle.

Both girls made the transition like the heroes they are. They are Jews, after all. Their *neshomos*—souls—were *also* starved for Torah. Once they were settled in our new life, they thrived and quickly caught up with their new friends. They became leaders in their classes, and today they teach others.

The Rebbetzin's late husband, our Rabbi, taught us *aleph bays*. We were like nursery school children. I have to this day the audiotape the Rabbi made for us in which he sings the entire *Haggadah*, the text for the Passover *Seder*. I listened to that tape literally dozens of times, singing along. That is how I learned to make a *Seder*. The Rabbi also put on tape for us the High Holiday services, so that we could familiarize ourselves with them beforehand. Do you realize what an investment of time that took for a busy man? And he had only just met us.

We all needed Jewish names. We had been Roy and Linda, the children Susan and Juliet. Zayda gave us all names. I became "Yisroel," named after my ancestor, the holy sage Rabbi Yisroel Salanter.

Linda became "Leah," Susan became "Sarah," and Juliet became "Yaffa." It is explained in our holy writings* that

---

* *Midrash Tanchuma, Haazinu 7*

our essence is described by our Jewish names. It changed our lives to use these holy names and realize that they reflected who we really are.

Then there was Shabbos.

Just hearing that word gave us hope. That first Shabbos at Kibbutz Lavi liberated us from slavery to the daily grind of life. Before we left Cornwall, Susan would ask us why the family never used the good china and silver and never sat down together in the dining room.

"That is only for special parties," we told her.

What an answer. Our children weren't special? Our family wasn't special? Who, then, was special? Some half-strangers who sat around and groped for conversation?

Now, every Friday night, we began a *really* special party. Our children were the featured guests. Our friends who shared Shabbos with us became part of our family. And every week the beautiful and pure Shabbos Queen joined us, along with her retinue of shining angels. She stayed with us for over twenty-four hours, and on Saturday night we were reluctant to bid her farewell, so we lit another candle and she tarried a while longer.

Instead of groping for conversation, instead of turning on the television or opening the newspaper, instead of going to the movies or the mall or in countless different directions, we turned to G-d. We discussed pure and elevating Torah thoughts. We sang ancient songs praising the holiness of Shabbos, and we got to know each other.

Linda tells me that sometimes preparing menus and cooking food for a party can be tedious, complicated, and difficult. But she loved to cook for Shabbos. It was no chore for her, even though we often had a house full of guests. She felt as if there was nothing she was missing out on or would rather do. Cooking for Shabbos was not just preparing food, it was elevating the preparation of food to the service of G-d.

Not only did she prepare the food every week, but she reminded me to prepare also. What was my job? To prepare *spiritual* sustenance. Part of the joy of sitting around the Shabbos table is the beautiful Torah thoughts that are expressed. And, like anything important, those thoughts had to be prepared in advance. Whenever I would drive somewhere on Friday, I tried to use the time just to think about that week's Torah portion and plan out what I was going to say at the Shabbos table. That became one of my favorite moments, because even the preparation felt like part of Shabbos. When else did we get to speak to the children without pressure, without deadlines? On Shabbos we didn't watch the clock. In fact, after hours at the table, it often seemed as if time had ceased to exist. I once heard a beautiful thought: just as the Land of Israel represents the sanctity of space, so Shabbos represents the sanctity of time. Israel is a holy land, a land created as a place to keep the Torah and become an earthly interface with the heavenly kingdom. Shabbos is a holy time, a time created to be an earthly interface with the heavenly kingdom.

Out came the best silver, beautiful china plates, and sparkling glasses. The wine flowed—and so did the blessings. The food nourished our souls as well as our bodies. Sarah didn't need to ask those questions anymore.

When I was a little boy, we would get bread delivered every week that we called "Friday bread," a braided loaf with a golden crust. We didn't order it because of Shabbos; we didn't know about Shabbos. We ordered it because it was good. It happened to be available only on Friday.

Now, every Friday night, we ate warm *challah*, fresh from the oven. And just the way the *challah* was braided, so the family was braided together by Shabbos.

The nourishment remained with us for three days after Shabbos, and then—the last three days of the week—our appetite returned and we were hungry for Shabbos again.

How truly is it said, *"If I safeguard Shabbos, Hashem will safeguard me."**

Leah learned to go to the *mikveh* every month. This changed the nature of our marriage. Gradually, anger and alienation were dissipated in the holy way of life that saturates a Jewish home.

Personal relationships between husband and wife are so close. If they are not on the highest level, there is a danger that they will deteriorate into conflict. I mentioned earlier how the Talmud shows that, if G-d is not with husband and wife, there will be destructive flame and fire. The *mikveh*, the pure waters into which the Jewish wife submerges herself every month following her menstrual period, calms the flames. It is a vital instrument G-d has given the Jewish family to bring purity into the home. Each month becomes a new wedding, a new honeymoon, a new beginning for the Jewish couple. The same freshness the young couple had when they first met, they have every month. They are never bored with each other or take each other for granted. Their relationship becomes much more than just a physical union.

The *mikveh* is referred to as "the waters of Eden." It recreates the Garden of Eden every month for the Jewish couple.

---

* From *Ki Eshmerah Shabbos*, a *zemer* (Shabbos song) traditionally sung at the Shabbos table

We thought to ourselves: *How could we have left these diamonds untouched all these years? These were the secrets of happiness in the world, and we had come so close to never knowing about them. Thank you G-d; thank you Zayda, Mama, and Rebbetzin Jungreis for bestowing these boundless riches upon us and saving our lives.*

We also needed a new wedding.

When we were first married, I had demanded a secular ceremony. Do you remember how full of hatred I was toward everything Jewish? Can you imagine? I could not stand the idea of even hearing a Hebrew word at my wedding.

So in North Woodmere, at the Rabbi and Rebbetzin's home, our rabbi set up a *chupa*, a marriage canopy, and got together a *minyan* of ten men. We had a new wedding, all according to Jewish law.

After eleven years of "marriage," we finally got married.

As I said at the time, "It's wonderful to get married twice . . . to the same person."

Let me tell you about my *bris*.

Every Jewish male, if he is healthy, is circumcised on the eighth day of his life. Why didn't G-d create us circumcised? The *Midrash* teaches us* that G-d gave us the privilege and obligation to join with Him in perfecting the world.

A *bris* inducts the baby into the family of Abraham through holiness and sanctity. It's the sign on his body that he is a Jew, a legacy passed down from father to son. For thirty years I had lived without a *bris*. I was approximately 11,000 days late. But in G-d's world it is never too late. Every year we have Yom Kippur. Every day can be a new beginning.

---

* *Berayshis Rabbah* 11:6

My *bris* took place in Zayda's modest living room in Canarsie, Brooklyn. The family's old friend, the legendary *mohel* Rabbi Mordecai Zimmerman, performed it. He was quiet and fast. Before you knew it, it was over. In my case all that was needed was a tiny pin prick to draw a drop of blood, followed by the required blessings. The medical work had been done in infancy. But I was still nervous. Everyone was whisked out of the room.

I am probably one of the few people in history who was reading during his *bris*. Zayda handed me something, saying, "Read this, Yisroel. Don't get nervous."

▲▲▲

In the transition to a Jewish life, some things were harder than others. I was a little nervous about wearing a *yarmulka* to work. I was afraid of what people might think. So in the beginning, when I first started working at *The Long Island Press*, I would take it off in the car at the company parking lot. But I felt like a hypocrite. Was I more afraid of people than G-d?

Yom Kippur came a few weeks after we moved, and the Rabbi gave an amazing sermon. He told us not to be embarrassed at our Jewishness. (Did he know what I was thinking?)

"Even the Pope wears a *yarmulka*," he said.

I felt like an idiot. *What was I embarrassed about? My allegiance to the Torah was my greatest achievement. Why should I be afraid?*

The morning after Yom Kippur I said to myself, "I am not taking this off my head when I get out of the car. I don't care what anybody says."

Guess what? Everyone had something to say. As in

Cornwall, the non-Jews were all respectful. Almost all of them asked me about it, and they were all genuinely interested in my response. I told them straight that as a religious Jew it is my responsibility to keep my head covered at all times.

But the assistant editor at the paper, a Jew, was not so happy. When I walked in, he took one look and stormed over to me.

"What are you doing? Why are you wearing that?"

I was stunned by the ferocity of his tone. I hesitated a second, then I said, "Well, yesterday was Yom Kippur. It was such a special feeling that I decided I wanted to try and keep that feeling." I didn't know how to complete the thought. He did it for me.

"All year?"

"Exactly. All year. That's it!"

He eyed me as if he never wanted to see me again, then turned on his heel. It was like Cornwall all over again. From then on, I would never be allowed to take a "*Mincha* break," ten minutes for afternoon prayers. You know the famous phrase, "If I catch you praying."

Fortunately, the presses were huge, loud, and far from his office. Behind them, I could find a little "peace" to say my prayers.

Years later, I had another "*yarmulka* experience" with another Jewish boss. I was employed at the elegant offices of a real estate empire in New York City. On my first day of work, I passed the patriarch himself, a tall man in his late eighties. Looking down at me, he asked "What is that on your head?"

"A *yarmulka*."

"We don't allow that here."

The non-Jewish employee who was showing me around almost collapsed with embarrassment. She looked for a hole in the carpet.

I said to the patriarch, "Sir, it is your office and you can do as you wish. I want you to know, however, that if you look around you, you will see successful people, many in your own business, who walk around with *yarmulkas* just like me."

He was not impressed and I was not going to yield. I compromised by buying a made-to-order toupee so that I could cover my head but not look as if I were covering my head. I told him, because I wanted him to know that I insisted on keeping my head covered at all times.

I said to myself: I must thank G-d for these experiences, because through them I am able to atone for my former life. The pain helped me understand that I had brought pain into the world through my rejection of the Torah. I could not have atoned for my former life without experiencing pain. It was a gift from G-d that made the transition real.

What is most troubling about these vignettes, however, is the glimpse they provide of why the Jewish people are in exile today. If we attack each other for our Jewishness, our adherence to G-d's commandments, then what do we expect from the others surrounding us? If we behave like Hitlers to each other, how can we be surprised when a Hitler behaves like us?

▲▲▲

OK. You have heard about the *yarmulka* episodes in the office, but what about wearing a *yarmulka* in that big wide world out there? It's dangerous, right? You don't just go out into a hostile world and advertise that you are a Jew! If you do, you expose yourself to danger.

Well, G-d has protected us for thousands of years among the most hostile enemies. And why? Because we stuck to His Torah! We stuck to our mission in this world. When we try to pretend we're not Jews, the nations remind us who we are. "In every generation they rise up against us to destroy us."* But when we act like loyal Jews, G-d always protects us.

The following story tells about a little Jew—me!— with a *yarmulka* on his head. Maybe I was too stupid to take it off when I should have. But with all the happiness at my new-found Torah, I wanted to show my allegiance to G-d, and G-d protected me.

Maybe He was proud of me. I hope so.

When I worked at *The Long Island Press*, I used to arrive each morning around 3:00 A.M. A few hours later, after the first edition went to press, there was a break. By that time it was daylight, and I would sometimes use the break to have my car serviced. I would drive about a mile to the service station and take the subway back to work. At noon, when work was finished, I would take the subway back to the service station, pick up the car, and drive home.

A few months after I started wearing my *yarmulka* all the time, I brought my car in for service. After work I went to pick it up. *The Press* was located a half block from the terminus of one of the city's long subway lines, at 168th Street and Jamaica Avenue in Queens. At that point the "subway" was actually not a subway any more, but an el-evated railway on a trestle high above the street. A train

---

* Passover *Haggadah*

would come to the end of the line there and wait until the next train arrived on the opposite track. Then the first train would leave.

At twelve noon at the end of the line the trains were empty, and I mean empty. As I entered, there was not a soul to be seen. The train sat in the station a few minutes and then I heard the rumble of the next train coming in. The doors closed and we were off.

These cars were constructed with one long row of seats down each side of the car, two rows facing each other, with standing room in the middle. Just little old me, sitting alone in the big car, in the middle of the big train.

Well, almost alone.

A few seconds into the ride, the door at the end of the car opened. Two tall young men entered.

You know how sometimes you just get vibes when someone enters a room. Not with everybody, but certain people emanate vibes. Sometimes good vibes and sometimes bad vibes. I got very bad vibes when these guys entered.

They walked through the car and—guess what!—they decided to sit down right opposite me. And they were singing a song. The clatter of the train prevented me from understanding the words, but I was somehow sure that it was a "serenade" intended just for me. I strained to hear the words and couldn't. Then all of a sudden, through the clatter, I caught them.

"Hitler killed six million Jews. Why didn't he kill them all?"

A nice song.

They were sitting directly across from me, but I was looking to the right, toward the end of the car, pretending I didn't even see them. And I was praying, "G-d, you got me out of so much before. Please get me out of this. I don't know how You are going to do it, but please help me."

One of the guys got frustrated because I wasn't paying attention to them. So he called out to me, "Hey mista."

I looked around.

"Oh, hi!"

"Hey mista, how come Hitler killed six million Jews?"

This was it. The setup. How was I going to escape?

And then, all of a sudden, a feeling came over me. Nobody could have seen it, but I felt it. It wasn't a question; it was a certainty. A feeling came over me that I was absolutely protected. Nothing could hurt me; an army of angels was surrounding me.

I got up out of my seat, and I walked slowly over until my face was a few inches from "Hey mista's" face. I was perfectly calm. But he wasn't. He jumped backwards in his seat, away from me, and began to tremble violently. All of a sudden, as soon as he saw I wasn't afraid, he became terrified, a mass of quivering jelly. I realized he was a nothing, a total coward.

I said to him in a voice as soft as you can use on the subway, "Do you really want to know why Hitler killed six million Jews? I'll tell you. It's because he was so sick! Only someone who is really sick could have done something like that."

"Bbbbbutttt I thought the JJJews were stealing everyone's mmmmoney and rrrrobbing everybody. . . ."

"Come on," I said, "you have no idea what you're talking about. You don't even know what a Jew is. You've never met a Jew in your life."

"Bbbbbutttt. . . ."

And then a funny thing happened. The train stopped and the doors opened.

"Hey guys," I said, "you know, I'd love to talk to you some more, but this is my station, and I've got to go. See ya."

I walked out of that train onto the elevated platform and looked down at the street. I felt I could jump off and fly!

G-d saved me! He sent angels to protect me. I was not alone.

▲▲▲

As we swam deeper into the ocean of Torah, G-d's presence began to become obvious in our lives in surprising ways.

It was a frigid Sunday night in February 1975, some six months after we had begun our new life. Around 11:00 P.M. Yaffa, then three years old, developed a high fever. Leah was worried and called our pediatrician, who happened to live one block away. Could she bring Yaffa over?

"Come right over," said the doctor.

I was asleep. Work at the paper began the next morning at 3:00 A.M.

At 11:15 the telephone rang. I jumped out of bed.

"Mr. Neuberger, this is Doctor X. I'm sorry to inform you that I believe your wife just had a heart attack. She is lying on the floor of my office. I can't get a pulse. I am a pediatrician and I cannot treat her. Please come over immediately and call an ambulance."

In the blink of an eye the whole world fell apart.

I grabbed a coat and was running out the door when I suddenly realized . . . there is a five-year-old girl in this house fast asleep. How can I leave? I quickly grabbed the phone and dialed the Rebbetzin.

Barbara Janov, the Rebbetzin's right-hand lady, answered. By incredible good fortune, the Rebbetzin had just walked in from a speech in New Jersey.

"Yisroel, you stay home with Sarah," Barbara said, "I'm going over to Doctor X to see what's happening."

Barbara was about to hang up when I heard a voice in the background. It was decades ago, but I remember the Rebbetzin's exact words as if it had happened five minutes ago.

"Barbara, don't hang up. I want to speak to Yisroel."

The Rebbetzin said my name twice.

"*Yisroel, Yisroel. Mazal tov!* Your Leah is pregnant. She is going to have a beautiful baby and everything is fine. Don't worry. Barbara will be over with her in just a few minutes."

Stop! Hold everything! The world has just been put back together. Humpty Dumpty is whole.

As soon as the Rebbetzin spoke, I had perfect peace. I didn't speculate. I *knew* she was right. I *knew* everything was OK.

Five minutes later Leah walked in, supported on one side by Barbara and on the other by the doctor. (We switched pediatricians after this.)

The doctor was shaking.

"Doctor, may I get you some coffee?" I asked.

They put Leah to bed.

The next morning she felt fine. She went for a pregnancy test.

That is how we found out that Miriam was coming.

Don't ask me how the Rebbetzin knew. Don't ask me to explain. I don't know any more than you do. I'm just telling you what happened.

▲▲▲

As we got into Torah life, our entire outlook changed. Life wasn't depressing any more. The world suddenly got bright. We wanted to have more children. There was hope.

One Shabbos morning two years later, I walked into synagogue. Before prayers, the Rabbi came up to me. The Rabbi was a dreamer. He had amazing dreams all the time. He had a direct line from upstairs.

"Yisroel, I had a dream last night that you have a baby on the way."

The following Monday, Leah went for a pregnancy test. But we didn't need it. The Rabbi had told us. That's how we found out about Aharon Yaakov.

Our next child was also announced in an extraordinary way.

There's a tradition which tells us that Elijah the prophet attends every *bris*. It's considered a very advantageous time to ask his help in getting prayers to G-d. Leah was attending a *bris* a few years later, when she suddenly got this feeling that she was pregnant. Maybe Elijah was delivering a message. In any case, a visit to the doctor showed that her "feeling" was accurate. About eight months later Nechama Bracha was born.

▲▲▲

Each time we do a *mitzvah*—whenever we knowingly and willingly do something that G-d commanded us—an angel is created* who will come to our defense on the Day of Judgment, when all our actions are weighed before G-d. Sometimes, it seems that those angels help us out on earth also, guarding us as we go through life.

---

* Ethics of the Fathers 4:13

Each night before we go to bed, we repeat the verse from the Torah in which our father Jacob said, *"Hamaloch ha-go-ayl . . .* May the angel who rescued me from all evil bless the children. . . ."* We ask G-d to send His angels to protect us on the road through life.

I used to stand in front of our house when the school bus came for our children. I would watch it go off into the distance and ask the angels who had accompanied us until then—certainly we had not been alone—to accompany the children wherever they went. I am still asking this today, even with our children grown up and in some cases living in the holy land of Israel, even when they are sending their own children off to school.

▲▲▲

We soon found out the greatness of our beloved rabbi, Meshulam ha-Levi Jungreis, the Rebbetzin's late husband. It takes a special man to encourage a wife who is in the world limelight. Most men would be jealous. But that was only part of the picture. Many of Rabbi Jungreis's acts of kindness were known only to the recipients and to G-d. At his funeral and during the *shiva* period some of those acts became public knowledge. But we found out soon enough how great a person he was.

It was during the spring of our first year in North Woodmere, after Passover, when the world was warming up and the flowers were beginning to appear. Yaffa was at nursery school. At three years old she was still a little girl with small, delicate limbs. But Yaffa was always an adventurer. That morning found her at the top of high monkey bars in

---

* Genesis 48:16

her school playground. All of a sudden she lost her grip and fell a long way to the ground.

It was shortly before noon when our phone rang. I had just come home from *The Long Island Press*. The school office told Leah and me that we had better come over quickly.

I had been in the ambulance corps in Cornwall, and when I saw that Yaffa's right elbow was blue, with funny shapes bulging against the skin from inside, I did not like the looks of what I saw. Not at all.

In their concern, school officials had moved Yaffa before calling trained personnel. In addition, they had given her apple juice while they waited for us to arrive. These mistakes were to have consequences.

I was scared, but I was also too busy to realize it until later. We had no time to lose. I slid Yaffa onto a board and tried to immobilize her arm. Then we drove—slowly and very carefully—to the hospital. Leah sat in back, holding Yaffa on the board.

We had called our pediatrician from the school. He was waiting for us at the emergency room. Fortunately, he had called upon a team of great orthopedic surgeons. Dr. Walter Lerman and Dr. Stewart Berger were angels sent by G-d. Today they are distinguished physicians with great reputations. At the time we knew nothing about them. We were just grateful that someone was there for us.

They had bad news.

They tried to set Yaffa's elbow. Nothing doing.

Inside her tiny arm things were not good. At the wrist there was no pulse. The hand could feel no sensation. The reflexes were shut down.

They tried traction, hoping the bones would move into place. Nothing doing.

I remember her agony. We could give her no anesthetic to permit surgery, because the school had given her that apple juice right after the accident. It was now early afternoon and it would not be possible to operate until nine o'clock that night.

I called the Rabbi to ask if Sarah could stay at their house when she got off the school bus. I was full of urgency, busy with countless thoughts and details. But there was silence on the phone.

Why is the Rabbi not answering me? That is so unlike him. Doesn't he care?

Suddenly, I heard the sound of sobbing.

Oh G-d! The Rabbi is crying!

I had been so busy that I forgot what was really going on. That's when *I* started to cry.

Don't ask what that afternoon was like. Mercifully, I don't remember. I don't want to remember.

The Rabbi had a Talmud class that met each week at a different person's house. That night, the Rabbi taught for fifteen minutes and then said, "Gentlemen, I apologize, but I must leave you now to go to the hospital. There is an emergency that requires urgent attention."

Shortly before 9:00 P.M. Rabbi Jungreis arrived at the hospital. Also there was his brother-in-law, Rabbi Jacob, Rebbetzin Esther's brother. The four of us—Leah, myself, and the two rabbis—were alone in the waiting room. The vigil began.

Have you ever driven in the middle of the summer? The pavement becomes burning hot and you see shimmering heat waves ahead of you. The air looks as if it is rippling and the scenery is swimming in front of your eyes.

The air above the rabbis' heads was shimmering and rippling as the *Tehillim* (Psalms) ascended to Heaven. I believe we could really see the waves in the air. For four hours they stood there, *Tehillim* books in their hands, with uninterrupted prayers of total intensity and devotion.

Four long hours we waited. Just the four of us. All alone in the waiting room.

At 1:00 A.M. the doors opened. Drs. Lerman and Berger, in their green surgical gowns, walked in. Our hearts were in our throats.

The doctors spoke.

"This operation," the doctors said, "should not have been a success. This was the most difficult surgery of its type we have ever performed. Your daughter's arm is so tiny that it was like operating on a watch. The bone was splintered and razor-sharp; the nerves and vessels were stretched over the sharp bone. Logically, there was no way we could have repaired this damage.

"But somehow we did repair the damage. The pulse and sensation have been restored to Yaffa's right hand and arm."

Please listen, my friends, to the following words of the doctors: "The surgery was a success. We can attribute that success only to the prayers of the rabbis. There is no other explanation."

It is unusual for doctors to be humble, but these great doctors humbled themselves by refusing to take credit for the successful surgery. Those words were a *kiddush Hashem*, a sanctification of G-d's name.

We returned home in the middle of the night with prayers of thankfulness on our lips.

A few hours later, at 6:30 A.M., I stumbled into the synagogue for morning services. I was, of course, exhausted.

The Rabbi was smiling at me.

"Do you know where I just came from?" he asked me.

How could I know?

"I just came from the hospital. I knew they wouldn't allow you. Only a rabbi can get in at all hours. I wanted to see Yaffa when she woke up, so she wouldn't be afraid. I said the morning prayers with her. I told her where she is and that everything is all right. She is doing fine."

Hold on! This was beyond the call of duty. Beyond everything. Beyond human kindness. We were new to the community. We were new to the Jewish world. We weren't big shots. Yaffa was just a tiny girl.

Why did the Rabbi do that?

Yaffa was in the hospital for a whole week.

Every day, except Shabbos, the Rabbi visited her at six o'clock in the morning, so she wouldn't be afraid.

We were beginning to get to know our Rabbi. Was he a man or an angel?

By the way: seventeen years later Yaffa became the Rabbi's daughter-in-law.

Explain this to me. The workings of G-d are beyond comprehension.

There are sequels to this event.

Rebbetzin Jungreis was in South Africa when this took place. On her way back, she stopped in Israel. The first news she heard on her return to New York was about Yaffa's accident. Before her coat was off, she called, so she could hug Yaffa "with the air of Jerusalem" still on her coat. Such are the actions of a person of *chessed,* of kindness.

We were all scheduled to go to Israel with the Rebbetzin in a few weeks, but we assumed the trip would be off for us with Yaffa's arm in a cast.

"You're coming," said the Rebbetzin. "Yaffa will do a big *mitzvah* in Israel with that arm."

And so it was, a few weeks later, at a military hospital in Nahariya, near the Lebanese border, that the Rebbetzin called Yaffa on stage after her talk and showed the soldiers her tiny arm, recounting the miraculous success of the surgery. Little three-year-old Yaffa showed the soldiers how she could wiggle her fingers, after having lost all sensation and movement in that hand.

In the audience was a soldier who had been shot near the elbow, in the same spot where Yaffa's fracture had been. He had lost all movement in his hand and despaired of ever using it again. But when he saw little Yaffa moving her fingers, he thought, "I am going to move *my* fingers."

All of a sudden there was a yell from the audience.

The soldier was moving his fingers!

Sometimes all we need is a little ray of sunshine to restore our will to live.

What a trip that was.

▲ ▲ ▲

As we learned more and more *mitzvos*, our lives changed. Each week we had guests in the house. We never concealed from our children or our guests any aspect of the change in our lives. Our children were always aware that their parents had different backgrounds from their friends' parents, and that taught them the possibility and the necessity of examining one's life every moment, always looking for ways to become closer to G-d and observing His Torah more perfectly.

I once heard a beautiful explanation of the prayer we say three times each day, which begins, "G-d of Abraham, G-d of Isaac, G-d of Jacob." Why do we repeat the name "G-d" three times? Why don't we economize and simply say, "G-d of Abraham, Isaac, and Jacob"?

This explanation tells you a lot about life. Isaac, Abraham's son, grew up in the greatest home a Jew could live in. What could be better than the home of Abraham and Sarah? What better place to learn about G-d? But it was not sufficient for Isaac to learn from his parents. That was vital, but Isaac also had to feel the need for G-d *within himself*. He had to know *from his own experience* that he could not live without G-d, that he could not survive without sticking to His commandments like glue. So G-d had to become for Isaac "his own" G-d; Isaac had to make his own personal path to G-d. Of course, his parents taught him, but he had to go through the process personally.

In each generation we have to go through the process again and follow for ourselves the footsteps of our ancestors. It is the same G-d, but each of us has to "find" Him for ourselves.

Rebbetzin Jungreis tells the heart-rending story of her last visit to her grandparents in Hungary before the coming of the Nazi murderers. A little girl, she sat on her *zayda's* lap and saw tears falling onto his *Gemora*. Frightened, she ran to her father.

"Why is *Zayda* crying?"

Her father answered by taking her for a walk in the deep snow outside. He dressed her up in boots and a warm coat and told her to follow in his footsteps. After a while he stopped and asked her, "Why did I tell you to follow in my footsteps?"

"So I would have a path to walk in."

"That is why *Zayda* is crying. He is making a pathway for us in the Torah with his tears."

We each need those footsteps to walk in. But we ourselves have to walk, to put one foot in front of the other and make the journey toward G-d— the G-d of Abraham, the G-d of Isaac, and the G-d of Jacob.

▲▲▲

What has it been like since 1974? Has it really made a difference that we've been living a Torah life? Has the thrill worn off? Are things really different from the way they were before?

When we were very new at this life, Leah and I went to speak at a Jewish center. No matter where they are on the scale of observance, Jewish people usually love to hear how and why other people got into the Torah way of life. They are strengthened and encouraged by it. So people enjoy hearing us speak about our experiences, and we have spoken publicly quite a bit over the years.

During the question-and-answer period, a lady asked me whether we really thought we would "last."

"You guys have been religious now for about a year. Do you think you'll still be so excited about it ten or twenty years from now?" That was the gist of her question.

To tell you the truth, it was a mean question. I imagine that this lady was a somewhat bitter person and was not pleased to see us so happy in our Torah life. The question seemed intended to deflate our balloon. Well, you can't let such things get to you. At least, you've got to try to not let them get to you.

I told her that after thirty years of searching the world and finding nothing to live by, we did not intend to leave the beautiful garden we had discovered. We hoped that life would not only continue to be exciting but would become ever more so. And it has.

Just as a married couple finds their spiritual and physical relationship constantly renewed through the Torah laws of family purity, so it should be with all of life. If we are really connected to G-d and His Torah, then each day, each second should bring new insights into its greatness. Each moment should be another rung on the ladder.

There is an endless quest in fulfilling the Torah. Even Moses did not reach the ultimate. It is G-d's Torah after all, and we cannot even comprehend G-d, let alone reach anywhere near Him or fulfill His Torah completely. But therein lies the greatness. There's always more to do, always a higher peak to scale, always more to improve in our character, always more we can do for our brothers and sisters, always more we can do to make this world the place that G-d intended it to be.

Do you think that's depressing? No, it's exactly the opposite. Life is never boring; there's never a time when there's nothing to do, and each "thing to do" is of ultimate importance. The famous Greek myth about Sisyphus is a story of a man who was continually doing something that made no sense, endless meaningless work. The Egyptians tortured the Children of Israel in ancient times by having them build the cities of Pishon and Raamses, huge projects that kept continually sinking into the desert sands.

But when your life is filled with meaningful work, and the goal is above you, guiding you ever higher and higher, then you are exhilarated because you are climbing the ladder. Each rung brings understanding and elevation, and you know the next rung will add even more.

Just prayers. Let's start there. I want you to know that I consider it a tremendous victory if I can say even part of the *Shemoneh Esray*, the central prayer of each service, with concentration and feeling. Sometimes, my mind is wandering for the whole thing. But if I can feel the meaning of even one blessing and think about what I am asking for, that is a tremendous thing.

Can you imagine if I can do that for two blessings, or three or ten? If I can do that, then I will be asking G-d to help me and to improve the world. I am confident that He will indeed improve the world, and that G-d is happy to have us asking Him for such important things. Then I can act on that blessing in my daily life. That's a high.

"Heal us G-d and we will be healed. Save us and we will be saved. . . . Bring a complete recovery for all our ailments . . ." To say those words with feeling, and to have in mind people who need a recovery, and then perhaps to go to the hospital and visit these people. This elevates us. And this is one microscopic aspect of fulfilling a Torah life. Can you imagine filling the entire day with such *mitzvos*?

This is living on a constant high, working for the Boss of all Bosses, who sees and rewards all our sincere efforts to fulfill His will.

How about making a living? How can that be a high? But there's a way to do that also. We can have in mind that we are working so we can live a Torah life, so we can serve G-d, so we can give charity, so we can raise beautiful children imbued with Torah values. If we have the right *kavanas*, the right thoughts and intentions, then everything becomes holy and full of meaning.

That's how I would answer the lady's question.

And that's what we have tried to accomplish since we were introduced to the Torah life.

▲▲▲

I was never a natural businessman like my father. So what did I do? First, after we moved to North Woodmere, I worked as an editor for *The Long Island Press*, as you know. When the *Press* closed about two years later, I began my "career" in education. I became English principal and then administrator at Yeshiva Ateres Yisroel in Brooklyn, the Jungreis family's *yeshiva*. I was able to use my training in English language and literature to upgrade the elementary curriculum. I was able to use the administrative experience I had received running *The Cornwall Local* to upgrade administrative practices at the Yeshiva. That was also the period when I became Zayda's right-hand man, spending every morning in his company.*

In the spring of 1991 I decided I needed to earn more money. It was very difficult to live on the small salary a *yeshiva* can afford to pay. So I followed my father's footsteps into Wall Street.

I was not a kid when I started. But I have always been adventurous, and I was not afraid to try something new. So I became a sort of apprentice in a big firm for a few years. There was a problem, though. I couldn't remember numbers. In Wall Street you have to be good with numbers. Not only do you have to remember them, you have to understand them.

I would meet with a company or spend the morning looking at an annual report, and within a few minutes I had forgotten every number I had read. Maybe if they had made sense to me I would have remembered them better, but they didn't. I wanted to succeed in this game, but the num-

---

* That period is described in Chapter Four.

bers were a problem. It was also a little hard to take seriously all these very serious people who talked about how many cents per share their company was going to make in the third quarter a year from now.

What I did love to do was to talk to my boss about Torah. He saw I was more passionate about that than about Wall Street, so he told me, "Why don't you go into that full-time?"

But I wasn't ready to quit yet. I wanted to make zillions of dollars, and I was looking for a way.

I discovered "technical analysis." That means you look at charts and graphs instead of numbers. I am very pictorial, so I thought that just might work for me. But my boss wasn't interested in technical analysis, so we parted company and I opened my own fund, where I could use any strategy I chose.

I was able to raise some money, enough to do well if my method worked. I set up shop in the office of another fund. The boys who ran this fund were religious, and we got along well. I was proud of how honest they were, how properly they spoke and acted. Besides all these things, they were brilliant and successful.

My fund went on for a few years, but after a while Wall Street became too difficult for me. My method was good for a few years, but it was not consistent. When I began to have difficulty with the market and was under constant tension, I decided "I don't need this any more" and liquidated the fund.

Then I had to decide what to do. I was very fortunate in that I had enough to live on; for that I am very grateful, but one wants to be useful in life. It is frustrating and embarrassing to be unsure why one is in this world, to feel one is not accomplishing anything. That is when I started to devote all my time to writing this book.

I feel that writing the book is one reason G-d put me in this world. I am so happy I wrote it. Through it I feel that my life makes sense and that I can communicate my deepest thoughts to you, and express my gratitude to G-d and His messengers, especially Rebbetzin Jungreis and her family. I feel such a desire to thank G-d for His kindness to us and to share my experiences with you. I sometimes feel that I have had certain experiences precisely so that I could write about them and pass that on.

What do I mean about my life making sense? When you look at it in perspective, as you must if you want to write about it, you see that everything that happened had a reason. Even unpleasant experiences were part of the plan. They were necessary because G-d wanted to steer me in a particular direction. This is one explanation of the Hebrew expression "*Gam zu l'tova* . . . Even this is for the best."* When you look at all your experiences, you see that everything had to happen; there was a reason for it, and it was all for the good.

For example, not being good with numbers. Sometimes you feel you have to do what everybody else does. I thought for a while that I was a misfit because I couldn't remember those Wall Street numbers, just the way I thought I was a misfit as a kid because I wasn't socially "cool." Now I look back and realize that everyone is different. I wasn't supposed to be in that world at that time and so G-d was showing me the direction in which He wanted me to go. This is similar to what happened to my father in Paris; he found

---

* Talmud, tractate *Taanis* 21a

out he wasn't made to be an artist, and that is how he got into Wall Street.

It is important to be sensitive to the signals we get in life. They tell us which way to steer. G-d is always sending us messages.

But that was not all that happened for twenty-five years. From the very beginning our priority was getting higher and higher, deeper and deeper into the world of Torah. That sounds like a contradiction, but it isn't. As the saying goes, your head should be in heaven but your feet should be on the ground. We did that through our constant and unceasing involvement in Hineni. After a while, we also got very involved in the workings of our synagogue, Congregation Ohr Torah in North Woodmere. Rabbi Jungreis was our spiritual leader there, and we wanted to help. We love this family; they saved our lives. What less could we do?

After a while, I became the president of the congregation and Leah of the sisterhood. Those presidencies lasted for twelve years, until after the Rabbi's death.

The Rabbi and Rebbetzin, with our help, were able to accomplish something great, to build a harmonious community, a vibrant synagogue family from which our members derived life itself. People loved our synagogue, some walking forty minutes several times every Shabbos to attend services there. We all felt honored to be in the presence of the holy Rabbi and Rebbetzin, not only to pray with them on a regular basis, but to be privileged to speak with them as family members.

It wasn't always smooth sailing. There is the ever-present worry about money in every synagogue. And there is the tendency among Jews toward division and strife. The Talmud* tells us, in fact, that this is the cause of our present exile, which continues today precisely because we have not yet learned to love each other as brothers and sisters; we have not healed the wound opened when Joseph was sold by his brothers.

The amazing thing, however, is that in those golden years at Ohr Torah we were able to overcome those divisive tendencies and create a model for how Jews should get along.

We used to have beautiful *kiddushes* after synagogue on Shabbos morning. People would stay to talk and eat the beautiful food prepared by Leah's Sisterhood. Imagine, just to be in the company of the famous Rabbi and Rebbetzin, to derive comfort and happiness from their presence and speak to them as if they were our father and mother. It was so special.

Kiddushes on Yom Tov—Simchas Torah for example—were full meals for several hundred people. Yes, it was food, but the food brought people together . . . to synagogue, to blessings, to G-d. This changed people's lives.

There was plenty of hard work. I got calls sometimes at 11:00 P.M. Saturday night when the synagogue's air conditioner conked out in the middle of a wedding. For Leah it meant hours with the ladies in the kitchen every week. Synagogue work consumed a huge amount of time. But it made a difference in our community, and I always felt that the ripples spread from North Woodmere all across the world.

▲▲▲

* Talmud, tractate *Yoma* 9b

When Leah and I go out to speak about our life, we take questions at the end. Usually the first question asked is "What was your parents' reaction to the change in your lifestyle?" It's a very understandable question, because everyone, parent and child, imagines himself or herself in that situation.

I told you in Chapter Two about how our parents reacted to the initial announcement of the change in our lifestyle. They were good sports, plus they had a basic confidence in our good sense. But what happened next?

Of course, the drama plays itself out over many years, but generally speaking it was a gradual process of seeing that our lifestyle was not only normal, but better than normal. We became closer and closer to our parents. We did not discuss religion with them; they would not have felt comfortable with it. In fact, it would have been counterproductive. They just saw a beautiful family developing, a family that went out of its way to maintain the friendliest and warmest relationship with them.

There was, however, one touchy point that I felt compelled to discuss with my parents, and that was the matter of death and burial. To have neglected it would have meant opening the door to a tragedy that could never have been rectified, and so I proceeded to do what I felt I had to do. What compelled me to speak was my knowledge that many people in our family's milieu chose cremation rather than burial. According to Jewish law, a person who intentionally chooses cremation is cutting himself off from eternity. The eternal existence that is the goal of all conduct in this world is impossible if one chooses to have one's body burned. The laws of burial, like all Jewish laws, are very specific and complete. They are the final act of kindness we can render our loved ones, besides our basic responsibility to live our lives in such a way as to bring honor to them.

I felt I should speak to my mother first, so I arranged a quiet opportunity to talk. I asked her to consider the Jewish way "for my sake." I didn't go into complicated reasons. She knew how we felt. And, you know, she agreed to be buried in accordance with Jewish law, and actually changed her will to reflect that. To tell you the truth, I think that she was very moved by our concern. Shortly after that, I took steps to make sure that we had burial plots for our family. And when Mother got sick and passed away some eight years later, I am proud to say that she died and was buried completely in accordance with *halacha*, Jewish law. I was with her when she died, and I remained with her until the *chevra kadisha*, the burial society, came to escort her on her final journey.

On Mother's first *yahrzeit*, the anniversary of her death, I visited the cemetery. I felt so strongly that we had done the right thing for her for eternity. I asked G-d if I could just have some sign whether Mother was doing all right, some little message from the next world. The next morning our daughter Miriam told me that Mother had visited our family in her dream. Mother's face was radiant.

My father was very moved by the way Mother's funeral was conducted with such dignity. He was particularly touched by the sight of her coffin being lowered into the ground and the way in which family members, in accordance with Jewish law, shoveled the dirt into the grave. He was also impressed with the simple wooden coffin that Jewish law requires.

"So unpretentious. Just like Mother," he said at the time. I will never forget those words.

The world of Madison Avenue prefers to pretend death doesn't exist. But we want to live in reality. When you see that coffin being lowered into the ground and the dirt piled on top of it, and you are shoveling that dirt, there are no illusions about what is happening. The finality of death is brought home to you.

That also permits you to mourn properly, because you cannot mourn for one whom you think may still be alive. The Torah tells us that Jacob had no peace for the twenty-two years that his son Joseph was missing. Jacob assumed that Joseph was dead, but he never knew for sure, and during that time he could never come to terms with Joseph's disappearance. The fact that Joseph was not dead prevented Jacob from having any peace at all, either the peace of life or the peace of death. Life is not complete without death, and death is not complete unless burial is carried out in the way specified by the One Who created life.

My mother's life was brought to a satisfactory conclusion, and I am sure that she is now in the presence of G-d in the World of Truth. But we had many wonderful years in between. Mother would never have believed it before we became religious, but she actually went to Israel with us on two very memorable occasions. After Sarah graduated from high school, she went to seminary in Jerusalem for a year of advanced study. We decided to spend Passover in Israel that year, and we went several weeks early to tour the country. Mother, who had a heart-felt bond with Sarah, accepted the invitation to join us. Dad did not have the patience to spend several weeks in Israel.

This was to be a very special trip. I remember it fondly. After the frigid winter in New York, the beautiful land of Israel was warm in the spring sun. I will never forget the first night. We hadn't seen Sarah in about seven months.

After we picked her up at her school in Jerusalem, we headed east toward Yericho (Jericho) and then south, past the beautiful springs of Ein Gedi, where King David ran to escape his pursuers, past Masada, to S'dom at the southern end of the Dead Sea. That night, after everyone else had gone to bed, Sarah and I sat on the warm beach in front of our hotel, listening to the gentle waves and looking across the inland sea to Jordan. It was one of those scenes that never leave your memory. We knew we were part of the still unfolding drama of Jewish destiny.

We had hired a guide, and we spent the next week touring the Negev and southern Israel. It was a time of happiness for our young family, and my mother formed bonds with our children that were strengthened with each passing year, until her death some ten years later. Because of our unusual entry into Jewish life, our children have a vantage point that is almost unique. Discovering the Torah was and is an adventure we all shared. We discovered the Torah together, and we came upon it like a desert oasis. We drank the elixir with the knowledge that it was indeed the difference between life and death. Somehow, mother felt the excitement on that special trip.

Looking at these children, my mother knew her life had not been lived in vain. She didn't have to say it; she just knew it. And I think she found it out very deeply during those weeks we had together in Israel. The following year we returned, and on that trip we toured the north of Israel, including the beautiful Golan Heights.

CHAPTER FOUR

WALKING BESIDE THE MIGHTY ONES

I N THE BEGINNING *of G-d's creating the heavens and the earth—when the earth was astonishingly empty, with darkness upon the surface of the deep, and the Divine Presence hovered upon the surface of the waters—G-d said, 'Let there be light,' and there was light."*

In my beginning I felt astonishing emptiness, darkness. Then I found that Divine Presence was hovering over me. And there *was* light!

How fortunate were we to have opened our eyes and seen that the light was there. It shone upon the dark recesses of our existence and everything changed. It's not that we did different things—we continued to eat and drink, sleep, carry on a marriage, raise children, earn a livelihood, walk, run, read, and write—but we did everything differently. We were conscious that G-d was watching us.

---

* Genesis 1:1–2

We knew that we had to do things His way. His way be-came, insofar as we were able, our way. And this, far from being slavery, was freedom. The light penetrated every corner of our lives, bringing warmth, blessing, and growth where there had been only fear and stagnant darkness.

It's not even that the fears or weaknesses vanished. Our personalities didn't change, but now—because we had met G-d—we knew that He would not let the darkness domi-nate. We knew that light was stronger than darkness, and now we had found the source of light. Just living by the Torah, the simple act of doing *mitzvos*, carrying out the 613 commandments, was all that was needed to change the entire nature of our existence.

The question is always raised whether a "leap of faith" is required to adopt a Jewish lifestyle. After all, we don't see G-d. How do we know we are right? Do we just have to "jump" without thinking? To us there was no problem. There was no leap of faith because we didn't *need* faith. Does that sound insane?

Actually, it's totally logical. At Mount Sinai the Chil-dren of Israel said "*Na-ase v'nishma* . . . We will do and then we will understand."* Jewish life consists of actions, com-mandments. Once we started carrying out the *mitzvos*, we started to see the world differently. Where we didn't see G-d before, now we began to see Him everywhere. Doing His commandments brought our souls to life and the soul is what perceives Truth. The whole Torah is comprehen-sible only insofar as we are following it, that is, doing the *mitzvos*.

You don't need to have faith to do actions. Do you need

---

* Exodus 24:7

faith to drive a car? You don't know why or how it works, but you drive it. Do you need faith to go swimming? No, you learn how to do the actions and you do them.

Do you need faith to do the *mitzvos*? No, you learn how to do them and then you do them.

Every *mitzvah* we do permits us to perceive G-d more clearly and to better understand the nature of our existence. There's no more leap of faith getting into the Torah than there is getting into a car. You can't sit around contemplating and become a Torah-observant person. Thinking, contemplating does not help us comprehend G-d. He is completely beyond our comprehension. Sometimes He helps us comprehend some aspect of His existence, but if we are rebelling against Him by not following His laws, how can we expect His help? Once we submit ourselves to His authority, we can expect His help. And that is what happens when we begin to adopt a Torah life.

If a cult member, for example, comes to Hineni, the Rebbetzin will not speak to that person before class, only after. Why? Because the process of learning Torah in that class actually changes the person. His or her soul will be awakened and opened by the *mitzvah* of hearing words of Torah. You will see in the next chapter how the Rebbetzin would only speak to Reverend Mike and his friend after Shabbos, but by that time there was no longer any need to speak; Shabbos itself had done the speaking.

So Torah is not a theory. We can bring G-d into our lives by following His commandments. *"The heavens are G-d's, but the earth He has given to mankind."**

But who will teach us the commandments? How do we

---

* Psalm 115

know whom to trust? How could one have the assurance to commit himself or herself to the guidance of someone else in the eternal matters concerning the soul? Who was the Rebbetzin and where did she come from?

I have not disguised our belief that Rebbetzin Jungreis is the most trustworthy spiritual guide in this generation. That's our belief and will explain why we committed ourselves to follow her so closely. We wanted to attach ourselves to G-d. When one wants to accomplish something, one must learn how to do it. For that one needs teachers. Torah is not an ordinary subject, however. Its practice changes one's life and our "final exam" is in the World to Come. You cannot take a chance on the wrong teacher. You cannot afford to get a bad grade.

You may think this is an "advertisement" for Rebbetzin Jungreis and her organization. It is not. I'm not telling you whom to choose as a spiritual guide. I'm simply telling you how we chose. Every person who wants to come close to G-d should consider very carefully the spiritual guide he or she chooses. There is hardly a more important decision in life.

The Rebbetzin and her family are not supernatural beings incapable of error. They are ever so human, full of pain and human frailties as we all are. I sometimes think that the Rebbetzin suffers *more* pain and is *more sensitive* than anybody else. If she didn't feel the pain of others, she wouldn't be in this line of work. Her family has, throughout literally hundreds of years of history, brought that spiritual sensitivity to others with much love. That gift has been handed down through the generations, and that is what touched us on that spring evening in Newburgh, New York, when we first heard the Rebbetzin speak.

The process of choosing a spiritual guide is crucial to every person, and I would like to tell you something about how we approached it.

▲▲▲

At the very beginning, we wanted to be certain that the Rebbetzin was trustworthy.

We observed that when she spoke, she always seemed to be on the verge of tears. Not obvious tears, but just below the surface. I don't think you can fake that. She was full of emotion. Observing her face and actions, we felt that she had no ulterior motives. I am telling you this because you could apply the same test to *your* spiritual guide. Don't be taken in by people who are trying to inflate themselves at your expense. I'm not just talking money; I'm talking ego. There are people whose egos expand because they are considered spiritually powerful and have many followers. Those people cannot help you because their advice will be tainted by the desire for self-aggrandizement. In this world you cannot afford to be even one millimeter off the mark, because if you follow that little deviation for a few years, before you know it you won't even know where you started from. It's fatal.

From the beginning we noticed that the Rebbetzin does not attempt to impose a stencil-type way of life on anyone. She's not looking for clones. She's looking for people to be really happy, because happiness means that your soul is in sync with G-d. You are doing what G-d wants you to do, which comes down to doing what *you* really want to do.

Not imposing a stencil-type existence should not be construed as being weak on the *mitzvos*. Not at all. A com-

mandment is a commandment. But one must approach the
mitzvos in a way that will encourage rather than discour-
age their observance. Not every boy is going to be a Torah
scholar. That doesn't mean that Jewish boys shouldn't attend *yeshiva*—of course they should. But when people come
back to Torah, not everybody is ready for the same path. It
is actually possible that a young man might be turned away
from the Torah path if he is exposed to a curriculum for
which he is not ready or not suited. Everyone is made a
little different, and the Torah is a *shulchan aruch*, a table
set with different food for each different type of palate.

The Rebbetzin is a genius at knowing just what is right
for those who ask her guidance. She knew when she first
met us that if she had told me that I had to tie the left
shoelace first I would have fainted on the spot. It took me
probably ten years to find out that the Torah really does
tell you which shoelace to tie first. But there are people
who want to know about shoelaces in the first three minutes after they discover the Torah. People who guide other
people have to be able to know the difference. That can
only happen if there is no ego in the way. They have to be
looking at *you*; there can't be anything in between.

We stuck like glue to the Rebbetzin because we trusted
her and we believed that her Torah guidance came un-
adulterated. I want you to know that, without exaggera-
tion, in over a quarter of a century she never ever let us
down. Please, when you look for your spiritual guide, keep
this in mind. A life is not something to waste. It is too
precious.

Even when it came to choosing a partner for Torah study
I was very careful to seek the Rebbetzin's guidance. Just
the way a small child must learn proper behavior before

anything else, so must a Jew who is returning to the Torah be very careful about his study partners. One who is new to anything is very susceptible to influence. Your study partner must be in tune with your program of spiritual advancement, and everything should be under the watchful eye of your spiritual guide. Remember what I said earlier about the shoelaces. One must never lose sight of the goal; one must try to balance learning with sharing that learning with others and refining one's character traits. So if I am thinking about a study program, I ask the Rebbetzin first to tell me if it's the right time and then to tell me which person I should team up with.

Of course, much of our studying was done right in the family. I have told you that at first we studied with the Rabbi. In the beginning, he taught us the *aleph bays*, the ABCs of Torah. He got us started on everything.

And our children! I cannot begin to tell you how much our children have taught us. To this day, when someone writes to us in Hebrew, we cannot always understand the words, so we ask the children. Our children have become our teachers. What they have learned, they are giving to us.

I want you to know, from the day our children started attending nursery school, they were already teaching us. Do you understand how close that makes you to your children, when they completely understand your background and they help you? They know infinitely more Torah than we do, yet they know how to answer us with tremendous respect, because this is part of honoring parents. So at the same time as they are teaching us, they are not acting superior to us. This delicate balancing act is an integral part of any successful teaching, but it is especially vital for any

A new life! Rebbetzin Jungreis with Sarah and Yaffa in Chevron (Hebron) on our second trip to Israel, in '75.

Zayda and Mama just happened to be in North Woodmere at the very moment we drove home from the hospital with little baby Nechami. You can see in their eyes the joy tzaddikim *have at another person's happiness.*

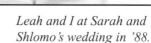

*Leah and I at Sarah and
Shlomo's wedding in '88.*

*The Rabbi. What a smile! In his
arms is Tzirel Gertzulin and
below is Yosef Dov Gertzulin,
his two oldest grandchildren.*

My parents on their fiftieth anniversary, with Ann, Jimmy, and me.

Yaki and Nechami's wedding, summer '99. Back row shows (left to right) Shlomo Lancry (Sarah's husband), Miriam, Leah, Nechami, Yaki, me, Ari, and Rabbi Osher Jungreis (Yaffa's husband). Center (left to right) is Sarah, Leah's mother; my father; and Yaffa with two of her children. On the floor in front are more of my beautiful grandchildren.

Jewish person who is anxious to adhere tenaciously to all the nuances of what a Torah personality should be.

This whole process is beautiful. Talk about dividends from investments!

▲▲▲

In the early 1970s, shortly before we met, the Rebbetzin started to become a very popular speaker. She needed an organizational structure to help her, but first she wanted to receive the blessings of great rabbis for her work. We Jews consider blessings to be very powerful. After all, the world was created with words that G-d uttered, such as "Let there be light." Words are spiritually powerful, and the spiritual rules the physical. When you perceive the world physically, you think the physical aspect controls everything, but that is incorrect. So a blessing, consisting of words from a holy person, is very powerful.

Zayda was very close to many great rabbis. Among others, he took his daughter to Rabbi Yosef Eliahu Henkin. Rabbi Henkin, who passed away in 1973, was the founder of the well-known charity Ezras Torah. At the time they visited him, Rabbi Henkin was very sick, but he gave the Rebbetzin a powerful blessing, which we have seen fulfilled. Rabbi Henkin blessed her that she should teach the Jewish people to have *rachmonis*, compassion, on their own souls.

Rabbi Henkin made the following analogy. In contemporary society we are obsessed with health. We exercise and watch our diets carefully. But one day, after a hundred and twenty years, we are going to appear before the Almighty for judgment on our conduct in this world. There will be no body at that time, just our soul "standing," as it were, before G-d. But will our soul be able to stand without a body? Will it have strength? Will it have spiritual "muscles," or will it fall apart like jelly? Did we exercise our soul in this world? Did we feed our soul? Our bodies were well taken care of, but what about our souls?

The food for the soul, said Rabbi Henkin, is study of the Torah.

The exercise is *mitzvos*.

Do we feed and exercise our soul? Do we even realize we have a soul? Rabbi Henkin gave Rebbetzin Esther the following blessing: May you teach the Jewish people to use our years on this earth to strengthen our souls with a proper "diet" of Torah and "exercise" in the *mitzvos*, so that after a hundred and twenty years we should be able to stand before G-d in dignity and strength.

▲▲▲

Hineni began decades ago with a regular column in *The Jewish Press* called "Ask the Rebbetzin." Then, in the fall of 1973, came a major event at Madison Square Garden's Felt Forum, designed to attract alienated or lost Jewish young people. It was a major success. Following that, the Rebbetzin began regular Torah classes for those who wanted to return to their Jewish heritage. Although now it is considered the norm, at that time it was unheard of.

What would we have done without those classes? Where would we be today? I shudder to think what would have happened if we hadn't met the Rebbetzin and there hadn't been that lifesaving Hineni School for us.

When we first started attending, Hineni School was at Shaare Zion Congregation on Ocean Parkway in Brooklyn. The Syrian Sefardic Jews there gave the Rebbetzin her first home, in a little classroom at the back on the second floor, and that's where we traveled from Cornwall during the gasoline crisis of 1974. A few months later, Hineni School moved to Zayda's synagogue in Canarsie. Zayda and Mama were always there, and Zayda would speak in Yiddish for a few minutes following the Rebbetzin's class each week. Many people didn't understand, but you didn't have to. You just looked at his face and were thrilled to be in his presence. (When Zayda spoke privately, he would speak in English.)

Those were the days when, after personal talks with whoever wanted to speak to her, the Rebbetzin would zoom off to Staten Island for her weekly 11:00 P.M. radio program. Today she reaches millions—including enthusiastic non-Jews—on nationwide cable television with a show on the weekly Torah portion. (Sleep has never seemed to be a consideration for the Rebbetzin, who literally operates around the clock.)

After leaving Hineni School in those days, Leah and I used to go over to Lewis's Bagel Store on Flatlands Avenue and buy bagels fresh out of the oven. Back then I could eat three warm bagels with butter at ten o'clock at night. I can still taste them. *Ahh.* That was before I had heard about cholesterol.

When Zayda got too sick to come to Hineni School, Hineni moved to Manhattan, first in rented quarters, then in our own building. After a few years, the crowd became so large that we had to rent space at the Ramaz School. I can't begin to tell you how many people have come home to Torah and a new life through these sessions. With almost two thousand people listening in total absorption on Tuesday evenings, you can hear the footsteps of *Moshiach.*

Tuesday evenings also gives these hundreds of young

people, mostly singles, a chance to meet in a dignified, wholesome environment. If they have questions—including asking, *"Do you think this person is right for me?"*—the Rebbetzin and her family are there for guidance, like parents. And with today's crazy family situations, a lot of people are looking for parent figures, someone trustworthy who loves them.

On Thursdays the same thing happens at the Hineni headquarters on the West Side of Manhattan.

All this was achieved with no publicity, through word of mouth, starting with a few people sitting around a table on the second floor of Shaare Zion.

Leah and I attend all sessions of Hineni School. We are there to greet people and to make them feel part of the family, to invite guests for Shabbos, and to teach whatever our experience has enabled us to impart to others. In addition to other subjects, Leah teaches the brides-to-be. Everyone who is getting engaged—and a lot of people *are* getting engaged at Hineni—needs guidance on how to live according to the commandments of the Torah. That means understanding not just the laws of family purity, but also *shalom bayis*, how to create an environment in which the husband and wife become loving friends. The lessons even get into raising children and cooking *cholent*.

As soon as Leah and I arrived on the scene, we started looking for a way to repay the immeasurable debt one has when someone saves your life. Just as the Germans can never adequately pay reparations for the evil they inflicted upon the world,* conversely, one can never adequately repay the debt one owes for the granting of life. So, unedu-

---

* I am not saying I am against reparations, although some Jews will not accept them because they want it to be understood that there is no way you can bring back a life—a mommy, a daddy, a *zayda*, a *bubbie*, a child.

cated as we were in Torah life, we immediately wanted to help. We got our chance. Sometimes, all that's needed is a smile and a kind word. You don't need formal education for that, although some educated people have unfortunately not learned it.

We have really not been absent from Hineni School for twenty-five years. We go there to get our own "spiritual adrenaline" going every week. For over a quarter of a century, fifty-two weeks a year (except Jewish holidays), we have not missed hearing the Rebbetzin speak. When you add that up, counting two sessions a week for the last five years or so, it comes to about 1,500 sessions.

Did we become bored? Just the opposite. We drank from the fountain of life, and this delicious wine tastes better each time, especially when you share it with others.

There were other activities at Hineni, especially in the early years, before the classes got so important that they became a draw in themselves. When the messianic churches, which were targeting Jewish kids, had a function on Saturday evenings, we would be there with the Rebbetzin to speak to the Jewish kids as they left. It was very fruitful.

When the missionaries started handing out literature to Jewish kids on the streets of Manhattan, we would also go out with pamphlets and talk to the kids. It was not easy at first. You had to overcome your aversion to sticking your neck out, otherwise known as laziness. But the Rebbetzin wouldn't let us be lazy. After a while, we got into the habit. Some wonderful things were accomplished out there on the streets. We distributed literature, offering classes and information for people who wanted to learn more about their heritage. We made sure to dress nicely, look normal, speak politely and try to present a perfect image. Many people, if not most, were extremely appreciative, and many came back to a Torah life in this way.

I do believe that the very difficulty of these encounters increased their value and made the *mitzvah* greater. The more effort you have to put into something, the more reward. *"L'fum tza'ara agra,"** the reward is in proportion to the exertion.

I remember an Israeli guy we met outside a Reverend Moon rally at Yankee Stadium. (We were careful never to venture inside these events.) He spent many a Shabbos with us and was famous in our family because he didn't like carrots, so we called him *bli gezer* ("without carrots" in Hebrew). Bli Gezer had been interested in Reverend Moon. If we hadn't been there, he would never have returned to earth and Hashem's Torah.

When the Rebbetzin spoke in the New York area, we would always try to accompany her. This was exciting; it made us proud to be associated with such a special person. We were able to help her, to learn from how she spoke to people, and to meet and speak with people ourselves. Just watching the Rebbetzin in action was an education. She constantly refines her approach, and it is amazing to see how she is able to deal with every kind of situation.

I will tell you one thing. Before she opens her mouth at any event, Rebbetzin Jungreis prays that Hashem will give her the right thoughts and the right words. Before every *Shemonah Esray* prayer we say the words "My L-rd, open my lips, so that my mouth may declare Your praise."** That's

---

* Ethics of the Fathers 5:26
** Psalm 51:17

what the Rebbetzin says before every speech. Once, at Hineni, she literally lost her voice in the middle of a class with eighteen hundred people in attendance. I don't mean for three seconds. I mean for more like three minutes she literally could not speak. Leah suddenly realized what was happening and ran out for a glass of water. A little while later the Rebbetzin remembered that she had been distracted at the beginning of the class that evening and had forgotten to say that prayer!

Sharing the Treasure

Soon after we moved to our new home, the Rebbetzin sent us our first Shabbos guests.

We protested.

"Rebbetzin, how can we have guests when we ourselves don't know what we are doing?"

"Yisroel," she answered me, "that's just the point. Just as someone reached out to you, you must reach out to someone else. You didn't return to Torah so you could enjoy this beautiful life all by yourself. If you eat a steak dinner alone every night, it will soon lose its flavor. The same goes with Shabbos and every other *mitzvah*. You came back so that you could share with others. That's the only way you can try to repay Hashem for His kindness to you.

"Furthermore, no one will ever feel uncomfortable with you, because they will know that you have been through what they are going through. It is precisely your newness to Torah that makes you and Leah such ideal hosts. You will learn together with your guests, and, if you come across a question, you have many rabbis in the family to help you, right down the block. That's how you will learn."

Thus began the tradition of having regular Shabbos guests and sharing our home with others. Hardly a Shabbos has passed in over a quarter of a century without guests, some for the first time and some again and again. The blessings accrued to them and to us. Here is a letter we received from a Shabbos guest who stayed with us more than twenty years ago. Notice, please, the effect our children had upon this person. Imagine the effect that being hosts had upon the children.

Thank you so much. I really felt at home and enjoyed being with you and Sarah and Yaffa and Miriam Basya. Sarah: Thank you for taking me to shul and being so nice to a guest. Yaffa, thank you for being so nice to a guest.

Sarah was seven years old and Yaffa five at the time. Today, those "little girls" have homes of their own to which they invite their own Shabbos guests.

People ask us how we could have "exposed" our children to the "danger" of such outside influences. Nothing could have been better for our children. They learned from an early age that a Jew's imperative is to care for his brother and sister. They learned to share their home and room and food. They learned to teach, not just to give over information, but to communicate a way of life with love. Our children, from the time they were little, found it natural to teach blessings, prayers, and Torah to others.

Holy Calories

Since we moved to the Rebbetzin's community, I figure, we have asked the Rebbetzin an average of two questions a day for over twenty-five years. That should be about twenty thousand questions by now, some of them very heavy and difficult, some ridiculously simple. I don't want you to think I am joking when I tell you that the Rebbetzin has never steered us wrong. Even if we didn't like the answer, we still followed the Rebbetzin's guidance, and it never failed to lead us on a path that bore delicious fruit.

People say to me, "You're so lucky that you are so close to the Rebbetzin," but it's not completely luck. We made an effort to be close; we moved to her community. Granted that we were fortunate to be able to do it, but everyone should endeavor, to the best of one's ability, to be as close as possible to one's spiritual guide.

How do you get close to people? My idea is that you just look around for things you can do to help, and you just do anything that comes along.

I'll give you one example. About twenty years ago, it came to our attention that every Friday trays of *challahs*, rye bread, rolls, cakes, pies, and cookies from the local kosher bakery went into the dumpster. The owner didn't know what to do with them, because he sold only fresh products and could not use them the following week.

The Rebbetzin said we must go to this bakery every week, just before Shabbos, and collect all the unsold bread and cake. What would we do with it? Easy. It would go right to Zayda and Mama's *yeshiva* after Shabbos. It would help feed the children for a week. Not only that, Mama's Russians (more on that later) would be able to eat.

Thus began twenty years of shlepping cake and bread. To this day it has not stopped. Leah, the children, the Jungreis family, we have all participated in what has turned out to be an incredible *mitzvah*. I sincerely hope that on the day all our deeds are weighed, they will put all that bread and cake on the scale. Then I'll love all those calories!

We also pitched in to help at Rabbi Jungreis's synagogue. We were willing to do anything to help. My first job was strengthening the *minyan*, making sure we had ten men for every morning, afternoon, and evening service. I had a whole schedule, with backups in case somebody couldn't make it. But each day we made phone calls, just to make sure. If I was out and couldn't call, Sarah or Yaffa would make the calls. It became a family affair. These are tremendous learning experiences for children, and our children were always so happy to do it. Don't forget, it wasn't just dialing a phone, it was speaking nicely to the man of the house and asking him to make a commitment of time. What better way is there for a child to learn both a sense of responsibility and the proper way of speaking to an adult?

For many years I worked at Zayda and Mama's *yeshiva* in Canarsie, Brooklyn. In the mornings I would be at their house. I wound up doing just about everything. Every autumn, for example, I wrapped up the air conditioner for Mama. Mama doesn't like cold drafts, so we had to make sure the air conditioner was covered from the outside with thick plastic. I would do anything just to be around that house with all the holiness in it, just to see how Zayda and Mama lived. After a while, if you make yourself useful enough, you feel at home and you become a member of the family. You fit right in.

The Meaning of Yichus

I have told you about how we tried to verify that the Rebbetzin was as solid and truthful as we hoped she was. The very fact that we had found someone who could fulfill the degree of trust we needed to get us through life was an indication that G-d was watching over us. Everything in life is so tricky; so few people are trustworthy.

We wanted to understand on what basis the Rebbetzin's solidity rested. Meeting Zayda and Mama began to answer that question. For two kids raised in the assimilated world of Manhattan and the Ethical Culture Society, Zayda and Mama were a new experience.

The first word I want to use is "comfort." There was an immediate, all-encompassing feeling of comfort from being in their presence. You felt the eternity and power of their lifestyle. You felt that it reached way back in time, perhaps to a distant world of truth, but a world that you could also try to attain. It was that glorious, then distant dream I had dreamt in the darkness of my childhood. You felt that you were "home" for the first time in your life. We found out some amazing things about Zayda and Mama and the family. They lent support to the feeling of confidence we had in the Rebbetzin. The more we got to know the family, the more we felt the power of its history. Don't get me wrong. I'm not saying the Jungreises are the only family with such a history. There are many Jews today who can trace their ancestry back through every generation to Biblical times. The amazing thing in this case is that the Jungreises made that entire history, with its rock-solid foundation and tradition of reaching out to all Jews, available to others.

The Jungreis family tree goes back thousands of years to King David. From there, of course, you can go further back, all the way to Abraham and Sarah. This line of descent, this genealogy, this noble and royal inheritance, is called *yichus*.

I would like you to hear a little about Zayda's own childhood. These stories inspired me because they taught me where the sanctity I saw before me came from and how it was transmitted. I knew Zayda and I know Mama, *may she be healthy and have long years*. Knowing them, made these stories come alive for us. We saw with our own eyes the reality of what we were hearing.

Zayda* was born in 1908 in a town called Boskowitz in what is today the Czech Republic. In 1914, on the eve of World War I, Zayda's father took him to the grave of their ancestor, the Shach, a famous rabbi who had lived some 250 years earlier. This old cemetery was in Holosho, Czechoslovakia. Zayda's father cried bitterly for a long time at the grave. Finally, he said, "Know, my son, that you will survive and the *rabbonus* [the legacy of serving as a rabbi] will continue through you."

Zayda was afraid to ask his father what this meant, but he understood that it was extremely important. Only after having survived Bergen-Belsen, more than thirty years later, did he understand. Out of some eighty-seven rabbis in Hungary named Jungreis, only he and his immediate family had survived.

As a young man, Zayda became the rabbi of Szeged, the second largest city in Hungary. Szeged is in southern Hun-

---

* The stories about the Jungreis family in Europe were told to me by Rabbi Jacob Jungreis, Zayda and Mama's oldest child and Rebbetzin Jungreis's brother.

gary, near the Yugoslavian border. In Yugoslavia the future Marshal Tito led a large partisan army against the Germans. Hungary was the last country in eastern Europe to be invaded by the Nazis. Many tried to get over the border to Yugoslavia, and Szeged was the gathering point. Before and during World War II, Zayda and Mama operated a one-family *hatzola* organization to save Jewish lives.

In 1943 the Belzer Rebbe was smuggled into Hungary from Poland. He was living incognito in a basement in Budapest. Zayda went to see him. Travel was very difficult in those days because, on the train or the street, Jews would be beaten at whim, or their beards would be pulled out from their faces. The trip from Szeged was four to five hours. Zayda took with him a briefcase full of *kvitlach*, pieces of paper with written requests for blessings from the Rebbe. Zayda climbed through the basement window.

The Rebbe was emotionally drained. He had seen his wife and children murdered by the Nazis. He told Zayda, in Yiddish of course, "Szegediner Rav, I have no strength to give blessings." No one thought they would survive in those days. The Rebbe made Zayda his *shaliach*, his representative, to give over blessings. And Zayda came back to bless all his people in the Belzer Rebbe's name. Later, the Rebbe was rescued and smuggled into Israel.

Do you see what kind of *yichus* Zayda came from? A family of royalty.

But we can go even further back in Zayda's lineage and understand even more.

This story begins late on a Friday evening in Hungary somewhere around the year 1800. A young man is asleep; his bar mitzvah is this Shabbos. His father, passing by his room, hears laughter from within. He opens the door and sees his son sleeping peacefully. Curious to understand the laughter, he wakes the boy.

"*Tattie*, I had the most amazing dream. I was standing in our *shul*. It was dark, but as my eyes got used to the light, I saw a glow in each corner. As I looked more carefully, I saw that in one corner stood Our Father Abraham. And then I looked and saw Isaac in the next corner. Jacob was in the third corner and Elijah the Prophet was in the fourth corner. But I had a problem. With such holy visitors, whom should I greet first? Then I remembered learning in *yeshiva* that one who sees Elijah the Prophet and greets him will receive a tremendous blessing.* In my dream I remembered this and ran to greet Elijah."

From that day on, the young boy was blessed with the power to cure sickness. As he grew older, his fame spread and people from around the world sought him out. Near where he lived there was a Hungarian nobleman who was a terrible anti-Semite. This landowner had vast estates and untold wealth. He also had a beloved son who had become sick. As the illness progressed, the distraught parents searched frantically throughout Europe for a cure. They took him to Vienna, to the greatest doctors on the continent, but to no avail. It seemed that the end was near.

A Jewish woman worked in the nobleman's palace. She summoned up the courage to approach her master.

"Your highness, not far from here lives a famous rabbi who is known for his ability to cure people whom nobody else can cure. Perhaps he can help your son."

Swallowing his loathing for Jews, the nobleman sent for

* It says, referring to Elijah the Prophet, in one of the special songs we sing Saturday night after Shabbos, "Fortunate is he who has seen his face in a dream, fortunate is he who greeted him with 'peace' and to whom he responded 'peace.'"

the rabbi. He came, spent some time with the boy, and then told the grieving parents that their son would recover and live. Miraculously, the son began to regain strength and before long was his former healthy self. The nobleman was overcome with gratitude.

"Rabbi, I must tell you that I do not look upon Jews the same way I did before I met you. Not only am I convinced that your blessing saved my son, but I am amazed by your kindness, dignity, and compassion. I want to reward you. Please tell me your desire and I will make you and your family wealthy beyond your dreams."

The rabbi was grateful for the offer but refused all remuneration. He asked only one thing of the nobleman: that it become a tradition in his family to pass down in every generation the story of how his son had been saved by the rabbi's blessing.

This rabbi later became known as the Menuchos Osher.* The Menuchos Osher was Zayda's great grandfather. (Our son-in-law, Rabbi Osher Anshul ha-Levi Jungreis, bears his exact name.)

We now travel many years ahead to 1943. Zayda, the Rebbetzin's father, is on a train, in the shadow of the German war machine, on a mission to visit desperate Jews throughout Hungary. It was dangerous for a Jew to travel in those days, and Zayda was alone, or at least he seemed to be alone.

On the same train was a squad of Hungarian *gendarmes*, militarized police. The German murderers had not yet entered Hungary, but the local militia was indistinguish-

---

* He was called the Menuchos Osher after the title of his book. Referring to a great rabbi by the title of one of his books is a venerable Jewish tradition. Thus, we call Rabbi Yisroel Mayer ha-Cohen Kagan the "Chofetz Chaim."

able from them in its vicious hatred. They forced Zayda into their compartment, where they roughly questioned him. It was commonplace then for Jews to have their beards pulled out and suffer terrible beatings by these thugs. Things were getting rougher and rougher. All the while the torturers were laughing.

A high-ranking Hungarian officer was moving through the train. Hearing the commotion, he opened the door to the compartment.

"What's going on here? Oh, you have one of those pigs, do you? But you are being too kind to him. Come with me, you Jewish filth."

With that the officer grabbed Zayda and pushed him through the train into his own special compartment.

Soon, the train made an unannounced stop. The officer had a convoy waiting for him, and Zayda was thrown into his private car, separated from the driver by a thick glass partition.

In hushed tones, the officer addressed Zayda in Hungarian.

"Rabbi, I am so sorry I was rough with you, but I was forced to do it so the others would not be suspicious. Don't be afraid, rabbi, I am going to take you home.

"I want you to know something. My great-grandfather was saved by a holy rabbi named the Menuchos Osher, and it became a law in my family that the story should be told in every generation. My father told me the story and warned me always to protect and honor all Jews. Now, rabbi, I feel I have paid back a little of our family's debt. Without the blessing of the Menuchos Osher, neither I nor my fathers would ever have come into this world."

And so it was that the great-grandson of the noble lord

and the great-grandson of the Menuchos Osher met on a train in Hungary.

Knowing Who We Are

We are discussing genealogy. The lineage must be pure; the seed must be uncorrupted in order for Torah to be handed down and take root in the next generation.

Jewish law stipulates that the identity of a child is entirely dependent upon the mother. In other words, if the mother is Jewish, the child is Jewish. This was brought home to us in an unforgettable incident. We should never think these laws are arbitrary or man-made. We should never take our lineage lightly, nor our responsibility to maintain the purity of the Jewish family.

THE SCENE: Zayda's synagogue in Canarsie, Brooklyn
THE TIME: A Saturday night in the early 1970s

Saturday is the night for *Melave Malka.* On Friday night we welcome the Shabbos Queen with light, and on Saturday night we escort her out with light. After Shabbos, we light a candle and serve a special meal to bid her farewell. This meal was originated by King David and dedicated to his descendant, the Messiah, who will lead us back to Torah and the Land of Israel in the end of history.

In those days, Russian Jews were starting to trickle out from behind the Iron Curtain, and each new arrival was greeted with emotion. The religious community was anxious to lead them on the path of their ancestors so that they could undo the havoc inflicted by decades of Communist repression.

This Saturday night, Rebbetzin Jungreis was speaking to about one hundred Russian Jews in her father's synagogue. Candles on the floor provided a flickering light. The Rebbetzin spoke, and Avi, a Russian Jew who was active in Hineni, translated.

The Rebbetzin sketched the panorama of Jewish history, from the days of Abraham to the darkness in eastern Europe and the emerging light of Torah. There were few dry eyes. There were many questions. Then came time for refreshments. The lights were turned up and we broke into smaller groups and continued to talk.

Suddenly, there was a commotion. Somebody was yelling in Russian.

"This whole thing is so stupid. I don't know what you people are all excited about. This is ancient baloney that our grandparents rejected. Nobody believes in these fairy tales any more. You people are fools to let this woman get to you. Don't fall for it. It's a trick."

The Rebbetzin was standing in the middle of the synagogue.

"What is going on?" she said to him.

"This whole thing is a fake."

From across the room Zayda was observing. He walked over to his daughter and whispered something in her ear.

"What is your Jewish name?" she asked the young man.

"Alexi."

"Your *Jewish* name."

"What do you mean?"

"Tell me about your parents."

"What do you mean?"

"Your father. Tell me about him."

"He is a tailor. What should I tell you?"

"Is he Jewish?"

"What a stupid question. Of course he's Jewish. What kind of place is this, a courtroom? Am I on trial?"

"And your mother?"

"My mother is a mother. Why are you asking me all these stupid questions?"

"Is your mother Jewish?"

"What do you mean? What business is it of yours?"

"Alexi, answer straight: Is your mother Jewish?"

"So she's not Jewish. You are all really crazy people around here."

By this time there was absolute silence in the *shul* as one hundred pairs of eyes and ears focused on this confrontation.

The Rebbetzin looked up at the crowd.

"Now you see, *kinderlach,* why the Torah states that the Jewishness of a person is entirely dependent upon the mother. If your mother is a Jew, you are a Jew. And if your mother is not a Jew, you are not a Jew. It's as simple as that. There is no half and half. Here we have a boy who does not feel what we feel because he is not a Jew. He has been told he is Jewish, but he is not. And since he made a public declaration, we have an obligation to declare the truth in public also.

"Alexi, as a non-Jew you can receive great blessing by recognizing and publicizing the holiness of the Jewish nation and performing those commandments that the Torah obligates all people to perform. There is nothing wrong with not being Jewish, but you must know who you are."

Alexi turned and left the room.

The Rebbetzin continued.

"Zayda saw Alexi's eyes from across the room, and he came here to tell me that he is not one of us. That is why

Alexi was the only one in this room who could not feel what we felt. All the rest of us felt it, because we all stood together at Mount Sinai."

Applying Torah Values to Life

From being with Zayda, I learned how one applies the Torah to everyday life. I began to feel the truth of how the holy Jews of Europe lived, the infinite kindness, patience, and love that could exist between Jew and Jew.

I am not telling you stories designed to make the Jungreis family appear to be saints. They would be the first to tell you that they are ordinary Jews who are only doing what the Torah requires. But the Torah elevates us human beings from the level of animals to the level of G-d's servants. We have seen its effect on our personal lives, and we learned it by observing the activity of Zayda, Mama, and their family.

Zayda and Mama saw their world go up in flames, and yet they did not lose their Torah values, their humanity. They saw their family disappear in the crematoria, and they themselves, with their children, disappeared into the dark night of Bergen-Belsen. Even in those dark days, when they themselves were prisoners of a world that had gone crazy, they carried on a life of *mitzvos*, saving others and preparing for the sunrise that they knew would come. They lived with Torah values, both in "normal" times and in times of crisis. Nothing can match the lessons learned from this *yeshiva* of real experience.

I was always impressed by Mama's self-discipline. When her Hungarian newspaper arrived or some major article appeared about Rebbetzin Esther, she would never read it right away no matter how interested she was. She would put it away for Shabbos. Mama was always busy, and everyone else's needs came first.

We were all soldiers in Mama's army. Many hundreds are the frozen chickens I shlepped down Mama's back stairs to the basement freezer, where they remained until needed by the *yeshiva*. I have often thought that blessings I received in my life are the result of the perspiration I shed shlepping those chickens or huge bundles of used clothing under the disciplined eye of Mama. Sometimes I "needed" to have this in mind to give myself strength as I was struggling on that staircase.

Whenever I had to stay late, Mama would make me a huge hot dinner, with chicken and potatoes and all kinds of vegetables, *kugels*, soda, and cake and cookies for dessert. Mama always wanted me to eat, and the food was delicious. She wasn't proud about her cooking; she didn't mind if you drowned the food in ketchup, just as long as you were enjoying it. Everyone was her child.

Mama and Zayda did not let one drop of food go to waste. This is literally a *mitzvah*. In America, we acquire and throw out food and other precious necessities without a second thought. But each crumb is a gift from G-d. It's not "coming to us," even though we may think it is. That is one reason why we make a blessing before and after every instance of eating and drinking, even going to the water fountain. For Mama and Zayda, who lived through daily starvation for years in the ghetto and the concentration camps, each crumb was a discrete present from the Al-mighty.

These lessons came home to me especially around the time of the *yeshiva's* annual dinner. Before the dinner, Zayda would have me shlepp up all the liquor from the garage. This was another perspiration-and-blessing producer. You can get an idea of how much liquor there was in the garage by realizing that Mama and Zayda had no car. The liquor, which filled practically the entire garage, came from gifts they had received and which they carefully saved for the *yeshiva's* use. Over the years, my station wagon became holy by transporting many objects, from Torah scrolls we took to the *sofer* (scribe) for repair to the liquor we transported to the catering hall prior to the *yeshiva* dinner.

Immediately after the dinner, Mama went on patrol in the caterer's kitchen. Every morsel of unused food, every ounce of beef and chicken and vegetables and salad and cake, everything was packed for *yeshiva* lunches and needy families. And of course, all the half-empty liquor bottles had to come home to Zayda's garage for storage until the ritual was repeated the following year.

Saving Lives

Today, in the twenty-first century, the story recounted in the Passover *Haggadah* could seem like a fairy tale. It is tempting to sit around that beautiful Passover table and romanticize it. But we are supposed to feel its pain and reality. That's why we eat *maror*, bitter herbs.

The same is true of the events of the Second World War. Today, a half-century later, the Holocaust takes on a surrealistic air. Our enemies claim, in fact, that it didn't happen.

But our generation grew out of those bitter times, and we have to understand their reality in order to understand ours. The fact is that we are still in exile. It is tempting to forget about that in the comfort of America. Until *Moshiach* comes we Jews will always be in danger. It is very dangerous to forget that fact. *"Esav sone es Yaakov . . .* Esau hates Jacob."* In general, we are hated by the other nations of the world. This is not only a historic fact, it is a law of humanity, and is so stated in the Torah.

Zayda, Mama, and the whole family had to face terrible tests. I learned how a Jew faces trials by hearing how they reacted during the periods of darkness. It is not too much to say that Hineni was born in the cauldron of war-torn Europe.

The German plan was to create a ghetto in Szeged, the city where the Jungreises lived. They would do it by herding all the Jews from the surrounding countryside into the Jewish part of town. Many families were crowded into each apartment. There was no hospital.

A pregnant lady, whose husband had been deported to a slave labor camp, was very close to giving birth. She went into labor. The only place where there was privacy was in the synagogue, so Zayda and Mama made it into a hospital.

Zayda found a hospital bed, and the lady gave birth to a boy. Mama and other women were there to help her. Eight days later there was a *bris*. It was May 1944. Everybody at this *bris* was crying bitterly. People felt guilty, as if the *bris* had killed the child because the Germans would know he was a Jew.

There were no diapers. Mama told Rabbi Jacob, who was then about ten years old, to take off his *yarmulka* and yellow star, jump the fence, and go outside the ghetto. For years afterwards the family could not believe how naïve

---

* Rashi on Genesis 33:4 based on the Sifri

they had been to let him go. If the Nazis had caught him, he would have been shot on the spot. It was a very dangerous mission. He ran like a madman for about three blocks, bought the diapers, and ran out of the store. His heart was beating wildly. He jumped the fence and came back, knowing he had done something very dangerous.

By some miracle this mother and baby, instead of being taken to Auschwitz, ended up in Theresienstadt. Theresienstadt was not really a concentration camp but a showcase, which the Red Cross used to inspect. The Germans used it to demonstrate how "happy" the Jews were in concentration camps. They even had street names. The mother and baby survived.

This baby is the present Tselemer Rebbe. When Zayda passed away, the Rebbe came during *shiva*, the mourning period, and Mama told him, "I gave you your first bath."

Another well-known chassidic *rebbe* was given life through Zayda and Mama's efforts. The current Satmar Rebbe was a young man before the war, the rabbi in the town of Zenta. Zayda was very close to him. Several times he was imprisoned by the Germans and several times Mama went to the prison and somehow succeeded in getting the future Satmar Rebbe out of prison at the risk of her life.

Maybe the miracle happened *because* she risked her life.

Is it possible to understand what it means to risk one's life for others? Through having known Zayda and knowing Mama, at least I get some idea of how one is supposed to live. Maybe, because I've met people who have actually put their lives on the line, I'll give up something in order to make the world a little better. Maybe I'll give up eating shrimp or pork, or going to the movies on Shabbos. Maybe I'll give money to charity, more than I was planning. Maybe

I'll try to discipline myself in some way so that I can try to become a better person or benefit someone else. Maybe Zayda and Mama's example has taught me that, if nothing else. Maybe a little smidgen of them rub off on me.

▲▲▲

Hungary was the last country in Europe to be overrun by the Nazis, and although conditions weren't good, at least people were not yet being deported to concentration camps. So they would smuggle Jews from other countries into Hungary.

Many of these Jews would come to Szeged, stay a few days, and then try to get over the Yugoslavian border. If a visitor from out of town came to your house, the law in eastern Europe then was that you must report him to the police even if he was your cousin or uncle. A Jew would come to the railroad station, usually at night, maybe at 10:00 P.M. or even 2:00 or 3:00 A.M. Where could he sleep? He usually had almost no money. At the railroad station there would be a taxi or a horse and buggy. The drivers would say, "Don't worry; I know where to take you."

They would arrive at the Jungreis's apartment in the middle of the night. This was very scary. If it had come to the attention of the police, they could literally have shot the family for putting up strangers. It frightened Zayda that every taxi and buggy driver knew that their home was a "hotel."

You see, Zayda was not an ascetic "holy man" who had no fear. He was a human being who had fears just the way you and I do, but his greatness was that *despite his fear* he and his family risked their lives for their brothers and sisters.

In Zayda's apartment house, as was common in Szeged,

the superintendent had the only key. He locked the door at 10:00 P.M. If you came in after that, you had to ring the bell, wake up the super, give him a hefty tip, and then he'd let you in. Zayda's people would come in at midnight or 2:00 or 3:00 A.M. and wake up the super. He knew what was going on, and he was not a friend.

When a man entered in the middle of the night, Rabbi Jacob would go to the door with Zayda, who greeted every Jew with a kiss and a hug, no matter how dirty and disheveled he was. He immediately gave the person a chance to take a shower and eat some food. Mama fed them all. Zayda was crying with every Jew. Rabbi Jacob never knew where he would sleep. Most of the time it was on the floor together with another two or three dozen people. This was a regular occurence in an apartment of four or five rooms.

Once, in the spring of 1943, a young man came from Poland with a horrifying story. Zayda was sitting at the large table in his library and the man sat down with him. Rabbi Jacob was standing. (*Please, friends, note this fine detail*: it is a lesson to all of us in twenty-first century America how far we have traveled. It was not considered *derech eretz*, proper behavior, for him to sit with the adults. How many children today would even think about that, let alone understand it or follow it? How many parents would have the courage to expect their children to act that way, let alone train them to do so?)

Mama came in and stood at the other end of the table. The man started to speak. He had just escaped from a concentration camp in Poland. At that time in Hungary they didn't understand what a concentration camp was.

He spoke in Yiddish: "Rebbe, you know they *mach zeif fun menschen* [make soap from people]."

Zayda's face turned white. His face fell down onto his chest. He did not answer.

Mama said, "It cannot be."

Mama couldn't believe such things could happen. Zayda believed it.

Then Mama said, as it started to sink in, "But here it cannot happen." They still thought Hungary was a civilized country.

Rabbi Jacob pretended not to understand the significance of what he had heard, but no one could get it out of his head. Rabbi Jacob says that's when he became a bar mitzvah. At that moment his childhood ended.

When we hear these stories, we wonder if we really have any problems today. I think that in America we are a little spoiled. We sometimes forget that Torah is a life-and-death matter. When you're comfortable, it can happen that you think this is the permanent situation and it always was this way. This is a dangerous belief, because reality is never far away. Such is the responsibility of a Jew: to uphold these Torah standards of goodness and proper behavior even when it seems that the sun will never shine again. Please read a little further, to see the extent that goodness and kindness can extend. Then you will begin to understand what heritage was transmitted to Rebbetzin Jungreis and why she was so committed to bringing the Torah to our brethren here in America, where such a holy lifestyle and such self-sacrifice were almost unknown.

As more and more refugees fled to Hungary, Zayda and Mama's responsibilities increased. The closer the Germans came, the more anti-Semitism increased in Hungary. Szeged became the embarkation point for the infamous Bor mines in Yugoslavia. Young men, drafted into slave-labor battalions, would be sent down the River Tisa in boats to mine copper there for the German war machine. They seldom came out alive.

Zayda and Mama had a double-edged strategy to help these boys survive.

Unbelievable as it may sound, their primary strategy was to make them sick. They found that certain compounds mimic the symptoms of communicable diseases. The last thing the Hungarian authorities wanted was for a plague to sweep through the ranks of their slave battalions. Any boy suspected of carrying an infectious disease would be rejected from the draft.

Zayda consulted doctors. As a result of his research, about a dozen concoctions were made in Mama's kitchen, which would then be sewn into the children's coats or the boys' pants and long socks. Mama also found places to conceal things. Then the family would visit the boys who were waiting to be shipped out to Bor. Zayda would be searched, but Mama and the children were not. Discovery would have meant instant death, but they felt they had to risk it.

The two most effective concoctions were raw milk and soy paste.

Raw milk straight from a cow, when injected into the bloodstream, causes a high fever lasting forty-eight to sixty hours. Mama and the children concealed syringes and raw milk in their clothing. Can you imagine? Boys with this fever would be quarantined in a military hospital and not be allowed on the boat. This bought time and sometimes salvation.

The soy paste, which the boys would put under their eyelids, produces an instant reaction that mimics trachoma, a highly contagious eye disease that can lead to blindness. The Hungarians were very afraid of this disease, and boys suspected of having it would also be quarantined.

But that was not all. What about the boys who were well enough to go on the transports?

Here was the second part of the strategy.

The transports would leave late in the afternoon. At about 1:00 A.M. the previous night, Zayda would hire a horse carriage. With the young Rabbi Jacob accompanying him, he would go to the docks. Thousands of boys were waiting. For the next twelve hours, Zayda would speak to each boy individually and give him a special blessing and an amulet that was designed to give him strength for the ordeals that lay ahead.

The amulet consisted of a Hungarian coin with a hole in the center, comparable in value to an American quarter. Zayda would tie a string through the hole and hang it around each boy's neck.

Zayda's blessing to each boy consisted of verses from Psalm 91: "Whoever sits in the refuge of the most High, he shall dwell in the shadow of the Al-mighty. I will say of Hashem, 'He is my refuge and my fortress; my G-d, I will trust in Him' . . . beneath His wings you will be protected . . . no evil will befall you . . . He will charge His angels for you, to protect you in all your travels. . . . "

Once, during this scene, a Hungarian officer started to make fun of Zayda. He danced and jumped around, singing, "This will not help them, rabbi. You are wasting your time." Zayda ignored him and went about his business.

A few weeks later, the family was stopped by a Hungarian officer. This had never happened before. They were afraid that they had been betrayed and were about to be arrested.

"Don't worry, rabbi," said the officer. "I just wanted to ask whether you heard what happened to that officer who made fun of you?"

"No."

"He got on the boat to Bor. After they arrived, it was very warm and he decided to go for a swim. He drowned. The whole camp is talking about it."

Despite their bravado, they sensed Zayda's holiness.

Why do you think Zayda took the ten-year-old Rabbi Jacob with him to the docks? Wasn't it cruel? Don't you think that poor boy was exhausted? Is it good for a kid to stay up all night and the next day? Isn't it unhealthy? How could he learn his lessons? What would the Board of Health say?

I think I know the reason. Sure he was exhausted. So was Zayda. But I want to ask you: could there have been a greater school than that? Was that scene not etched onto Rabbi Jacob's soul with letters of fire? Could he grow up after that without the deepest feelings of compassion for his brothers? Could he ever forget the look in their eyes? Could he ever forget the look in his father's eyes? We know how you teach math and French. But how do you teach a man to feel for his brother? Zayda knew.

Again, friends, I am telling you that Hineni was born there, in the crucible of Nazi Europe. OK, Rebbetzin Esther was not physically at the docks with her father and brother, but do you understand what kind of household this was? In such fire and flame is the sword of Torah forged. From such tears as they shed comes the water to cleanse us all.

There is a sequel to this entire episode at the docks. It shows with startling clarity the foresight—I am tempted to say "prophetic vision"—of Zayda in bringing his young son with him.

Many years later, after the family had settled in America and Rabbi Jacob was in his twenties, he went to Israel for a year of study. In the 1950s it was still very unusual to fly to Israel, so he traveled by ship. The ship docked in Naples, and Rabbi Jacob got off to stroll on the pier. He saw a warship and walked up to it, amazed to see that it flew the flag of Israel. At the end of the gangplank was a sailor.

The sailor had a gun in his hand. For Rabbi Jacob, coming from the Holocaust, it seemed as if he were looking at the angel Gabriel. This was the first time he had ever seen a Jew with a gun.

He went over and asked the sailor, "Where are you from?"

"Hungary."

So he asked in Hungarian, "Can I go up on the boat?"

"You cannot."

Rabbi Jacob noticed a Hungarian coin hanging around the sailor's neck.

"Where did you get that coin?"

"Nine or ten years ago I was in Szeged and there was a rabbi and a little kid and the rabbi gave it to me."

Rabbi Jacob started to shake.

"I want you to know, that rabbi is my father and I am that little kid."

The sailor looked at Rabbi Jacob, and then he kissed and hugged him. Rabbi Jacob could not speak. Two "defenseless" Jewish children, at the mercy of the seemingly invincible nations, survive through miracles and meet again to embrace. Such are the wondrous ways of G-d. Such is the eternal story of the Children of Israel.

The sailor said, "I'm going to speak to the captain and get permission for you to go on the ship."

He started walking up the gangplank. Rabbi Jacob called him back.

"I have a second thought. I have experienced enough today to satisfy me forever. I want you to know that it's the first time in my life I ever heard a Jew say no. In the camps, even before the war, every time a German or a Hungarian spoke to us, we had to say, 'Yes, master.' It's the first time I ever saw a Jew with a gun, and he said no. That's enough for me. I don't need to go on the boat."

▲▲▲

When the Jungreises first came to America after the war, they lived in East Flatbush, Brooklyn. They had hardly any money and were living in a basement apartment. At one point, Rebbetzin Esther, still a young girl, developed a fever. A neighbor called her own doctor and paid for the visit. Until the end of this woman's life, long after they had left the neighborhood, Zayda insisted that the family call her regularly. She was invited to every wedding and family celebration. Zayda never forgot, and that's what he taught his children.

In those early years, Zayda had a synagogue in that neighborhood, and he was contemplating building his *yeshiva*. He befriended the president of the local bank, who helped him with both projects. Years later, the bank was bought by a bigger bank. Zayda maintained his relationship there and made friends with the new people also. He continued to use the bank even after a bigger bank bought the second bank. Why? Because his friends, who had helped him, were still there. And so on and so on, through three or four name changes at the bank, Zayda continued to come.

Even in my time, some twenty years after Zayda had left East Flatbush, he still returned to the same bank. I know, because then I had the honor to drive him. It was a big moment when Zayda entered the bank. The officers, black and white, Jew and non-Jew, would stand up when they saw him. And believe me, it wasn't because his balances were large.

Zayda would stop to see every officer and every teller and inquire about his or her family. Even though he was always busy, Zayda seemed to have time for everyone.

Before every holiday, Mama would bake cookies and cakes, sometimes very elaborate creations, and we would shlepp big cartons filled with everybody's packages. Some people would cry with happiness when this happened. They would tell Zayda they had been waiting all year for this moment.

But the ultimate version of package distribution took place at Brookdale Hospital. Between his frequent visits to sick people and, later, his visits for his own ailments, it seemed that Zayda knew everybody at this huge hospital, from the president to the security guards. Our trips to Brookdale before the Jewish holidays consisted of transporting dozens of cartons, each filled with many packages for Zayda's "following."

It was a tactical challenge to deliver these packages to the right people. Zayda and I would walk through office after office and he would tell me exactly which person got which package. Each box looked the same on the outside, but Zayda knew what was on the inside. Each package would be distributed with a blessing. Many were given to people Zayda didn't know so well; he did not want anyone to feel envious when their officemates received packages, so he would give them one also.

The doctors got a package, the nurses and office workers got a package, the security guards got a package. Even the tellers in the locked cashier's area opened up the door so that Zayda could bring packages. All doors opened for Zayda because Zayda was a giver. Doors seem to open for people who give.

Toward the end of his life Zayda had to endure great pain to distribute these gifts. Getting around this big hospital became very hard as walking became difficult. But as long as he could endure it physically, he continued to distribute his blessings. Zayda was willing to undergo pain in order to bring healing and happiness to others.

I don't say I had the kind of education that Zayda's family had in Europe, and none of us should have to live through such conditions again. But simply to see Zayda or Mama in action made an impression on one's soul that nothing could obliterate.

▲▲▲

On our rounds throughout the city Zayda would stop periodically to visit people. On the trip to Manhattan we would always pass through Brooklyn's Crown Heights and stop at a certain shoemaker's store on Utica Avenue. This was the most humble shop you could imagine. The shoemaker was an old European man who was a member of Zayda's congregation. Having Zayda in his store of course not only made the shoemaker's day, it probably made his whole life.

But Zayda's visit had a specific purpose. The store was

in a dangerous neighborhood, and Zayda was worried about the man's safety. He would use every visit as an opportunity to try to persuade him to sell his store and move to a safer neighborhood. Zayda never gave up on this.

There were many such stops along the way, and all business was interspersed with long personal talks, concern for the welfare of the people he met, and discussions of Torah topics where it was appropriate.

I remember not once but many times people whispering to me as Zayda was going about his business in their store, "Rabbi Jungreis saved my life in Europe." This was just the tip of the iceberg. How many stories did I not hear for all the stories I did hear?

We would visit many spots on the Lower East Side. We needed to buy cases of *yarmulkas, tzitzis, siddurim* (prayer books) for the children at the *yeshiva.*

A regular stop was the Kedem Wine Company's offices on Norfolk Street, where Zayda's friend Rabbi Herzog presided amongst the barrels. The two rabbis would spend a long time in deep conversation. Rabbi Herzog sometimes expressed his concern to me as Zayda weakened near the end; he would ask many questions about Zayda's health. Rabbi Herzog was not a young man himself, and he trembled constantly, but his mind was sharp and he was always worried about Zayda. Zayda would visit the winery especially before Passover, when he stocked up on wines that the members of his congregation and the *yeshiva* would need for the holidays.

▲▲▲

So you see, I really did attend *yeshiva*, the *yeshiva* of real life with an ageless *rebbe* named Zayda. I learned by observing how a Jew should act. I was privileged to begin to understand something about the genesis of Hineni, and the place from which Rebbetzin Esther had inherited her passionate love for the Children of Israel. This is what I am so anxious to pass on to you. After all, why should I keep this to myself? I learned from Rebbetzin Esther that I should share every good thing with my brothers and sisters.

And now I would like to explain, with G-d's help, how we tried to apply these timeless lessons to our new life.

CHAPTER FIVE

INTO THE FUTURE

IN CONSTRUCTING OUR NEW LIFE, we tried to build upon the foundation of previous generations. That is why I have described to you Zayda and Mama's life in Europe and how Hineni came about.

Now it was our turn. How would we carry on the challenge to the next generation? What would *our* edifice look like? What kind of life did we try to build? What should people who aspire to spiritual advancement strive for in the twenty-first century?

I would like to tell you how we have tried to incorporate some important building blocks into the structure of our new life.

If there is one thing we learned, it's that everything starts with proper behavior.

There is a widely used phrase, "*Derech eretz kadma l'Torah,*" which means that proper behavior precedes and underlies Torah observance. One cannot observe the Torah properly unless one behaves properly toward other people. One cannot be evil or mean and observe G-d's commandments. It doesn't work. The concept of treating others properly is not separate from the Torah. It does not exist "on top of" the commandments. It is more like a constant effort to apply all the commandments of the Torah *to oneself* on a constant basis—a continual, nonstop process of examining each word and action in an ongoing effort to accomplish everything G-d is asking us to accomplish. If we don't do that, if we don't at least *try* to change our lives on a continual basis, then we're not taking the Torah seriously.

We're not supposed to change the Torah to suit ourselves, we're supposed to change ourselves to suit the Torah. That's so basic. Why did G-d give us a Torah if not to use it to improve ourselves?

Observing Zayda, Mama, and the Rebbetzin gave us a grounding in how one applies Torah to daily life. If you see people whose entire being is defined by Torah, you can learn from them. You see that it can be done.

Finding One's Life Partner

In constructing a home, the first requirement is marriage, and in our world the process of meeting one's life companion has become very difficult. Even among Jews who are returning to Torah it is a difficult area, because there usually is no family to help and guide. This is one situation in which proper behavior has immediate consequences, because everything depends on the interaction between two people. How you act determines how you are going to get along.

The Rebbetzin always tells single people, if someone comes up to you and wants to talk, you must act like a mensch. *You may feel that he or she is not for you, but there is almost never*

*a reason to snub someone. Just speak to the person in a pleas-
ant manner. Give your full attention. Perhaps say, "I have an
idea for someone who would be great for you." In that merit
you will be helped to find your own* basherte—*that individual
you were destined to spend your life with—and you will have
helped the other person. But always smile and be respectful.
Act as if this is your brother or sister, because it is.*

We've got to have the right attitude to succeed in anything, especially dating. Often, the process is filled with
frustration, but one must fight the tendency to give in to
depression or despair.

Ellie was a little overweight, a little shy. She didn't fit in
that well in her suburban New Jersey high-school crowd.
Her older sister was popular and vivacious, but not all sisters are the same. If your social skills or appearance don't
measure up, then you're "out of it" in the secular teenage
world.

Being "out of it" turned out to be Ellie's biggest blessing.
Being a very resourceful girl, she thought about things
deeply and considered the following: If I don't fit in here,
where might I fit in? She decided to find out more about
her Jewishness.

She wound up at a Hineni *Shabbaton* at the Pine View
Hotel in the Catskills, and that's when we got to know
her. Ellie soon became a regular Shabbos guest at our home
and then moved in with us. She became part of our family,
and as she melded in, her dedication to Torah became ever
stronger.

You never know when you are going to have an experience that changes your life. These big events always seem
to come when they are totally unexpected.

One Shabbos in late spring, about nine months after we

first met her, Ellie was at our house with Alan and his family, the same Alan who was a disciple of "Reverend" Mike.* By that time Alan had been married for several years and had several children. Ellie loved to take care of the kids, and on this long Shabbos afternoon they were enjoying the climbers and other toys in the sunny backyard.

When you're watching little children, you frequently can't see everything at once. Before she knew it, Dina, Alan's three-year-old girl, had slipped and fallen, cutting her chin. Blood was gushing out. Her mother came running. There was a commotion, climaxing with a pilgrimage to the doctor around the corner.

It was one of those childhood injuries with lots of blood and some stitches. You say it was nothing if you look back years later, but it didn't feel like "nothing" at the time. It healed completely, and now it's only a memory, but Ellie was beside herself with self-reproach. She felt responsible for the injury to little Dina, whom she loved so much.

She went up to her room and cried the whole afternoon. We didn't see her the rest of Shabbos. She just wanted to be alone.

At *Havdalah*, the ceremony that marks the ending of Shabbos and the beginning of the new week, we pried her out of her room. She didn't want to come, but we convinced her. She didn't speak; she still wanted to be alone.

At that time, Hineni used to conduct monthly singles nights in Brooklyn for the thousands of Jewish young people who wanted an appropriate place to meet. Hineni gave them the right atmosphere and a sense of security. Zayda was always there, his notebook filled with the names and

---

* See "Doing Teshuva," page 224.

phone numbers of eligible girls and boys, and who would be right for whom.

The Rebbetzin would speak, to give the right theme to the evening.

This Saturday night a Hineni singles event was scheduled. Ellie was going to come along, both as Hineni staff and as a single.

"Ellie, please get ready. We'll be leaving in about fifteen minutes," I called out.

"I'm not going."

"What do you mean?"

"I don't feel like going. I'm staying home tonight."

If there's one thing I learned from the Rebbetzin, it's that depression is the enemy. If you sit at home and contemplate how messed up your life is, how bad your mistakes were, how impossible it is to get out of the pit, you will convince yourself and you will indeed not be able to get out of the pit. I knew that Ellie had to fight it.

"Ellie, you've got to come. Everybody is depending on you, and besides, you know what the Rebbetzin says about depression. You can't allow it to get the better of you. I know you're upset about what happened, but it's in the past. It was an accident. You learned from it. Dina will be fine. So be thankful. Now it's time to do a *mitzvah* and help some Jewish kids who are looking for a *shidduch*. Who knows? Maybe you'll find your *basherte* over there."

Ellie gave me a resigned look and went off to change her clothes. During the car ride to Brooklyn she never opened her mouth.

Before we got out of the car, I said to her, "Look, you can't mope forever. Even if you don't feel like it, put a smile on your face. Pretend you're happy even if you're not. You know what Rabbi Jungreis always says in the name of the Berdichever Rebbe: 'If you put a smile on your face, G-d will give you every reason to smile.'"

Ellie forced herself. She went inside, and before long I saw her helping everybody, setting out refreshments, cutting cake.

I noticed a young *yeshiva* guy who looked like he might be right for Ellie. His name was Chaim. I introduced them. We were very busy, so I really didn't have my eye on Ellie that much, but every once in a while I caught sight of her, and I noticed that throughout the evening she was talking to him a lot. Then she'd be hard at work somewhere else, but again, a little later, there she was talking to him.

Toward the end of the evening I caught up with her.

"So how's it going?"

"You know he's a very nice guy."

He took her number.

A few months later Ellie and Chaim were married. Such a *leibedik* (lively) wedding! She was a young bride, and he was a young *yeshiva* boy. Now, several years later, they are young parents. With G-d's help they will be young grandparents. He's still learning and working on the side. Ellie is somehow able to run a clothing business from her home as well as being a full-time mommy and wife. Her parents are delighted with such beautiful grandchildren and such a happy daughter.

Hineni provided a family setting for her. We all need parents, *zaydas*, and *bubbies* to guide us through life. One of the tragedies of modern American life is that children think it is to their advantage to get "divorced" from their parents. The other side of the coin is that parents think they have no right to "butt in" to their children's affairs. What good have the parents' lives been if they can't use their experience to guide their children?

▲▲▲

Here is another story about dating, illustrating the concept that one's basherte is definitely there. You just have to find each other. People who are dating must have faith in that concept. It is true. It works. Do you remember what I said in the first chapter about the two halves of one soul reuniting?

Dana, a brilliant twenty-eight-year-old, came to us when she was still in law school, lost in the swirl of the assimilated world.

An orphan for a few years, she had been very close to her father. His sudden passing left a void that was hard to bear.

Bored with her job in the brokerage industry, she decided in her mid-twenties to go to law school. There she developed a friendship with a girl who had recently found a path to Torah through Hineni. Dana soon started coming to Hineni, and from the very first day she found a perfect fit. The vacuum in her soul sucked in the timeless words; she had been famished for Torah without realizing it. Her previous restlessness had not resulted only from the desire for a more exciting job; it was a *"hunger and thirst for the word of G-d."**

Dana's life started to change. The vacuum was replaced by a sense of meaning. Her agile mind found answers to questions that until then she had not known how to ask.

She started coming to us for Shabbos, and before long there was hardly a Friday afternoon when she did not appear on our doorstep. She became our children's sister.

---

* Amos 8:11

Our family became her family. Dana was no longer an orphan.

With her life on a solid footing, she began to plan for the future. She found a job as an attorney, but what she really wanted was a home and a family, so she could build the eternal edifice her heart desired.

For so many singles in this generation, marriage is difficult. I am not speaking of the insanity of society in general, in which marriage has almost been discarded; but even among newly observant Jewish young people, it is hard to find a mate.

One reason is that the newly observant cannot work with their parents on this. In addition, contemporary attitudes concerning marriage have influenced them. Career has become an idol. With every passing year, one becomes more used to the singles' life, and it becomes harder to break out of it and find a mate. In the case of women, the biological clock is ticking, making it more problematic each year to contemplate having children.

Dana wanted more than anything to find her *basherte*. She went out with numerous guys, but no one was right. She became concerned. Already in her early thirties, she began to feel she would never find anyone, would never have a family, and was doomed to a solitary life. Between her pressure-filled job and her failure to find the right guy, she became depressed. She said to herself, "I will never get married."

A few miles away in Queens, Ben sat on the edge of his bed. A young, highly respected day-school *rebbe*, he had just returned from what seemed like the thousandth date of his life. It was Saturday night and he was crying. There was nobody for him. Nobody! He had met so many girls. So many good prospects had been set up by his parents and friends. Was he wrong to be so choosy? Why did nobody click? Was there something wrong with him? Were his standards too high?

His parents heard the tears through the bedroom door and their hearts were melting. What could they do? They were out of ideas. He was out of strength. All three of them felt they had reached bottom.

In nearby Far Rockaway, a group of young religious wives gathered every other week. They had recently formed a "*shidduch* committee." Each lady would make a three-minute presentation describing an eligible man or woman. The others would take notes. When someone thought of a suitable match, she would suggest the name and the two women would set up the date.

One of the wives came tonight with a three-minute speech about Ben. Yaffa, our daughter, was listening carefully. She had her ear tuned for Dana, and when she heard the description of Ben, a bell rang.

When she got home, she called Dana. Was it OK to give her name to Ben? Dana answered from the bottom of the pit. She was still depressed and thinking, "It will never work. Nothing ever works."

"OK," she said, with no conviction.

As I write, these two wonderful people have been married for several years. The second they met, they knew they had been destined for each other since the beginning of time. They exude a perpetual glow of happiness, and G-d has blessed them with a beautiful son.

This truly is a *shidduch* made in Heaven, and our daughter Yaffa was privileged to have been one of those through whose efforts it came about.

It is written* that before the birth of a child a heavenly voice announces that he or she is destined for a certain mate. G-d has worked these things out in advance, and each person is created to reach perfection with his or her "other half." Dana and Ben suffered until they found each other. But they stuck it out. They overcame depression, pitched into a life of *mitzvos*, and today they have a warm home filled with hope and dedicated to the ageless path of Torah.

Here is one more classic dating story featuring none other than Mama. It emphasizes the importance of being a good person, not taking yourself too seriously. Mama gave this boy a good test, and he passed it.

When Zayda and Mama went to a wedding in the "old days," meaning before their grandchildren were married, they would insist on bringing Chaya Sora, Rebbetzin Esther's oldest daughter. There would be many fine families at these weddings, and Zayda and Mama wanted to introduce Chaya Sora to them.

Chaya Sora later found a wonderful *shidduch* when she married Rabbi Shlomo Gertzulin, but the story of their first date tells you a lot about Mama. It was also a good test of the prospective bridegroom's character.

When Rabbi Gertzulin first met Chaya Sora, Mama was "standing in" for Chaya Sora's parents, who were at a rabbinical convention. When the young man came to the house to pick up Chaya Sora, Mama was the chaperone.

---

* Talmud, tractate *Sotah* 2a

As the couple was about to leave, Mama handed Rabbi Gertzulin a big bag of garbage for deposit in the container on his way to the car. That's Mama; no pretense! But what a test for a young man on a date. Needless to say, Rabbi Gertzulin passed the test.

Dating is a microcosm of life. We've got to approach life honestly and not put on airs. Not only do we have to be ourselves, but we'd better make sure that "self" is a good self.

Getting Married

How are Jews supposed to behave at a wedding? In such a way that it forms the basis for a beautiful life. For one thing, a wedding must be carried out according to Jewish law in every respect. A competent Torah-abiding rabbi must see that every detail is correct, because every detail in a wedding will influence every detail in the entire life to follow.

Aviva was getting older and she wasn't married yet. She had been engaged four years earlier but had broken it off. She was pretty and smart and vivacious, but she wasn't meeting guys she felt were right for her. She had one quality, however, which I thought was the most amazing of all. Whenever her friends would get married, she was always completely happy for them, keeping her own pain hidden. Her *"mazal tov"* was from the heart; her smile was full; nobody knew her suffering.

She kept a record. She went out with sixty-six guys before she found the right one. Number sixty-seven is her husband, and they are a match made in heaven. I have always felt that two things enabled her to endure the difficulty of this process: her faith in G-d and her incredible self-control, which allowed her to express such happiness for others while hiding her own pain.

Here is another story about two Jewish children who were destined for each other, but whose path was very twisted. What straightened the path was the fact that they embraced a Torah life. Their wedding—and its postscript—were unique.

It all started on a lazy Sunday afternoon. Todd was flipping the television dial when he saw a lady talking about the Bible.

She called it "the Torah."

Todd lived alone in a big house in Westchester County, north of New York City. A successful financial consultant in his early thirties, he had everything . . . and nothing.

What was the point of it all, anyway? His big house, his Mercedes? What did his life mean? He had no purpose, no satisfaction. Being single, he didn't even have anyone to share his emptiness with.

In college, he had surfed the Pacific Coast. Now he surfed the tube.

At the end of the show, a message came on the screen telling viewers how to contact Hineni. Todd jotted down the information and stuffed it in his wallet. A few weeks later, he was in Manhattan on a Thursday evening with nothing to do. He dug the note out of his wallet.

"I might as well drop in."

Todd had never before heard such words as he heard that night. The "lady," Rebbetzin Jungreis, was even more powerful in person than on television. Todd started feeling goosebumps.

He came to us for Shabbos and instantly became part of our family. He loved the kids. He loved the *cholent*. He loved the stuffed peppers. He loved the Shabbos songs. He loved forgetting about money for twenty-four hours. He loved the sleep of Shabbos, the perfect rest that refreshed his soul, giving him spiritual as well as physical energy to carry him through the week.

Each Saturday night, as Todd's Mercedes pulled out of our driveway, we would give each other the "V for victory" sign, as if to say, "This will be a good week. Shabbos will get us through."

Todd grew in Torah and prospered in his career, but one thing was still missing: the companion with whom he could share his new life.

Around the corner from the Hineni building lived a beautiful young girl named Catherine. Raised in France and America with no strong connection to her Jewish roots, she had become a successful career woman. Like Todd, she had recently begun thinking about the meaning of her success. What was it worth?

She often passed the Hineni building and wondered what went on there. But she had nothing in common with "religious Jews."

She was at a family bar mitzvah in Virginia when she struck up a conversation with some friendly strangers.

"You live around the corner from Hineni and you've never met the Rebbetzin?"

On their next trip to New York, Catherine's new friends called her up.

"We're picking you up and taking you to Hineni tonight."

So they brought Catherine around the corner and through the doors of Torah. Immediately, she connected with the Rebbetzin's words, and her own life started to change.

It wasn't long before the Rebbetzin introduced her to Todd.

Everything clicked. After the third date, they were engaged. Today they are the parents of two beautiful girls.*

When Todd started coming to us for Shabbos, he became very close to the Rebbetzin's late husband. Every Friday night he would accompany the Rabbi home from synagogue before returning to our house.

Todd and the Rabbi were special friends. The Rabbi was a giant in every way. When he needed shoes (size 13EEEEE!), there was no place to get them except at the specialty store in Westchester that Todd had discovered. They went together.

Of course, Todd and Catherine wanted no one other than "their rabbi" to officiate at their wedding. On the wedding day, however, the Rabbi lay in Memorial Sloan-Kettering Cancer Center, only hours away from his trip to the next world.

The wedding was so sweet . . . and so bitter.

From his hospital bed, the Rabbi had instructed his son Rabbi Yisroel to stand in for him. Not knowing if he would ever see his father again, Rabbi Yisroel performed the wedding service through tears. He danced one dance with the groom and then rushed back to the hospital.

A few hours later, Sloan-Kettering was witness to an unprecedented sight. The elevator doors opened, and into the corridor, crowded with doctors, nurses, and medical equipment, stepped a bride in a flowing gown and a groom in a tuxedo.

The Rabbi opened his eyes. Before him stood two angels.

---

* Our daughter Sarah tells me I say "beautiful" too often, but all the children really are beautiful.

With all his strength he whispered two of his last words—
"*MAZAL TOV!*"—and raised his hands to bless them.

Blessings are real. That is why houses that echo to blessings are full of light, and houses that echo to curses are full
of darkness. The Rabbi's blessing, especially since he was
so close to the Next World, was full of power. Todd and
Catherine have been blessed with beautiful children and a
true Torah home. We have seen it. It is not a fairy tale.

I want to tell you about what it was like going to weddings with Zayda and Mama.

Zayda would say that morning, "Yisroel, you must stay
late because we have a wedding tonight."

Zayda, Mama, and I would leave in the evening. Usually the wedding was in Borough Park or Williamsburg.
Zayda would tell me: "Yisroel, I must be at the *chosson's
tisch* (the room where the groom, his family, and the rabbis
prepare documents and make sure all is in order for the
ceremony). You must eat for me. Go to the smorgasbord
and eat double."

On the way home, after the wedding, he would check to
find out exactly what I had eaten.

The ceremony would usually take place outside. There
was one wedding hall that regularly held weddings on the
street. The police would seal off the block and the wedding would take place under the stars—and under the "el,"
with the trains clattering by every few minutes.

One memory that stands out from these weddings is
Zayda's voice. I have heard many people make blessings,
but I have never heard anyone make a blessing like Zayda.
There was so much power and purity in the way he spoke
that I would get shivers from hearing him. It sounded like
a voice from Mount Sinai. It appeared that Zayda was

making himself a conduit for the blessing that was ema-
nating from G-d. One heard hundreds of generations of
holy rabbis in Zayda's voice. It was ancient. I can hear it
now. Any couple who received Zayda's blessing will never
forget that voice and that blessing.

Remember, blessings are real. The world was created by
G-d through words. When we make a blessing, we are also
creating something. We are acting, in fact, as if we were
made in the image of Hashem, which we are. So blessings—and curses—are never to be taken lightly.

Setting Up a New Home

When Leah and I moved to North Woodmere in 1974,
we had two children: Susan, whose name was changed to
Sarah, and Juliet, whose name was changed to Yaffa. Before we moved, we had not been planning a larger family.
The idea of having additional children was very frightening, to me especially. I was frightened at the idea of having
any children at all! I felt unable to raise them because I
didn't know what to teach them. I felt that they might
become uncontrollable and that our entire life would be
ruined by them. The fact is that I wouldn't have wanted
children at all if it hadn't been for a kind of social pressure
to which I gave in.

But when we discovered Torah, everything was different. There was a framework for life. I saw religious people
who had beautiful children, respectful, mature, and yet
innocent. Suddenly, we wanted to have more children, and
G-d blessed us not only with new children who increased
the sanctity of our home, but even our two children from

"the old days" became totally committed to Torah, as you have read in previous pages.

I remember once climbing the Grand Teton in Wyoming. Suddenly, after a few hours of hiking through forest, we emerged above the treeline and were overwhelmed by a huge vista stretching far into the distance. How had we climbed so high? It seemed we had just been on the ground.

It was the same with our family. Suddenly, we looked around and saw that we were surrounded by holy and smiling children, children bringing sanity and hope into our home and into the world. Where had they come from? Surely, these are the blessings of G-d.

Derech eretz, proper behavior, plays a big part in marriage. Without *derech eretz* there can be no peace in the home. I want to paint a vignette for you that is etched in my memory. It will give you an idea of the mutual respect between husband and wife that should underlie marriage.

It was December 1974 and I was driving Rebbetzin Jungreis to the airport. She had a major program in Miami, and Barbara Janov, Hineni's executive director, had gone on ahead. I pulled up to the house and the front door opened. The Rabbi and Rebbetzin appeared. The lawn was covered with ice. The Rabbi had to hold on to the Rebbetzin so she wouldn't fall. They slid down the icy slope together and he helped her into the car. As we pulled away, the Rebbetzin looked back at her husband, who was giving a blessing from the sidewalk.

"You know, Yisroel," she said to me, "there's not a selfish bone in that man's body."

That's the vignette, just a little scene, but it speaks volumes about how the Rebbetzin regarded her husband, how he acted toward her, how they behaved toward each other.

Can you see what kind of a home they created? In what kind of atmosphere the children were raised?

I want to tell you a little about the Rabbi, because I think these incidents will illustrate the kind of personality that can create a proper atmosphere in a home. We can try to work on ourselves to attain these qualities and change the nature of our existence.

After the Rabbi passed away, the Rebbetzin and her family were sitting *shiva*. They noticed a little girl crying hysterically.

"Who will help me with my homework?" she sobbed.

Nobody could understand what she was talking about. The Rebbetzin asked her mother. It seemed that this little girl had trouble with her Hebrew homework. In the afternoons, when she got home from school, the Rabbi would come over to the house and do her homework with her. Nobody knew except the family. Why should anyone know? It was just . . . the Rabbi.

Who knows what else we didn't know?

How about the widows who received bread and cake every Friday afternoon? Did we know?

How about the sick people whom the Rabbi visited eight times in the hospital? Did we know?

How about the mourners whom the Rabbi visited not once but every day they were sitting *shiva*? They knew, but did we know?

The Rabbi was the chaplain of the Nassau County Police Department, a very large department. You would assume that he was the *Jewish* chaplain. Well, he was, but that didn't stop him from being everybody's spiritual leader.

When he visited the chief of police, all work came to a halt. First, the secretaries would gather around the Rabbi and tell him their troubles. He healed their hearts. There was no time limit. The chief waited. Then it was *his* turn.

When the Rabbi passed away, the chief of police came to visit the mourners. He told the Rebbetzin something that will go down in history as a great *kiddush Hashem*, a sanctification of G-d's name.

Remember, this is not a Jew speaking:

"Rebbetzin, I have known many clergymen in my life, but your husband was my bridge to G-d."

Bridge to G-d.

A title of royalty.

What an honor to be called "bridge to G-d."

The Rabbi passed away in Memorial Sloan-Kettering Cancer Center in Manhattan at about 3:00 A.M. on Tuesday, January 23, 1996. His body was taken to a funeral home in Brooklyn. The funeral was to take place at our synagogue in Long Island at 1:00 P.M., some ten hours later. In those few hours over two thousand people assembled.

How do you think the Rabbi's body was transported from Brooklyn to Long Island?

A cavalcade of twenty-three Nassau County Police cars escorted him, sirens wailing and lights flashing. A helicopter flew overhead. Do you think these were all Jewish cops? No matter. *This was their Rabbi, their bridge to G-d.*

Is not the entire Jewish nation supposed to be the world's "bridge to G-d"?

This is what we would call a role model.

The Rabbi was a dreamer. G-d spoke to him constantly in dreams. A few months before he knew he was sick, the Rabbi dreamt that he was standing in his living room, looking out the big window at the lawn below, the very same lawn he and the Rebbetzin had slid down when I picked her up to go to the airport. It was snowing and his entire family was gathered on the lawn. He waved to them and called, but they couldn't see or hear him. He was watching them all from above.

Today, he stands in his heavenly house, watching his children from above. We can't see or hear him, but he is watching us. His granddaughter, Shaindie Wolff, says that the snow in that dream represents this world, which seems so beautiful and all-encompassing for the brief duration of our lives. But in a moment it is gone, melted away.

Incidentally, do you think it is a simple thing to have a granddaughter like Shaindie, who can interpret a dream like that? She was a little elementary school girl when she said that. Simply understanding that a child can say that will give us some idea of what a Torah home can be like.

When we ourselves returned to Torah, the Rabbi became like our father. We learned Torah from his mouth, we who were like kindergarten children. Is this not what we mean when we refer to the Oral Law? This is how the Torah is passed down, from father to son, from generation to generation, beginning with Moses at Mount Sinai receiving the Torah from G-d.

How does a Torah home begin to take shape? You have seen some of the personality traits that can help create it.

In today's assimilated world, young people just meet and decide to live together. If they get married, they tell their parents about it, either before or after it happens. But that's not how it works in a Torah home. A structure must rest on a firm foundation. The previous generation should be involved constantly with the next generation. That's how the Torah is passed down.

That's where the idea comes from of helping others

find their *basherte*, the person who is meant for them. In our work for Hineni, we have been fortunate to meet many people. One of the most important things we can do for them is to help them find their soulmates. Hineni has introduced literally hundreds of people to their prospective spouses. And we run a "full-service shop." Leah instructs the brides before marriage. Either Rabbi Yisroel or Rabbi Osher Anshul, the Rebbetzin's sons, instructs the grooms, and one of them is always available to officiate at the ceremony. In the years that follow, the Rebbetzin's daughters, Chaya Sara Gertzulin and Slovie Wolff, teach "young married" and "parenting" classes.

Leah recently received the following note from three young brides-to-be: "Thank you for your guidance. You have taught us some of the most important things we need to live happy lives. It really means a lot to us that you took this time to talk to us."

Dealing with Illness and Adversity

There is another side to life.

"Everything has its season, and there is a time for everything under the Heaven. A time to be born and a time to die . . . A time to weep and a time to laugh."*

How should one act in a time of adversity?

I remember particularly going to funerals with Zayda. He would always be asked to speak, and I soon found out why. It wasn't only that everybody loved Zayda and needed

---

* Ecclesiastes 3:1-4

his consolation, but at funerals Zayda had a way of conducting himself that was so ancient and holy that one does not find it in our contemporary, sterile environment. It is painful to see how much we have been influenced by the cultures to which our exile has brought us. But Zayda was like someone who lived thousands of years ago.

Zayda cried.

Whether the funeral was for someone Zayda had known for forty years or only briefly, Zayda felt the suffering of the family. Zayda always, *without exception*, wept as he spoke at a funeral. It never occurred to him to be embarrassed about this. His emotion would bring out the deepest feelings of the family and allow the catharsis that only tears can bring.

Zayda was amazing at visiting mourners. I learned a big lesson from this. I would have expected him to spend a long time at *shiva* calls, and when it was necessary, he did. But most of the time, Zayda would be in and out quickly. He did his work with such intensity that he could visit, cry with the family, leave them feeling that an angel had come to comfort them, and be gone in just a few minutes. Zayda did his work with complete dedication; but he didn't have any time to waste, and as soon as he had done what he had to do, he went on to the next *mitzvah*. He was driven, I believe, by the knowledge that he had only a finite amount of time to accomplish things in this world.

I accompanied Zayda to the cemetery when he bought plots for himself and his family. I know from Rebbetzin Jungreis that he gave up the idea of being buried in Israel to enable his children to visit his grave whenever they wanted. He sacrificed even burial in the Holy Land for his family.

I remember thinking how peaceful the place was.

How distant death seemed at the time!

Zayda had his share of sickness. But I remember, when he was still alive, there was a time when Mama was in the hospital. The atmosphere in the house changed during her protracted absence. Zayda sat in his usual chair and everything was the same, except everything was different. The darkness was palpable. I was reminded of the *Midrash** that says when our Mother Sarah died, the light that used to burn in the house from Shabbos to Shabbos was extinguished, not to be rekindled until Rebecca entered the tent with Isaac. Mama brought light to the house, but now Zayda is not here to see it.

As I write these words, Mama herself is not well. May she have a speedy and complete recovery and be with us "until a hundred and twenty years."**

Examine, please, the life of Rabbi Meshulam ha-Levi Jungreis, the Rebbetzin's late husband. His own family was taken away from him in the depths of Europe's darkness. His father was a holy sage of Israel. His mother refused to sleep in a bed from the day the Nazis took away her eldest son. Seven siblings gone. He witnessed torture and depravity, a world gone insane. And yet he never seemed depressed, never showed anything but a smile. Who knew what he had witnessed? Who knew what was in his heart? If he was crying inside, we didn't see it. All we saw was kindness and love.

When he was in the hospital, in agonizing pain only a few days from death, he had only one complaint.

"I can't reach out to people from here."

---

* Quoted by Rashi in his commentary on Genesis 24:67

** This is the traditional Jewish blessing for a long life. Moses died at a hundred and twenty, and led the Children of Israel until his last day.

That's what bothered him.

Following is the obituary notice our synagogue placed in *The New York Times*:

Congregation Ohr Torah mourns the passing of our beloved founder and leader, Rabbi Meshulam ha-Levi Jungreis. Rabbi Jungreis arose from the ashes of the European Holocaust to carry onward the spiritual dynasty from which he had descended in Hungary. A man who had witnessed elemental hatred and cruelty, he was possessed of elemental compassion and love. He brought the greatness of Torah Judaism from Europe to America and planted it in Long Island, where it took root in one of the South Shore's first Orthodox congregations. He was legendary for his care of all those who were suffering. He was legendary in his love of Eretz Yisroel and Am Yisroel. He taught the meaning of selflessness to a generation of American Jews. For thirty-two years he piloted our congregation through all waters. He was our leader, our guide, our teacher, our father. His towering greatness of soul cannot be replaced.

How should one confront sickness? Please read the following story.

Roz walked into our synagogue one Shabbos, a look of fear on her face. Her husband, Henry, sat down in the men's section. I immediately went over to greet him.

They were scared.

A few months previously, they had been visiting their daughter's family. In the middle of the night, Henry heard noises. He awoke to find Roz in the midst of convulsions.

Petrified, he ran to wake their daughter and her husband. Roz was admitted to the hospital. Soon afterwards, tests confirmed everyone's worst fear: an inoperable, malignant brain tumor.

Roz was given the classic death sentence: *"Six months to live."*

Frightened by their doctor's "decree," Roz and Henry entered a twilight world. They wandered through life like people on death row. Life became death itself, without hope for this world or belief in the next.

Friends and "experts" told them they had better just accept the doctors' pronouncement and enjoy life while they were still together, but this advice depressed them even further. Who can enjoy life on death row?

They were at the bottom of a pit, devoid of hope. The prison walls closed tighter around their lives. Those who were supposed to help them, the doctors and friends, had failed them. There was nothing left, so they drifted aimlessly from place to place, like Cain, who became a "wanderer on earth."*

Nothing in this world happens by chance. When someone reaches the bottom of the pit, he sometimes cries out in desperation in a way he never would have done before. They drifted into our synagogue. Maybe, they thought, there is a G-d, a Power higher than man, higher than the doctors' decree.

We spoke with them, and it was not long before Roz and Henry showed up at Hineni to hear Rebbetzin Jungreis conduct her weekly class, where the Torah portion somehow happens to "hit the bull's-eye" every time. I always marvel how each week the Rebbetzin discusses exactly what is on everyone's mind.

Desperate people, afraid of death, can do big things, even

* Genesis 4:14

abandoning concepts to which they have clung their entire lives. Desperate people lunge for the life preserver.

With nothing to lose and everything to gain, they plunged into Shabbos, *kashrus*, the whole Torah. Roz jumped (OK, *walked*) into the *mikveh*, and, at the age of "forty something," started to practice the timeless laws of family purity. The Rebbetzin gave Roz special psalms to say every day, and she said them with devotion born out of a desperate desire to live.

Roz and Henry became the most dependable people in our congregation, regular *shul*-goers upon whom others depended.

Soon it was time for Roz's checkup. This was the moment everyone dreaded. With the Rebbetzin's help, she had found a new doctor, not only a top specialist but also a *mensch* who felt her pain and would not play G-d.

At regular intervals for months, Roz had gone for a brain scan. Each time, the tumor was larger. Roz suffered from unbearable headaches. Sometimes, between the effects of the tumor itself and the medication, she was unable to function.

With trepidation, she went for her brain scan.

Every time the routine had been the same, but this time the nurse took her aside.

"Mrs. Goldberg, we're going to have to perform still another scan."

"Wh-wh-what's wrong? What happened?"

"Please bear with us a few minutes. The doctor will discuss the findings with you afterwards."

Roz felt her muscles stiffen. What terrible new thing had they seen?

After what seemed an eternity, she was ushered into the doctor's office.

"Have a seat, Roz. I've got some very surprising news for you."

Roz's heart was in her throat.

"We can't explain this, and in fact I've never seen anything like it at such an advanced stage, but we're having trouble finding your tumor. To be more accurate, we *can't* find your tumor. *It's not there.* It was there a few weeks ago. It's not there today. I can't explain it. Maybe the Rebbetzin can explain it."

Roz sat motionless, silent, unable to assimilate the words she was hearing. She sat like a stone. And then, as with a certain stone in the desert, water started to flow. Roz started to cry. Water flowed, and it would not stop. These were tears of joy, tears of life.

In fact, Roz's tumor did disappear. At just about the time of her "sentence of death," she received a "sentence of life" from a Higher Power. Her treatments continued, and she had to deal with the threat of the return of her disease, but she was alive.

Their existence returned to "normal," except that it was different; she and Henry now lived the life of Jews in every respect. They became Rivka and Chaim, and they lived with hope for this world and hope for the Next World. Nothing could shake them, and their faces radiated a strength they had never known before.

Depression: Public Enemy No. 1

I want to tell you some stories about how depression can destroy a life, and to show you how family and friends can help combat depression.

A year ago, we received a letter from Israel:

"I hope that you will remember me, for I know that you have welcomed so many through your doors over the years. Go back about eighteen years and remember a girl from Brooklyn named Miriam. At that time I was at a 'confused' stage of my life. . . ."

What memories that brought back!

When we met Miriam, she was a beautiful eighteen-year-old who was living with a non-Jewish man. At that young age she already felt she had reached a dead end. She had almost given up on herself. But not quite.

One day, she chanced into Hineni and heard words of Torah. Something within her stirred, and she began to feel a sense of hope. Maybe there was a future. Maybe she wasn't a *shmattah*, a dishrag, after all.

Miriam came for one Shabbos and then another and another. After she got to know us, she confided that she was literally in fear of her life because of the man she was living with. So one afternoon I drove her to the building where she lived. She knew he wasn't home, but she was still terrified. She ran upstairs and grabbed all her belongings, praying that he would not return unexpectedly. She threw her few possessions in the trunk, and off we sped . . . to a new life.

We gave her a prayer book and took her in as one of our children. She stayed with us for a few months. We introduced her to several young men, but she never found exactly the right one. After a while we lost touch, but the memories would come back to us every little while, and we would wonder where life had taken her.

Time moved on. Eighteen years. And then came the letter:

"Our paths parted, but the warmth, wisdom, sincerity,

kindness, and light of Torah have been an inspiration to me always. I've thought of you often through the years and want you to know that what I received back then has carried me far. I am finally sitting down and writing these words that I've wanted to put down for some time. What I really want to say is 'Thank you.'"

Miriam had moved to Israel, where she is living with her husband and five beautiful children. Her children have the light of Torah in their eyes and she herself looks younger than she did when she was eighteen.

"Please give my warmest regards and deepest respect to Rebbetzin Jungreis. May Hashem give her strength to carry on with her wonderful work and may He bless you all.

P.S. I am still using the *siddur* you gave me."

Do you see how the seed grows in the ground? Under the soil, observed only by G-d, it sprouts and forms a magnificent tree, like the seed of Ruth, who descended from the family of Abraham, but whose lineage was hidden in the land of Moav for seven hundred years.* Ruth came back from that degraded land to become the grandmother of King David. So much is hidden from our eyes.

Miriam disappears for a few years and then arises as a mother in Israel, presiding over a household with a devoted husband and shining children. How did it happen? It happened because there was a Hineni to provide a family for her, a family that could guide her and give her support and encouragement to reach her potential.

"[G-d] raises the needy from the dust, from the trash heaps He lifts the destitute. To seat them with nobles, with

---

* *Book of Our Heritage*, Sivan (Chapter Two), by Eliahu Kitov, Feldheim Publishers, explains this story in fascinating detail.

the nobles of His people. He transforms the barren wife into a glad mother of children."*

Perhaps the ultimate story of depression is the following, concerning a girl who, although she was alive, was literally among the dead.

Lisa lived in a cemetery. She wasn't dead, but she wasn't exactly alive either.

Once a proud Israeli girl, she had no other place to go. This child of the Jewish people, daughter of kings and prophets, was a vagrant.

When she first arrived from Israel, she had worked as a nursemaid to an old man. When he died, she was alone, with no friends and no job. She became depressed. Rabbi Jacob Jungreis, conducting a burial service, found her in the cemetery.

Rabbi Jungreis brought her to Hineni, and soon she came to us for Shabbos. Shabbos turned into weekdays and she stayed on.

What a little Torah will do! As soon as she started keeping *mitzvos*—eating kosher, saying *Shema*—her soul returned to her. She began to see herself as part of Jewish destiny, and suddenly there was no longer a reason to be depressed.

Lisa became a new person. She cleaned herself up, got a job, put a smile on her face, and pitched into life.

One of our neighbors had a single brother who used to visit. The Rebbetzin thought he was a great match for Lisa. So after services one Shabbos, the Rebbetzin introduced them. They hit it off from the start. Today they are living in Israel, a happily married couple with thriving children.

For Lisa, life began in a cemetery, which we call in He-

---

* Psalm 113

brew *bays ha-chaim*, "house of life." The bodies buried there return to dust, but the soul lives forever.

The last of Maimonides' Thirteen Principles of Faith states: "I believe with complete faith that there will be a resurrection of the dead whenever the wish emanates from the Creator, Blessed be His Name. . . ."

If we keep that in mind, it will help prevent depression, because G-d's plan for us is all good. With the help of the Torah we can try to use each event in a positive way. But we've got to make the right choices. We have free will, and that means we can make mistakes. Everything that happens to us can be either good or bad depending on whether we act in accordance with the Torah.

And even if we've made mistakes in the past—and who hasn't?—we don't have to be prisoners of those mistakes in the future. One of the greatest gifts G-d has given us is the ability to recover from the past. If we are sincere about it, He will accept our repentance and wipe the slate clean. This process is called *teshuva*. What a gift! No matter how much we have messed up our lives, we can find our way back if we really want to.

Doing Teshuva

The week we moved to North Woodmere, with cartons all over the place, I got a call from Rebbetzin Jungreis.

"Yisroel, I'm sending over Michael Kransky for Shabbos."

"Wait a minute, Rebbetzin, we don't know what we're doing here. Shabbos? I never made *Kiddush* in my life."

This was our introduction to the *mitzva* of welcoming guests and our "crash course" in how to keep Shabbos.

Nothing like the pressure of real-life events to bring a lesson home forever!

Michael Kransky was a story in himself. As a young man in the army, his non-Jewish "friends" got to him in the lonely wilderness of their Alaska outpost. Mike didn't know anything about his Jewishness, so he was easy prey. Those long winter nights were very boring; there was plenty of time to talk. Not only did Mike "convert," but after his return to civilian life he himself became a clergyman in his community.

It was exotic in the early 1970s for a Jew to be a minister. He could feel superior to his fellow Jews who didn't understand, who were missing out. He felt sorry for them. They didn't know what life was all about.

On the surface everything seemed fine, but Mike had questions. Exotic lifestyles sound exciting until you begin to live them. "The grass is always greener" until you discover the weeds. The more he thought about his life, the more Mike realized his ignorance of the Torah and the more questions he had. Nights were long at home, too, and after a few months Reverend Mike began to wonder why he felt so empty inside if his new religion was "the real thing."

He didn't tell anybody about his doubts. That would have destroyed the façade and he might have lost his disciples, but secretly he started writing to rabbis. It suddenly dawned on him that he had embraced his new-found religion without knowing anything about what it means to be a Jew.

But nobody wanted to discuss those questions, even rabbis to whom he had written. Nobody answered his letters. It seemed that nobody was interested in Mike Kransky.

In the summer of 1974 he happened to pick up a copy of *The Jewish Press*. In it was a column by Rebbetzin Esther

Jungreis, with a refreshingly forthright tone. It was a kind of Jewish "Dear Abby."

"Dear Rebbetzin, I am having trouble finding the right husband. Can you help me?"

"Dear Rebbetzin, television is bringing alien values into our home. What do you suggest we do?"

"Dear Rebbetzin, should we send our son to Israel for a year to study?"

"Dear Rebbetzin," wrote Reverend Mike, "I am a minister. I am of Jewish descent. I have some questions for you people. I want to know how you can justify rejecting the truth of our testament. I have seen the emptiness of Jewish life and I am amazed at how many people blindly cling to it. You seem to be articulate and caring, and I am asking you to provide some authoritative answers for me about the attitude of Judaism toward our religion."

Reverend Mike couldn't believe it. He got an answer.

"Dear Reverend Kransky, I am so glad to have heard from you. I would be most happy to discuss all your questions, but face to face is the only way to do so. I invite you to spend a Shabbos weekend with me and my family at the Pine View Hotel in the Catskills. We will be able to explore all these questions in great depth. Please let me know when you can join us."

On a Friday afternoon in August, Reverend Mike and his young disciple, Alan, pulled up to the gates of the Pine View Hotel. Alan was also Jewish. For a few minutes they just sat there, taking it all in. Kids in *payos* running back and forth, mothers in *shaytlach and tichlach.** ("So many pregnant," noted Reverend Mike.) Men engaged in animated discussions on topics from the Talmud, *tzitzis* hanging from their waists.

"Pretty lively around here," thought the reverend.

As soon as he got to his room and freshened up, Mike went to find the Rebbetzin. He didn't want to delay their debate. Rebbetzin Jungreis said, "No problem, but not just at this minute. First, we are going to welcome the holy Shabbos, and tomorrow night, after Shabbos is over, we can debate until the sun comes up . . . or longer."

That was OK with Reverend Mike. He could use a good meal and a rest.

The Rebbetzin's father, her husband, and her brothers took Reverend Mike and Alan under their wings.

First to the synagogue, where afternoon prayers were recited, followed by the prayers ushering in Shabbos, and then evening prayers.

Nobody pushed them to pray. The two men just watched, listened, thought, observed as several hundred men *shuckled* back and forth in the rhythmic way Jews pray. They listened to the beautiful song *"L'cha Dodi,"* which welcomes the Shabbos Queen.

Just before sunset, the women lit up the gathering darkness with their candles, as the Shabbos Queen entered in her finery. The children's faces reflected the fiery glow.

Soon, services having ended, the men joined their wives in the dining room and the Shabbos meal began with the singing of *"Shalom Aleichem,"* the song welcoming the Shabbos angels. Reverend Mike and Alan couldn't keep their eyes off Zayda, who took his grandchildren's hands and made a circle with them around the Shabbos table.

Zayda was a man of deep emotion. When a troubled Jew came to him, Zayda's tears would wash away his pain. And now Zayda was crying with happiness as he welcomed the

Shabbos angels, and, for that matter, as he welcomed Reverend Mike and Alan.

Next came *"Ayshes Chayil,"* the beautiful song composed by King Solomon in honor of the Jewish wife, who brings light, happiness, and discipline—not to mention delicious food—to every Jewish home.

The two visitors had never seen anything quite like this. Something inside them started to warm up. Old feelings, dimly remembered, revived within their hearts. There was no debate as they heard *Kiddush,* made blessings, and ate the delicious meal in the glow of the Shabbos candles. It was pure pleasure, an absence of worry and fear, which they had never experienced before. They felt completely at peace.

Shabbos songs. A little wine. Good food. Stories and wisdom from the Torah. The warmth of the family. Soon, the blessings after the meal and to bed. Before they knew it, they were lost in the sweetest sleep of their lives.

It is said that a Jew receives an "additional soul" on Shabbos, which elevates him so that he sees life in perspective and is released from the prison of worldly anxiety.

The morning began with prayers and the Torah reading. Another meal with the family. A quiet walk around the grounds. A lecture on the lawn by the Rebbetzin. They even had a nap.

As the sun descended, Reverend Mike and Alan were sad. They wanted it to go on forever.

Shabbos begins and ends with light. A *Havdalah* candle and the aroma of sweet spices mark beginning of a new week.

Suddenly, the hotel's PA system comes alive. Weekday sounds are heard. Cars start. Young people are off for pizza.

Now, Reverend Mike, are you ready to debate?

To tell the truth, the two guests had forgotten all about that debate. But they did have a long talk that night with Rebbetzin Esther, Zayda, and the rabbis. A long talk about things half-forgotten in the mists of time. Shabbos had changed them. The next morning they publicly burned their missionary books on the hotel lawn. They would never be the same again.

Alan was going to go home, say goodbye to his non-Jewish girlfriend and then return to New York.

Zayda took him aside.

"Alan," he said, "If you go home and see your girlfriend, she will cry. Then you will cry, and we will never see you again."

Alan did not go home. He stayed. In fact, he stayed with us. In fact, he stayed five years. Much of the time he was living at Yeshiva University, where the Rebbetzin had arranged for him to receive his Jewish education and continue his secular degree program. But every Friday afternoon, he was "back home."

Alan became a part of our family. He grew up with our children, was an older brother to them, and stayed with us until the Rebbetzin found a wonderful girl for him. She had also been involved in non-Jewish religious practices. Today they have a family of beautiful, talented children.

What was it like to have a "stranger" live in our home? As soon as Alan arrived, he was no longer a stranger. He was healed through his contact with a Torah life. And we were healed by reaching out to him.

Sometimes it takes just a few seconds to reach someone's heart. We've got to be sensitive to each person. Don't you feel good when someone understands you and cares about you? We should try to do that for our brothers and

sisters, and bring some warmth into their lives. Everybody needs it.

Susan was trapped in a cult.

While attending university, she started listening to the
propaganda of the local "messianic" missionaries. They sent
her to Wisconsin.

What did she know? She had grown up in suburban New
York, like her friends, with an assimilated view of Jewish
life. She had attended "Sunday School," was "confirmed,"
and attended her friends' bar mitzvahs (as the saying goes:
more "bar" than "mitzvah").

It was just before Thanksgiving, and somehow Susan had
obtained permission from the cult to visit her family for the
long weekend. Ordinarily the "elders" didn't permit new-
comers to stray, but someone's guard was down and Susan
returned home.

She took advantage of the visit to ask her family rabbi
some tough questions. He didn't know how to answer, but
he was a humble man who at least knew when he was out
of his depth. He advised Susan's parents to take her to
Rebbetzin Jungreis.

In Wisconsin, they had warned Susan to keep away from
the "Devil Rebbetzin." But she felt strong. She wasn't afraid.

One evening, Susan's parents pulled up in front of our
house, and in she walked. I'll never forget that look. Eyes
glazed, she stared straight ahead. She had been hypnotized
by the cult. She was trying to save herself, but she didn't
know how. Frozen in zombie-land, she was like an addict
who couldn't break the habit.

In Wisconsin, they would have fainted. Here was Susan, doing exactly what they had warned her against. Her

addiction was powerful, but there was something deep within her struggling to burst forth. She was caught in powerful currents.

During the half-hour drive to Hineni School, hardly a word was exchanged among us. Susan's defenses were on maximum alert.

When we walked into the synagogue, Susan showed no hint of courtesy or respect as she was introduced to Zayda and Rebbetzin Jungreis. After the class, the Rebbetzin spoke to her. In those days, in Zayda's synagogue, the Rebbetzin would sit by the Holy Ark for private talks. Susan walked forward like a prisoner of war, wrapped in the icy garb of hostility.

This was one of the most memorable of the Rebbetzin's dialogues, and the shortest I am aware of. Susan herself, and the Rebbetzin later, described it. The entire exchange lasted only a few seconds. During that flash of time, Susan's life changed forever.

This is an example of how to reach someone. The Rebbetzin spoke softly, never debating Biblical passages or arguing. I learned from this that every conversation must be geared to the individual and the situation.

Rebbetzin: "What is your Jewish name, sweetheart?"
Susan, in an icy tone: "I don't have one."
Rebbetzin: "I'm sure you have one. Maybe you forgot."
Susan, thermometer descending toward absolute zero: "I don't have a Jewish name."
The Rebbetzin took a long shot: "Come now, didn't you ever have a *zayda* who called you 'Sara-le'?"
Silence. A long silence. The eyes began to cloud up, becoming moist. A tear formed. All of a sudden, a choke.

A sob and "Susan" was crying hysterically. The Rebbetzin was holding her in her arms.

Ten seconds! That's how long it took. No debate, just an arrow that hit its mark, and a mental image of a *zayda* who used to wrap his "Sara-le" in his *tallis* when she was a little girl, long, long ago. An image forgotten until the Rebbetzin's words opened her heart and she remembered her own past.

Following that fateful conversation, Sara-le moved in with us and stayed for two months. In our home, she began to learn a new way of life. Rebbetzin Jungreis helped her enroll in a *yeshiva* for young women who are returning to a Torah life. Not long afterward, she was introduced to a young man from Borough Park.

Today Sara-le is the mother of seven beautiful children. Her eyes are clear and calm. The world from which she escaped is a distant memory, far in the past but not completely forgotten, just the way we don't forget that we were once slaves in Egypt. Its memory, rather than disturbing her tranquility, strengthens it, because she knows exactly how she arrived at the truth and security of the Torah.

When we arrived in North Woodmere, a young lady named Rena was living with the Rebbetzin's family. Rena had become the leader of the so-called "messianic Jews" in the South. Nobody could reach her. Her parents called the Rebbetzin and begged for help. When, shortly thereafter, the Rebbetzin spoke in her city, Rena's group picketed the auditorium. Afterwards, the Rebbetzin found her. They talked all night, and by morning Rena had decided that she wanted to try a Jewish life. She accompanied the Rebbetzin on the plane to New York.

Rena stayed for two years in the Jungreis home, and she became a strong and vital part of the Jungreis and Hineni families. The Rebbetzin found a wonderful young man for her and they were married amidst great joy, with her proud parents in attendance.

Making the Best of Every Situation

The threat against our way of life comes from every con-ceivable angle. In the desert, when Moses led the Chil-dren of Israel out of Egypt, Amalek attacked the old and weak at the rear of the line. Today, missionaries attack the sick and the ignorant, but our people have surprising strength. It's up to us to help our brothers and sisters in every situation.

The following story describes how our children partici-pated in reaching out. In my opinion, the greatest weapon in strengthening Jewish children is to make them aware of their responsibilities. We are a society of entitlements; we demand services and complain if they are withheld. But that is a false view of life. We are owed nothing. We have an endless debt to our Creator for having given us life and everything we need to sustain it. We are also indebted to people who have helped us. Even if we give of ourselves ceaselessly we cannot repay that debt. This is vital to teach our children, lest they think that G-d or man owes them something. By teaching Malka bas Rivka, our children gained more than they gave, and they gave a lot.

In 1980, the Rebbetzin received a phone call from dis-traught parents whose son was afflicted with cerebral palsy. Missionaries in his nursing home were trying to take advantage of the Jewish patients' vulnerability by influencing them to abandon their heritage. The Rebbetzin asked Leah and me if we could follow up on this situation, and the results were far more than we bargained for. One Sunday morning, after checking in with the administrator, I showed up in his room and told him I wanted to start Torah classes. He was hostile.

But I persisted. After a while I got the names of other Jews in the home. By the next week we had a nucleus of about five people. One of them was a girl we came to know as Malka bas Rivka. Her room was a few doors away, and she was delighted.

Malka's body was twisted. She never left her bed or wheelchair. It was hard at times to understand her words. When we met her, she was in her thirties, a victim of cerebral palsy since birth.

But what a soul! It only needed Torah to soar to the heights. Malka bas Rivka became a person of profound faith because she possessed possibly the greatest gift a person can have: she was content with her lot in life. She never complained; she always smiled.

"Ben Zoma says . . . Who is rich? He who is happy with his lot . . . "*

Malka, who had *almost everything* to complain about, never complained. She, who had *almost nothing* to smile about, always smiled. She could soar beyond her twisted body and reach the heights.

When I first approached, her face lit up. She volunteered her private room for the classes. I affixed a *mezuza* to her door, and we had an instant study hall.

---

* Ethics of the Fathers 4:1

Shortly before we had met, Malka's beloved "mum" had passed away. Already hurting, Malka had lost her best friend on earth. Instead of cracking, however, she somehow survived this trauma. I told Malka that I was sure her mum in Heaven was beseeching the Master of the World to strengthen her daughter so that she could survive her trials. Her cries were answered when the Rebbetzin received that phone call.

In Malka's "study hall" we started a weekly class on the Torah portion. This went on for years, and I am happy to say that this group of Jews was strengthened in every aspect of their lives. Many were saved from the missionaries. But no one matched Malka in her zeal and fantastic memory.

Rabbi Eliezer ben Hyrkanos is compared in Ethics of the Fathers to "a cemented cistern that does not lose a drop."* Despite other limitations, Malka's mind was like a cemented cistern; not one lesson was forgotten.

Malka could be confused by time sequences, however: If I told her that Abraham went down to Egypt and so did his descendants hundreds of years later, she had trouble sorting out what happened when, and then she would get very upset. "I'm *fermisht* [confused]," she would cry out. "I don't *fershtay* [understand]." Then I would try to unravel the confusion.

Every week, until she passed from this world, we played a game. At the end of each session, Malka would say, "I want you to put your hand over your eyes and repeat after me, "*Shema Yisroel* . . ." Every week she would "teach me" the prayer that a Jew says twice every day. I can just imagine her entering the Heavenly Courts and proudly, in front

---

* Ethics of the Fathers 2:11

of G-d's throne, putting her hands over her eyes and uttering these words, her passport to that Eternal Kingdom, with tears of happiness, in the presence of her beloved mum.

Malka's zeal never diminished. And she was the epitome of concern for others. She would inquire every week about Rebbetzin Jungreis and her parents. She would always pray for them. The prayers were fervent and, I am sure, totally pure.

Our conversation about Mum led to the high point in her spiritual life. We learned that there is a World to Come, where all souls who merit it reside forever in the presence of G-d. We also learned that, after the coming of Messiah, all who have passed away will be resurrected and reunited.

When Malka heard about the resurrection of the dead and the World to Come, her eyes lit up. She looked as if *she* had just been resurrected from the dead.

"Do you mean I'm going to see Mum again?" she whooped.

"Of course," I said, "and you'll dance with her. You'll be one hundred percent healthy with no physical limitations. I hope to be there with you, so please don't forget to introduce me."

She looked at me with a smile that reached beyond the end of time.

"I always thought that after this world there is nothing. You know: goodbye is goodbye. I can't believe it. I can't believe it."

From that moment she became a new person, full of hope, praying passionately and continually for the speedy advent of *Moshiach*. Her prayers elevated her soul to a great height. I am sure they have already hastened the arrival of *Moshiach, may he come speedily, in our days.*

Malka was blessed with a devoted father and stepmother,

who had become a second mother to her. G-d sent extra sustenance to a very special soul so that she could survive her continual tests.

Over the years, Malka moved from one nursing home to another, all relatively close to us. As our responsibilities grew, our children took over the teaching, each one committed to increasing the depth of her Jewish knowledge.

In the spring of 1994, Malka broke her hip. Her spirit was as strong as ever and she never complained, despite the additional pain. But the surgeons had found that this was no simple accident. Cancer had weakened her bones, and this had caused her fracture.

Her family did not tell her, and we continued our visits as always. Our son, Aharon Yaakov, often walked to her nursing home on Friday afternoons from his *yeshiva* in nearby Long Beach, New York. He would spend well over an hour with her before returning for Shabbos.

Months passed and she was again in the hospital. The cancer was spreading.

On the ninth day of the Hebrew month of Av in the year 1995, we visited her for the last time. The Ninth of Av (Tisha b'Av) is the lowest point in the Jewish year. It is the only full-day fast besides Yom Kippur, a time of deepest mourning for the two Temples that were destroyed in Jerusalem and for countless other tragedies that befell our people on that very same day throughout history.

Malka was painfully thin, but her spirit was as strong as ever. We discussed the significance of the day and talked about Mum. Of course, she did not forget to "teach me" *Shema Yisroel.*

Ten days later the phone rang. Malka had been called to her reward in Heaven.

I was privileged to be asked to speak at the funeral, along with Malka's brother, a successful businessman whose handsome face made me realize how beautiful Malka would have been if her body had been normal.

But her soul was beyond normal; it was exceptional.

It is not what happens in life that is most important, but how we react to it. Misfortune and good fortune both present great challenges.

Malka accepted her lot with contentment. She was an example of what a Jew should be like, smiling at adversity—and she really had it—surviving the trauma of her very existence, surviving the trauma of her mother's death, and holding on to the essence of life by gripping the Torah with all her strength.

Now she's in Heaven with her mum. She doesn't have to worry about that twisted body any more. She's straight as an arrow.

Fighting Against the Odds

Here is another story of teshuva, *in which an old* Yiddishe Bubbie *plays a heroic part. If our life is to mean anything, then we must take a stand. This story also demonstrates the power of prayer.*

One day in 1975, Rebbetzin Jungreis got a call about a kid named Bob.

Bob had been living in California, where he got mixed up with a missionary group. Later, he had the good fortune to meet the legendary Rabbi Shlomo Carlebach. Many Jewish kids' lives were transformed by Reb Shlomo's songs and stories in those days, and Bob became inspired with love of Torah and the Land of Israel. To complete his return, Bob wanted to go to the Holy Land. He had no money, but he had the will, and so he started on the way. The first leg of his journey led him to the East Coast, where—at Reb Shlomo's suggestion—he looked up Rebbetzin Jungreis. That's when we met him.

Bob had a grandmother in New York, an old lady who had come from Russia as a young girl. She was very pious and smart, but her life had been filled with deep tragedy.

A young widow, she had brought up a daughter, Deborah, from whom she had great *nachas*. Deborah had married a successful businessman, a liberal Jew whose life had gradually become more Jewish through the influence of his wife. Her warm love of tradition had been inherited from her mother. Their home was filled with the laughter of young children.

Then tragedy struck.

Deborah was pregnant with their third child, but near the end of her term something went wrong. Deborah became sick. Her baby was healthy, but the young mother did not survive. Her devastated family was in shock, the father and older children were alone, their lives shattered. The baby was named Robert.

Their *bubbie* kept the family together, trying to fill the void left by the death of her daughter. In her heart, the tears never ceased; she was bereft of both husband and child.

Like generations of *Yiddishe bubbies* before her, she went on against the odds and held her head high, but this was not to be her last test. A greater tragedy was yet to strike.

The young widower, now a father of three, was lonely. In the course of time he met a young woman who soon became his wife and the stepmother of his children. She was Jewish, but she hated her ancient heritage and everything connected with it, including the old *bubbie*.

Bubbie became *persona non grata* in her own family. She, who had nursed children and father through the greatest of trials, was cut off completely from her own grandchildren. Her days were bathed in tears; her nights were utter loneliness. She could have collapsed, but being a stubborn fighter, a true *Yiddishe bubbie*, she did not allow that to happen. She had lived through too much already to succumb to self pity.

She immersed herself in community work. A natural linguist, she became a skilled translator of books into English from her native Russian. As more and more Russians escaped from behind the Iron Curtain, she would help them cope in their new environment. She was particularly active at a nearby hospital, where her talents saved lives when she translated for patients who were unable to describe their symptoms in English.

Her tenacious religious belief enabled her to hang on to life with the timeless strength of the Jew who never gives up even when there is no logical reason to hope. She beseeched G-d. She would not let Him alone.

Through her many *mitzvos* and ceaseless prayers, the *bubbie* must have penetrated the gates of Heaven. Something unexpected happened. One of her three "lost" grandchildren realized that he was on a dead-end road. That's when Bob, lost among the missionaries, encountered Shlomo Carlebach.

Before we knew it, Bob was a guest in our home for Shabbos. We were about to leave for our second trip to Israel with Rebbetzin Jungreis. Bob was anxious to join us, but besides being broke, he was physically weak from years of cult life.

"I have a *bubbie* in New York City. I don't know if she would talk to me. I have let her down in the past. I don't know if she would believe me if I told her I want to go to Israel."

The Rebbetzin suggested that I speak to Bob's *bubbie* on his behalf. By an amazing coincidence our family knew her from the past, when we had attended the same school as her grandchildren. All these "coincidences" played a part when I finally summoned the courage to pick up the phone.

"Do you remember me? My brother went to school with your grandson."

Her voice, filled with Jewish history and personal tragedy, was kind and gentle.

"Of course I remember you. How are your mother and father? And to what do I owe the pleasure of this call?"

She always spoke in perfect, though accented English, with precise grammar and unfailing politeness. You would never have guessed her troubles.

I told her the story of how her grandson had come to us. There was silence on the other end, a silence full of emotion, throbbing with tears and pain.

"I can hardly believe your words. Are my prayers being answered? Can it be true? Is he sincere? After his life 'on the streets,' I am somewhat skeptical."

She asked me many questions, and then she arranged for a reunion with her grandson. They had a long, emotional talk. The Rebbetzin's trip to Israel was in a few weeks. There was much to do. Even if she agreed to pay his way, he had no passport. But that was a minor matter compared to the big issues that were being weighed.

Yes, she would do it. She would sponsor her grandson's passage to Israel.

"*Bubbie*," he told her, "you will be proud of me."

All this time he was living in our home. We rushed out the next morning to the passport office, standing on line for hours until the paperwork was completed.

People do not just get years of idol worship and street life out of their system in a flash. Often, they do not realize how deeply ingrained those habits have become. Bob's *bubbie* sensed that, but she was willing to give him a chance.

I will never forget the plane trip. In those days there was still a pioneering feeling in Israel. On El Al, the loudspeakers would burst forth with "*Hevaynu shalom alaychem*," a joyous welcome to the Holy Land, just as the plane crossed over the coastline. Every flight seemed like a rediscovery of the Land, as if we were the first Jews to return after two thousand years and had just trekked hundreds of miles over mountain and desert. There was always clapping, and a tear or two in most people's eyes.

The "fasten seat belt" sign had just signaled our imminent landing when I heard a familiar voice.

"Yisroel, come here please."

"Rebbetzin, the 'fasten seat belt' sign just came on."

When the Rebbetzin called you, it didn't help to argue.

"Yisroel. We are entering the Holy Land. This is a land that cannot tolerate sin. I want you to go over to Bob immediately and tell him he must do *teshuva*, he must repent—right now. He cannot enter the Land of Israel with idol worship in his heart."

The Rebbetzin can sense what is going on in people, and she knew what had to be done. The stewardess wouldn't like it, but when the boss gives an order, you do what you're told.

I gave Bob the message. He looked at me in shock and didn't answer. A message like that is heavy. You just hope it sinks in.

The next day was Friday. Just before we were about to walk to the Western Wall to usher in the Holy Shabbos, the Rebbetzin spoke to us as a group. She again warned, though this time in general terms, that before we went to this holy spot at this holy time, we had to root out all idol worship from our hearts. Such impurity cannot be tolerated in a holy place.

Bob was still in shock, but now, a quarter-century later—when I contemplate how his life turned out—I see that the Rebbetzin's words found their mark. I can only assume that the idol worship that the Rebbetzin had sensed was indeed purged from him as he entered the Holy Land.

His *bubbie* lived to see her prayers answered. Bob returned to his people. His *bubbie* had the *nachas* of holding Torah-observant great-grandchildren on her knee.

We used to call her every week. Every Purim we would drive up to see her with *shaloch manos** and reminisce about the "old days." She would thank G-d for His great miracles and show us the pictures of her daughter, her grandson, and his family.

One day the phone rang. It was Bob.

"I'm so sorry to tell you that my *bubbie* died today."

We cried. The world did not realize what a righteous woman had passed away, a woman whose prayers had ascended to the throne of G-d. The obituary columns could not comprehend who she was, let alone do justice to her.

---

* *Shaloch manos* is food that is exchanged by Jews on Purim, as described in the Book of Esther (9:22).

I will never forget the funeral. The main speaker was Bob. We all listened as he poured out his heart.

Many family members were embarrassed. After all, they had put this holy lady in "exile." I couldn't help noticing one relative who kept looking at his watch, at first every minute, then every few seconds. It looked as if he was about to explode. All of a sudden, he jumped out of his seat and started shouting.

"Bob, you are taking too much time. We all want to leave."

I couldn't believe it. To interrupt a funeral! Their *bubbie* had shed a lifetime of tears for them, and now they couldn't spare another minute.

But Bob just went on speaking, quietly finishing the praise of his beautiful *bubbie*, who had braved the entire world in life and now had to do so even in death, carrying the Holy Torah onward, across continents and into the next generation.

"*Yisgadal, v'yiskadash shmay rabba. . . .*"*

Children at Risk: The Rebels

What happens if something does go wrong in the Jewish family? Here's the story of a child from a very religious home who had a dangerous violent streak. This extreme type of case is rare, but today we are seeing an unprecedented infiltration of the outside world into the Jewish home. All one has to do is read the paper, hear or see the news, or walk down the street. Television and the

---

* The beginning words of the *Mourner's Kaddish*.

Internet bring everything into the home. How does one guard against alien values and pure filth? One way is to realize the frightening dangers that are in store for one who leaves the safety of G-d's protection. The following story gives some idea of what can happen and how hard it is to return.

The drama begins for us in a famous gambling mecca.

A handsome young man is in the casino. He calls himself Sal.

Sal is in his twenties. He is dark, with a crewcut. He is playing cards. He seems to have a habit of winning.

He has a few other businesses on the side. The police know about them. It's probably better not to mention them. Actually, the police know a lot about Sal. They had left him alone until a certain young lady got beaten up. This young lady, however, besides other activities, was a police informer, and the cops didn't like it too much when she got beaten up. In fact, Sal was accused of beating her up, and when Sal started messing with the cops, the cops started messing with Sal.

Sal the card dealer, Sal the man of many careers, suddenly found himself behind bars. Six felony counts. The prospect of being locked up for life swam in front of his eyes. He was just a kid. All of a sudden the tough guy was scared.

A phone rang in Williamsburg, Brooklyn.

This is a community that looks more like a European *shtetl* than a neighborhood of the Big Apple. Young mothers with hats on top of their *sheitlach* walk with eight or ten children, children with innocent, shining faces. The streets are thronged in the early morning with bearded men carrying *tallis* and *tefillin* to *shul,* and late at night returning from Talmud studies.

A phone rang in Williamsburg.

"*Tattie.*"

"Who is this?"

"*Tattie,* this is Ezriel . . ."

"Ezriel. EZRIEL. Is it you? Is it really you?"

"Yes, *Tattie.*"

"Ezriel! Mama . . . Ezriel is on the line. Where are you, Ezriel? It's been years since Mama and I heard your voice. Where are you?"

"*Tattie,* I don't have too much time to talk, but I'm in a little bit of trouble, *Tattie.*"

"Ezriel, what happened?"

"*Tattie,* I'm calling you from a . . . a jail, *Tattie.*"

"A what? I thought you said 'jail.'"

"Yes, *Tattie,* I did say 'jail.' I need a little bit of help."

"*Ribono shel olam.* Ezriel, what happened? A jail? Mama. He's OK, Mama, just a second. Ezriel, your mother wants to speak to you."

"Ezriel. Where are you? What happened to you? I didn't stop crying for years. Where are you?"

"It's far away, Mama. I can't explain too much right now, but what I need right now, Mama, is a lawyer. Do you know a good lawyer, Mama?"

"A lawyer? Ezriel, what about food? Can you get kosher food in the jail?"

"Mama, what I need is a lawyer. Do you know a lawyer?"

"A lawyer? I can't think right now. I have to think. *Tattie,* do we know a lawyer?"

▲▲▲

Robert Goldsmith, Esq., stepped off the flight from New York. Attaché case in hand, he blinked in the brilliant sunlight. Then he hailed a cab.

"County jail, please."

The plea bargain was a straightforward deal: Sal leaves town . . . forever. Detective Lieutenant Hobson, chief of the vice squad, escorted him onto the plane. Lieutenant Hobson spoke ever so slowly, pausing between each word as if he had all day, so each thought could sink in very deep.

"Son, I want you to understand very well what I'm going to tell you. If ever—and I repeat that word 'ever'—you show your face in this town again, that will be the last time. I would hate to see anything terrible happen to you. Be glad you got off easy, son. Remember my words."

Sal was standing in a synagogue in Canarsie. What was he doing here, anyway?

"Mama, *Tattie*, stop hovering around me. I'm not a two-year-old. I can take care of myself. After all the rabbis I've seen in the last two weeks it's like . . . enough. Give me a little breathing room."

Soon, Zayda and the Rebbetzin entered the crowded room and there was a hush. The Rebbetzin began to speak. After the class was over, Sal's parents escorted him to the front. The Rebbetzin had been expecting him.

He looked like a bum.

He hadn't shaved in weeks. He had a glowering, furtive look that, together with his dark glasses, helped him avoid direct eye contact. He looked like someone not to be trusted.

He drew back as Zayda reached out and put his arms around him, as if he was afraid of Zayda's touch. But Zayda drew him close, and Zayda's tears fell on his jacket. For all his tough demeanor, Sal had never expected this, and it broke through the cold exterior. Just a small breach, but it was an opening.

"What is your Hebrew name?" said Zayda.

Silence.

"What is your Hebrew name, Sonny?" Zayda persisted.

"Ezriel."

"Ah . . . Ezriel."

The Rebbetzin and her father looked at each other. The name "Ezriel"* is a Jungreis name, after a great and holy sage who was a direct ancestor of both the Rebbetzin and her husband. How did it happen that this punk was walking around with the name of a *tzaddik*?

It seems that Ezriel was born prematurely. He was very sick, so sick that his parents thought he wouldn't make it. Desperate to save their child, the parents spoke to their rabbi, who told them, "There was a holy sage who was able to work miracles, to cure people on whom the doctors had given up. You must add his name to your son's name. Perhaps, in the merit of the *tzaddik*, the baby will live."

And so it was the little boy became known as Ezriel. Little did the parents know that the name of the miracle sage would save their son not only at his birth but also now, at his rebirth.

"Ezriel," the Rebbetzin said, "I want you to meet Yisroel and Leah Neuberger. They are my neighbors and close friends. They have guests in their home every week and they have room for you this Shabbos.** Will you join us?"

---

* This name is fictitious, in order to protect "Ezriel's" identity.

** Ezriel, of course, could have spent Shabbos with his own family, but that was the whole point. Somehow, he had not managed to absorb Jewish values from his parents. The Rebbetzin felt that he needed an entirely new perspective, perhaps from people who had once been completely secular and had come back from the "wilderness" just like Ezriel.

Again, Ezriel was thrown off. Every rabbi his parents had "dragged" him to see over the last few hectic weeks had attempted to engage him in a long, searching conversation. This he could deflect because he expected it. What he didn't expect was an invitation for Shabbos.

Ezriel showed up at our house that Friday afternoon. His dark, resentful glare made us feel as if we had a wild animal in the house. How could we do anything for him? He hated us.

He stayed two years.

Somehow, the icicles started to melt.

He responded to family. It all started with Zayda, who had welcomed him back into the Jewish family with a hug—no speeches, debates, or harangues. Zayda's tears brought Ezriel back. And through Zayda and the Rebbetzin we invited Ezriel into *our* family.

It took a while for Ezriel to shed the rebellion, the scars, the resentment. But our children adopted him as a brother, and today we can look in our photo album and see a picture of him carrying our two-year-old son on his shoulders and, for the first time in his life, feeling like a *mensch*.

We involved him in every phase of our life. When Hineni showed up outside a meeting house for messianic Jews, Ezriel participated. No confrontation, just conversation, but Ezriel felt like a Jew for the first time. There's nothing better for one rebel than straightening out another rebel.

When the Rebbetzin went to speak on college campuses, Ezriel, wearing his Hineni windbreaker, was in charge of security. He was a pro.

The Rebbetzin found job opportunities for him. He was a good salesman. He had a good line.

It wasn't all "peaches and cream." There was the little matter of a divorce. In his old haunts, Ezriel had been married to a non-Jewish girl, so that when it came time for him to think about establishing a Jewish home, he had to free himself from this entanglement. Rebels often get so deeply mired in the quicksand that without the help of Torah sages like Zayda, it is impossible to get out.

We had to extricate Ezriel from this mess, and that meant a trip to his old stamping grounds. A trip out there was not a simple matter. It was like taking a reformed alcoholic to a bar. One drink and he's gone. But we had no choice.

He thought he could do it, but he underestimated the strength of his evil inclination.

I was his chaperone.

The trip was planned so that we would literally not have one minute to spare. Our plane was scheduled to arrive about midnight. We would go straight to a motel, go to sleep, and leave at 8:15 A.M., right after morning prayers, for our appointment with a local lawyer. The lawyer had told us over the phone that he could get us to the judge and arrange the whole thing by early afternoon. We would be out before evening.

Not so easy.

First, we didn't count on the weather.

It was a blazing Sunday afternoon in August. We said goodbye to the Rebbetzin. Then to the airport. Airborne. Uh oh. Weather reports indicated a huge thunderstorm in our flight path, meaning that the plane had to land and sit it out until the storm moved or we had clearance to fly hundreds of miles around it. So here we were on the ground again. When we were finally able to take off, it was discovered that our flight crew had been up too long without sleep, so we had to wait until a new crew was called in. By the time we arrived at our destination, it was 6:00 A.M.

So much for a night's sleep.

It took a while to find the lawyer. Then there were complications with documents. "Maybe it can't all be done today," said the attorney. "You may have to come back."

As things became more complicated, I noticed a strange look on Ezriel's face. His eyes had become glazed. He seemed to be drifting away into a different world.

Walking the sweltering streets between one office and another, I was reminded of the way he had looked when we first met, more than a year earlier.

"Ezriel."

He didn't answer me. He was lost in thought.

"Ezriel."

"Yeah."

"What's wrong with you?"

"Nothing."

"Ezriel, I think we'd better get out of here right now. We'll finish this up next time."

"I'm not leaving. You can go."

"What?"

"I'm not leaving. I have a few things I need to do here."

"You *are* leaving. In fact, you're leaving a lot sooner than you think."

I sounded tough, but I was scared. This guy was my responsibility and I could lose him here. I was all alone. I had no leverage. On the streets of this town he was a zombie.

G-d, this is your child. Tell me what to do. We have come this far. Must it end like this? After all that has happened?

All of a sudden, in my reverie, my eyes opened and I saw before me, on the sweltering street, the answer to my prayer: *a telephone booth.* G-d was reaching out to save His child.

"Ezriel."

"Yeah."

"I'm just stopping by this phone for a minute. Got to make a call. To a friend of yours."

"What friend?"

"You know, your friend Lieutenant Hobson. Remember your friend that you told me about. He'll be so interested to know that you're in town."

"You wouldn't . . ."

"I wouldn't *what* . . .? I *am*."

"You wouldn't call him."

"I just told you that I *am* calling him. *Right now*. I don't even think I need a quarter. I can just dial 911."

He looked at me. A kind of killer look began to creep into his eyes. He was going to stop me. And then his eyes softened a little. Maybe he remembered something. Maybe he felt Zayda's arms around him. Maybe he remembered Zayda's tears falling onto his jacket. Maybe he remembered carrying our little boy on his shoulders. Maybe he heard the Rebbetzin's voice: *"May angels of mercy go with you."*

He wanted to stop me. But something stopped *him*. He owed me a little too much.

"Let's get out of here."

Not one word was exchanged between us on the trip back to New York. For days and even weeks after that, the cold look still flashed in his eyes from time to time.

Several months later, the legal process having achieved its desired result, we returned for the final court appearance. This time we came prepared, spiritually prepared, the Rebbetzin having fortified Ezriel for weeks in advance to give him the strength necessary to withstand the coming test.

Everything flowed smoothly this time. No thunderstorm.

No problems. No phone booth necessary. The papers were signed, the divorce was complete, and—as we were about to board the plane home—we made a "victory" phone call to the Rebbetzin.

Ezriel was a free man, like the Jews on Passover, free to worship G-d and live by His commandments.

The Power of Shabbos

As you have seen, there is a recurring theme throughout many of these stories. So many are tied up with Shabbos. Often the first contact we had with people was on Shabbos. Shabbos is a healer, a refuge from a mixed-up world. When we wanted to bring someone close to G-d, they came for Shabbos. We didn't do anything for them; Shabbos itself did it for them.

Would you like to read some letters from guests we've had over the years? It will give you a taste of what Shabbos meant to them. The guests stepped into the Garden of Eden through Shabbos, and it restored their souls.

"I loved Shabbos so much. I felt more at home and at peace with myself and the world than I do in my own house . . . When we were *bentsching* and doing the blessings for the meals I thought that we could do it forever and ever. It seemed to be an everlasting joy."

"I felt so completely at home . . . it makes me think that perhaps *Moshiach* will come to a world that has paved such a righteous street for him to walk on. I will always remember. . . ."

"Shabbos was a fantastic experience that inspired us tremendously . . ."

"I have been exposed to our religion before, but never have I witnessed its true beauty as I did Friday evening . . ."

"The inspiration from Shabbos I couldn't get elsewhere. I felt like I was tasting the Garden of Eden."

"Shabbos has made a difference in my actions . . . Until last Shabbos Judaism was largely a closed book for me . . . Shabbos opened the book."

"The singing and festive meal was so beautiful. We felt that G-d was in the room with us."

"My introduction to a meaningful and traditional Shabbos service . . . gave me a new understanding of what G-d had in mind when He commanded us to rest on the seventh day . . ."

"Thank you for walking me through this past Shabbos . . . My first Shabbos and one that I will always remember . . ."

"Shabbos rekindled my spirit."

"The spirit of the Shabbos angels was palpable . . . I was more rejuvenated than if I had returned from a two-week vacation. . . ."

And so it was that, right from the very beginning, we had guests in our home every week. Every guest became part of the family. Even when we lost touch, our lives were intertwined, and the seed of Torah grew amongst us, sprouting in new places and in new generations, ever stronger and more vigorous.

Homecoming of a Nation

The fact is that in this generation we are witnessing a homecoming of epic proportions among the people of Israel. Some-

thing unprecedented and mighty is happening. It is obscured by
the problems that are occurring concurrently—intermarriage;
infighting among Jews; the overall lack of derech eretz, which
afflicts the entire world; and the mighty allure of the material
world. But it is happening. Jews around the world are awaken-
ing.

During the last few hundred years, Jews have been given the
opportunity as never before to taste the wine of assimilation.
We have been invited into other nations as if we were no different. Some of us have allowed ourselves to believe that was ac-
ceptable, and those people have disappeared or are disappear-
ing as distinct Jews. But others have refused to allow themselves to be submerged in the surrounding culture. Their souls
longed for a different kind of success than the material success
that beckoned the rest of the world.

It is possible that those who have tasted and rejected the alien
wine will be the leaders of a new generation that will bring in the
Age of the Messiah, who will lead us all to the Promised Land in
a spiritual as well as a physical sense.

Did you know there are Jews in China? Not Jews who
look like what you would expect Jews would look like, but
Jews who look exactly as if they were Chinese. The only
way you could tell that there is something different about
them is by the eyes. If you look into the eyes of a Jew, he
looks different. He stood at Mount Sinai long ago and saw
G-d. No one who has seen G-d looks the same again. Even
today, thousands of years later, you can still see the awe of
that ancient event in the eyes of a Jew.

Abraham is a Chinese Jew. His mother, Elena, is from
Russia. Her parents were killed in a pogrom. During the
years after World War II, she made her way to Moscow,

where she found menial work as a housekeeper at the Chinese embassy. There she met a young diplomat.

She had Jewish feelings, but being alone in the world, she allowed herself to be influenced by him. He begged her to marry him and return with him to China. Finally, she consented.

She never felt comfortable in China. She was determined that her children should learn their heritage, but it was so difficult in this strange and alien land.

Her older daughter was not the kind of girl she could speak to confidentially. And in Communist China private conversations were theoretically under the surveillance of the state and subject to control and outside discipline. It was not unheard of for children to turn their parents over to the authorities.

But her younger son, Abraham, was different. There was something about him that was soft yet also strong. You could see it in the eyes, a special look.

Elena had to be cautious. She had to test the waters. She observed her son.

He *was* different. When all his contemporaries were starting to meet girls, he was not interested. Not that he was unpopular or unfriendly; he just wasn't going to start a relationship. Elena felt there was an unspoken, maybe even unknown reason behind his actions. Abraham seemed to feel that he was different from other young people. He himself may not have understood why or how, but he felt something.

Elena never served pork. Every Chinese family ate pork, but not Elena's. Somehow she managed to sustain them without it. She never explained it to them; it was just a fact, an unwritten rule.

She made a promise to herself: whatever the personal
danger, she was going to tell Abraham on his twenty-first
birthday who he was. That was the only hope for him . . .
and for her.

Shortly after his birthday, Elena took him aside.

"My son, there is something different about us. Are you
aware of it? We are not the same as everyone else. We are
Jewish.

"You know that I come from Russia. Your father met me
there and brought me here to China. I have never spoken
about my past, but I cannot keep it from you any longer.
Now you are a man. You will go out into the world and
build your life and family. You must know who you are
before you do it. You are a Jew.

"My parents, your grandparents, were very holy. They
were killed long ago in Russia because they were Jews. It
seems like a different planet, but I can never forget the
way of life we lived and the greatness of my parents and
their parents and all the people I grew up with, the holy
Jewish community.

"I couldn't live if I had not passed this on to you, my
son. I would like to pass it on to all the children, but somehow you and I are the closest. I feel you understood me all
these years, before we ever had this talk. You always knew
inside your heart that we were different.

"The longer we live in China, totally divorced from all
that I knew when I was growing up in those happy days
with my family, the more I miss those blessings of a Jewish
life. You, my son, could be mistaken for a Chinese young
man, but in your eyes I see your Jewish soul. In your actions I see your grandparents alive again.

"From now on we must have a goal. We are going to

fulfill our destiny as Jews, no matter what sacrifice it entails. If your father and the other children will join us, well and good. But we cannot desert our Father in Heaven. We must somehow leave China; we must go where our Jewish brethren live and fulfill our destiny.

"There are some very practical things I want you to do right away. First, I want you to go to the hospital and become circumcised. They know how to do it here because of the Muslims in this region, so it will not be a completely strange request. It will be painful for you, but it was painful also for our Father Abraham, and you will receive the greatest reward. It will not be correct according to Jewish law, but we will take care of that in the future, if G-d will permit us. In the meantime, it will be a first step.

"Our next step will be to communicate with some international agency to arrange for passage out of China. I hope the authorities will not punish us, but it is a risk I am willing to take, and I think G-d will assist us.

"Of course you understand now, my son, why we did not eat pork all these years. There are many things that Chinese families do that we do not do.

"And now, my son, I have told you our deepest secret, the secret of our existence. May G-d help us fulfill our destiny as Jews."

Abraham followed his mother's instructions. He went to a regional hospital, where the doctors did not reject his request for a circumcision. They thought it strange at his age, but he could have been a Muslim. He had taken his first step toward fulfilling the Torah.

Abraham was very clever with electronics. Communist China was a closed society; one could not know what was happening beyond the borders. But Abraham was curious; he built a shortwave radio.

One night, very late, turning the dial, he heard something that made his hair stand on end. He heard music that sounded like something his mother hummed, and then he heard the following words in Russian: "This is the international voice of Israel, broadcasting from Jerusalem."

"Oh my G-d," he cried out. "It is true."

"Jews all over the world, we are speaking to you from your ancient homeland, the land to which we have returned after two thousand years. We invite you to join your brothers and sisters here and renew the land with us."

Abraham was shaking. He could not believe his ears. He had heard from his mother about being Jewish. He had heard stories about Jews returning to their ancient homeland, but they were like fairy tales. Now this voice crackling out of his radio was alive. This music was actually coming from Jerusalem, the city of his dreams and prayers, the place where his fathers had lived.

Israel is real.

At that moment, Abraham's life changed forever.

They had to leave. They would live as Jews. They would seek the Holy Land. They would leave China. Somehow they would do it. They had to penetrate the Bamboo Curtain.

Elena wrote a letter addressed to the United Nations refugee organization. Like a castaway stranded on a desert island throwing a bottle into the sea, she dropped the letter at the post office. Would the letter ever make its way out of the city, let alone out of China? Was there really a way out of this vast country, with its fanatical dictatorship? Would the reply be a visit from the police? Perhaps the letter would result in the persecution of her family. Count-less fears plagued Elena, but she felt she had no choice.

Just as our ancestor Joseph, alone in an Egyptian prison thousands of years ago, was rescued, Jews in "impossible" situations throughout history have been rescued against all odds. Elena was determined to put her trust in G-d and pray for a redemption that was, logically speaking, almost impossible.

Life went on. The years dragged by and Elena began to despair. Abraham grew into his mid-twenties. Every day was an eternity. Even though she prayed, she felt she could not really expect to be rescued.

"Not only people, but even letters can't get out of here. This really *is* like ancient Egypt."

And then one day a big envelope arrived at the house. It was very official, bearing the return address of the United Nations Commissioner for Refugees in Hong Kong. Elena's hands trembled as she opened the clasp.

"Dear Madam: Your request for assistance in seeking re-ligious freedom has been received and is being discussed with the government of the People's Republic of China. The government is prepared to make the following arrange-ments. . . ."

Tears streamed down Elena's face as she read these words. G-d had heard her prayers even from the depths of this enormous prison called China.

Quickly, the family made plans to leave before some anonymous official changed his mind. Abraham's sister would also leave, but their father would remain in China. He did not understand what this was all about. He would not stand in the way, but his heart was in China.

Soon, mother and her children were on a train, bound

for the nearest border crossing, where they were met by a United Nations official who escorted them to Hong Kong and freedom.

FREEDOM!

Freedom to serve G-d, freedom to be a Jew, to take upon themselves the "yoke of Torah," freedom such as the Jewish people had gained thousands of years before when we left Egypt to serve G-d.

There were relatives in New York. Several months later Abraham, his mother, and his sister arrived in Rockland County, in the Hudson Valley, to start a new life.

They took Elena's maiden name, the name of those holy parents who had perished so long ago in Russia. Elena's parents had been watching over her all these years from the Next World. Now a new life had begun. This time she would do everything right.

One night Abraham attended a lecture sponsored by Hineni. The speaker was Leah, my wife. She described the trauma of Jews growing up without knowing who they are. She described the joy of finding G-d and how everything could change.

After the lecture, Abraham spoke to us, and before long he was at our house for Shabbos. Abraham embraced his new life and prospered.

Soon Rebbetzin Jungreis was asked to come to Israel to speak to the soldiers. We went along, and so did Abraham, overjoyed at the thought that he would finally visit the land from which that fateful radio broadcast had originated.

Also on the trip were the Rosenbergs and their daughter Judy.

As we traveled the mountains and valleys of the Holy Land, visiting military bases and hospitals, walking in the footsteps of our holy ancestors, we noticed that the footsteps of Judy Rosenberg and Abraham were usually close to each other. Something was "developing."

Abraham caused a sensation in Israel. It's not every day, even in a land of constant miracles, that a "Chinese" guy turns out to be Jewish. It's always exciting when a Jew returns, but here was a man literally from the other end of the world—and he looked it. He had revolutionized his entire existence to embrace his Jewish past, against all the odds. It was amazing.

At thirty-one years of age Abraham celebrated his bar mitzvah at the Western Wall. A major Israeli magazine did a story on him. Bar mitzvah at thirty-one? *"It's perfect,"* said the Rebbetzin. *"31 is 13 backwards!"*

Everyone was going nuts over Abraham.

Including Judy Rosenberg.

What do "typical" Jewish parents from Brooklyn think about their daughter marrying a Jew who looks Chinese? Well, it took a little hard swallowing, but Abraham is a truly gentle person. His winning ways, molded by so many trials, won over the family.

Today Abraham and Judy are a happily married couple, living a Jewish life with children who are growing up in a Torah home far from the fearful pogroms that claimed the lives of their great-grandparents in another age, another land.

▲▲▲

Abraham comes home from China and we come home from Central Park. Is it really so different? The Jewish Nation *is* coming home today. There are big problems, I know that, but what is new is that we have never come home like this in the entire sweep of our history.

Rebbetzin Jungreis once told me a startling thing. I asked her, if the great sages and holy Jews throughout our history could not bring Messiah, how could we expect to bring Messiah in our present weak and divided condition.

Her answer: *there has never before been a generation in Jewish history when it was not unusual for children to be more religious than their parents.*

Think about that. Throughout our long history parents have always taught the children, passing the Torah on to the next generation. Each generation has been a step farther away from Mount Sinai, a step weaker than the previous generation.

In our generation the parents are weak. But many children, instead of being weaker, are returning, and in many families we are seeing that the children are more observant than the parents. This unprecedented situation seems to be a fulfillment of the very last prophecy in the Bible: *"Behold, I send you Elijah the prophet before the coming of the great and awesome day of Hashem. **And he will turn back the hearts of fathers with their sons and the hearts of sons with their fathers** . . . "**

Throughout the Jewish world the children are looking for a way to return to their ancient heritage. Throughout the world at large people are looking for meaning. The train of history has reached the end of the line. We have seen science and technology transform our lives, and we have seen that it is not enough. Now we are reaching toward G-d. We want to live. We want truth. We want happiness—not the happiness of a steak dinner, which lasts only as long as the taste of the steak—but the happiness

---

* Malachi 3:23–24

that doesn't disappear, the happiness of a life lived according to eternal truths.

We are willing to adjust our lives if we find something
we can trust, and we *are* finding something we can trust,
something ancient, not created by man. From a Source
greater than we are and before Whom we must subordi-
nate ourselves, we are rediscovering G-d's Torah.

"*Na-ase v'nishma* . . . We will perform it, and then we
will understand."*

We are lost, but we are coming home.

---

* Exodus 24:7

RIPPLES
ON THE POND

ALMOST THREE DECADES have passed since our fateful meeting with the Rebbetzin and the transformation of our lives. We have seen much in those years. We have seen our own family take root in new soil. We have seen the birth of children. We have seen those children grow up, marry, and raise their own families. And we have seen countless others returning to their roots.

Life is full of choices. We *must* make the right ones. The implications of each moment's choice are beyond calculation. A whole world, many worlds depend on the answer each time we ask ourselves: "Should I go right or left?"

The ripples on the pond extend to eternity.

G-d runs the world in the intricacies of each detail. At the moment we met the Rebbetzin we were ready to hear her. Please focus on that word "moment." The moment came and the moment went. It had been designated from the beginning of time. We were infinitely fortunate to have grabbed it, because *that moment would never recur.* I don't say that we could never have returned to Torah any other way or at any other time, but that was the designated moment, the precise millisecond when we were ready to hear and the voice spoke.

When G-d rescued the Children of Israel from Egypt, they were at the lowest point, but *exactly* the lowest point before they would have ceased to exist as a holy and discrete people. He scooped them out with not a flash of time to spare.

It is like the moment when a man meets his *basherte*. Will he see that she is "bone of my bones and flesh of my flesh,"* or will he miss the moment forever? If he misses the moment, maybe he will marry, and maybe he will even marry *her*.

Maybe.

But maybe not.

If we miss the moments that G-d has prepared for us, life becomes a game of roulette. Why play roulette?

Hillel said, "If I am not for myself, who will be for me?"**

I am not telling anyone how to live. My purpose has been to tell you the incredibly exciting things that have happened in our life. Please draw your own conclusions. You may be Jewish or non-Jewish. If you are Jewish, you may be a *Kohayn* or a *Levi* or a *Yisroel*. You may live in the Holy Land or outside. You may be Sefardic or Ashkenazic. Each has its own implications.***

Don't let your moment pass.

---

* Genesis 2:22
** Ethics of the Fathers 1:14
*** You may have noticed that I did not include "you may be Orthodox, Conservative, Reform" in this list. That is because these distinctions are artificial. We Jews are one nation and we have one G-d and one Torah. Any distinction that purports to divide us in this way only brings confusion.

Listen for the voice of G-d.

Can you hear it?

Turn off the radio. Put down your newspaper.

G-d is calling us.

If you listen carefully, you can hear the sound of a *shofar* in the distance.

"It shall be on that day that the L-rd will once again show His hand, to acquire the remnant of His people . . . He will raise a banner for the nations and assemble the cast-aways of Israel; and He will gather in the dispersed ones of Judah from the four corners of the earth."*

"G-d is my shepherd, I shall not lack. In lush meadows He lays me down; beside tranquil waters He leads me. He restores my soul. He leads me on paths of righteousness . . ."**

▲▲▲

Well, here we are, almost at the end. Before I leave you for now, I want to tell you about two incidents that occurred after I finished this book but before it was published.

It is an interesting writing experience to get a book published. It is not a simple matter for a first-time author, and with a book like this, which doesn't fit neatly into any category, it's even harder. Many publishing houses are reluctant to take chances. Publishing a book takes money and guts; any book may succeed, but it also may fail.

It's not even easy to find an agent. An agent stakes his or her reputation on your book. I was fortunate enough to find Erwin Cherovsky, who immediately loved this book,

---

* Isaiah 11:11
** Psalm 23

and we formed a close bond. Since the story represents my entire life, I am emotionally very bound up with it. So therefore, on the day Erwin first met with the publisher, I was very concerned and worried that everything should go right. I asked G-d for His help, because this book is dedicated to bringing His name into high repute in the world.

The day before the fateful meeting I encountered a friend, Rabbi Zalman Mindell, who has been a great source of encouragement to me in writing this book.

Rabbi Mindell, among his other talents, keeps up on *yahrzeits*. The *yahrzeit* is the anniversary of the Hebrew date of someone's death, a day when we reflect upon the life of our beloved one, light a candle, and visit the cemetery.

Many people keep track of the *yahrzeits* of great people in addition to their relatives. For example, people observe the *yahrzeit* of Moses and his brother, Aaron. Rabbi Mindell keeps up on the *yahrzeits* of many holy people.

Rabbi Mindell said to me, "Yisroel, do you know what tomorrow is?"

"No."

"Tomorrow is the *yahrzeit* of your *zayda*, Rabbi Yisroel Salanter."

I started to shake.

Yisroel Salanter!

This story began with him, and now I find out that my *zayda* is holding my hand when I am walking into the publisher's office. It is too much to believe. Of all days in the year, the meeting with the publishers should occur on his *yahrzeit*.

If there's one thing I have learned, it's that there are no coincidences.

But that, as the saying goes, ain't all.

The following Shabbos, I got up early to study. I was drinking a cup of coffee in the kitchen and thinking, "I wonder if this is the right publisher for my book. Maybe I should continue looking." I am a good worrier, and since this book is so important to me, I was mulling these things over in my mind.

Then I decided, "It's time to stop worrying and start studying," so I opened up the Bible and started looking over the *haftara*, the reading from the Prophets for that day.

I almost fell off my seat.

The name of my publisher is Jonathan David. And what was this *haftara* all about? The deep friendship between two great men: Jonathan (son of King Saul) and David (future king of Israel).

All I saw in front of my eyes was "Jonathan/David . . . Jonathan/David . . . Jonathan/David"!

A sign from heaven.

I would like you to hear the last beautiful sentence from that *haftara*.

Jonathan said to David, "Go in peace. What the two of us have sworn in the Name of G-d—saying: 'G-d shall be between me and you, and between my children and your children'—shall be forever."*

This is a prayer for all of us. Since the days of Joseph and his brothers—no, since Cain and Abel—there has been nothing but strife in the world. Enough. Enough already! Enough fighting. Enough rivalry. Enough hatred.

Peace, it is time for peace.

Like Jonathan and David, may we and all our children be friends forever and ever, a friendship sealed with the name of G-d.

---

* I Samuel 20:42

▲▲▲

I can't quite leave you yet. I have one more story for you, a story that I don't think you'll ever forget.

Just before dawn you hear the birds singing. Their finely tuned senses are aware of the approaching sunrise. They can sense light over the horizon. If you listen in the Night of Exile, you will hear the birds singing; you will hear the footsteps of *Moshiach* approaching. The dawn is very close, closer than we can imagine. It will come suddenly, with light bursting upon the earth and all things renewed. We must be ready for the dawn.

Now it is night. Not only are we Jews exiled to the "*four corners of the earth*," but we are exiled from our G-d and from each other, our brothers and sisters.

But the dawn is very close. I don't think we realize how close it is.

A few years ago, our daughter Miriam was attending seminary in Israel.

The girls took a trip to Tiberias, the holy city on the Kinneret, the Sea of Galilee. There is a road around the Kinneret, where the vans stopped briefly to rearrange the luggage. Then they went on to their hotel. At the hotel, Miriam looked for her bag. Filled with all her belongings, including valuables, it was nowhere to be found.

She said to the van driver, "Perhaps we left it where we rearranged the luggage." He agreed to search for it, so Miriam, her friend, and the driver drove back along the road.

Soon they came upon the most massive traffic jam they had ever witnessed. They could see, for miles down the road, that traffic was at a complete standstill. What was going on? They decided to park the van on the shoulder and walk up to where they had shifted the luggage.

After a while, they saw ahead a cleared area filled with police and soldiers. All cars were being held back. In the middle of the road was a little blue and yellow bag. Attached to the bag were electrical cables strung down from nearby overhead power lines. A soldier was bending over the bag.

Chayfetz chashud, a bomb!

"*Ha-tik sheli*," Miriam yelled in Hebrew. "My bag."

Soldiers and police came running from every direction.

"That is your bag? Identify it. Where was it? How heavy is it? Is it soft or hard? What's in it?"

Suddenly, the soldier stepped back from the bag. Everybody looked at each other, and everybody started to laugh. All the soldiers, all the police, all the drivers got out of their cars and started to laugh and sing. On the road around the Kinneret, in the middle of a monster traffic jam, all the Jews were laughing: the ones in black hats, the ones in knitted yarmulkas and the ones with no yarmulkas; the ones with purple hair and earrings in their lips; the ones with payos and black coats; the ones in shorts and no shirt; the kibbutzniks and the Likudniks; the Sefardim and the Ashkenazim; the young and the old; the men and the women; the parents and the children; the wise son, the wicked son, the one who is simple, and the one who doesn't know how to ask a question. They forgot about hating each other and they suddenly remembered who they are and how miraculous it is that together, throughout history, we survive against all the odds, all the predictions, and all the "premature reports of our death and destruction."

This is a preview of the coming of Moshiach.

With great respect, I would ask the Jewish people and

the world at large to think about this story very deeply. The Jewish people are very holy; we are "a kingdom of Priests and a holy nation . . . the most beloved treasure of all peoples."*

We are very close to the time of *Moshiach*. The Jewish people should treat each other with that in mind, and the world should remember that "*all the families of the earth shall bless themselves by you* [the Jewish people]."**

The way back is very easy. It is very sweet. If you are a Jew, it is what you have been searching for, even when you didn't realize you were searching. If you are not a Jew, it is for you to bring healing and goodness into the world and to encourage your Jewish friends to return to their holy Source. That will be *your* greatest blessing.

The dawn is approaching. The birds are singing in the darkness. The footsteps of *Moshiach* can be heard. And we are coming home to G-d. It will be very, very soon. There is a light in the sky. We must hurry! There is so much to do before Moshiach comes!

---

* Exodus 19:5–6
** Genesis 12:3

Glossary of Hebrew and Yiddish Terms

ad may'a v'esrim—"To 120," a Hebrew blessing to live to be 120 years old, like Moshe Rabbeinu.

aydim—Hebrew for "witnesses," required for many contractual relationships in Torah law. A Jewish wedding, for example, is not kosher without G-d-fearing Jews in the role of witnesses.

aleph, bays—First two letters of the Hebrew alphabet, representing the alphabet as a whole.

Am Yisroel—Hebrew for "the nation of Israel." We are called "Israel" because we all come from Yaakov (Jacob), whose name was changed to Yisroel (Israel). So we are also referred to as Bnai Yisroel (the Children of Israel).

aron kodesh—Hebrew for "holy ark." In a synagogue, this is the place where the Torah scrolls are kept. In the Holy Temple, this is where the vessel containing the Two Tablets, a Torah scroll, and a container of manna were kept.

Ashkenaz (plural, Ashkenazim)—Refers to those Jews who traveled north and west after the destruction of the Second Temple, settling in northern Europe. *See* Sfard.

avos—Hebrew for "fathers." The Patriarchs—Avraham, Yitzchok, and Yaakov (Abraham, Isaac, and Jacob).

ayshes chayil—Hebrew for "an accomplished woman," the classic praise of a Jewish wife, written by King Solomon as part of Proverbs (31:10-31). The husband sings this every Friday night at the Shabbos table.

baal teshuva (plural, baalay teshuva)—Hebrew for "one who has returned." A *baal teshuva* returns to G-d, asks forgiveness for sins, and embraces the Torah more completely.

Balaam—A heathen prophet who tried to curse Israel (Numbers 22:2ff), but the curses came out as blessings. So it is with all who try to curse Israel.

Balaam's donkey—A talking donkey belonging to Balaam (Numbers 22:28ff).

bar mitzvah—Hebrew for "son of the commandments." This term refers to a Jewish boy who has reached his thirteenth birthday, at which point the obligation for Torah observance is passed from his father to him.

bas—Hebrew for "daughter of," as in "Esther bas Rachel," Esther the daughter of Rachel. *See also* ben.

basherte—A Yiddish word for that which is destined to happen or that person who is created to be your mate.

bays ha-chaim—Hebrew for "house of the living." Bodies decay, but the soul is with G-d eternally. Thus, we call a cemetery *bays ha-chaim*.

Bays ha-Mikdosh—The Temple in Jerusalem, the center of Torah life, which has been destroyed, rebuilt, and destroyed again. All that remains today is the Western Wall. The Temple will be rebuilt when *Moshiach* comes. The use of the word "temple" for "synagogue" is incorrect; there is no Temple today.

Bays Lechem—Bethlehem, the town between Yerushalayim (Jerusalem) and Chevron (Hebron) where Our Mother Rachel is buried on the roadside. Thousands pray at her gravesite daily with great emotion.

ben—Hebrew for "son of," as in "Moshe ben Maimon," Moshe the son of Maimon. *See also* bas.

bentsch—Yiddish for "bless." "Bentsching" is the common name for the blessings recited after a meal. Jews say to each other, "*Zai gebensht* . . . May you be blessed."

Bergen-Belsen—The Nazi concentration camp in which Rebbet-zin Esther Jungreis and her family were incarcerated.

braocha—Hebrew for "blessing."

bris—Hebrew for "covenant." Frequently used as a short form for *bris milah*.

bris milah—Hebrew for "covenant of circumcision," a Torah commandment through which an eight-day-old boy becomes part of the Covenant with G-d.

bubbie—Yiddish for "grandma."

Cain—Pronounced "Kayin" in Hebrew. Son of Adam and Eve, who killed his brother Havel (Abel).

chacham—Hebrew for "wise person." A *talmid chacham* is wise in Torah. Sefardim refer to a Torah sage as a *chacham*.

chachma—Hebrew for "wisdom." *See* chacham.

Chafetz Chaim—Considered by many the greatest rabbi and holiest *tzaddik* of recent history. Yisroel Meir ha-Kohayn Kaygan lived in Poland and died in 1933 at the age of 95. A great part of his lifelong work was to eradicate the sin of *loshon hara*, slander and gossip.

challah—An offering taken from dough, but what most people know as *challah* is the braided loaf of bread upon which a blessing is made on Shabbos and *yom tov*.

chassid—Hebrew for "pious person." Disciple of a *rebbe*. Also, a general term for one who is passionately devoted to G-d.

chavrusa—Aramaic for "study partner." The classic method of studying in *yeshiva* is with a *chavrusa*. *Chavrusa* also has the connotation of "friend," which tells you something about the way Torah is absorbed and studied.

chayfetz chashud—Hebrew for "suspected object." In Israel, such an object is immediately assumed to be a bomb.

cheder—Hebrew for "room." The term is used to refer to a *yeshiva* for young children.

cheshbon—Hebrew for "calculation, reckoning." Refers to the thinking process through which one decides on the right course of action.

chessed—Hebrew for "kindness." Treating another person the way you would want to be treated.

chevra kadisha—Hebrew for "holy brotherhood." Religious Jews who perform the *mitzvos* related to preparing the dead for burial.

Chevron (Hebron)—The ancient city south of Yerushalayim (Jerusalem) in which four holy couples are buried: Adam and Chava (Adam and Eve), Avraham and Sarah, Yitzchok and Rivka (Isaac and Rebecca), Yaakov and Leah (Jacob and Leah). Rachel is buried in Bays Lechem (Bethlehem).

cholent—A stew traditionally served on Shabbos day. Having been kept warm overnight, *cholent* demonstrates the Torah law that we cannot cook on Shabbos but we may keep food warm.

chometz—Hebrew for "leaven," which Jews may not possess on Passover.

chosson—Hebrew for "bridegroom."

chosson's tisch—The table at which the bridegroom sits with his rabbis, his father, future father-in-law, and friends before the wedding ceremony. Documents are prepared and his friends sing in a festive mood. *Tisch* is Yiddish for "table."

Chumash—The Five Books of Moses: Berayshis (Genesis), Shemos (Exodus), Vayikra (Leviticus), Bamidbar (Numbers), and Dvarim (Deuteronomy). *Chamaysh* is Hebrew for "five.

chupa—Canopy under which a Jewish couple stands at their wedding. It is said to represent the Jewish home.

daven—Yiddish term for "prayer." "Where do you *daven?*" means "What synagogue do you pray in?"

derech eretz—Hebrew for "way of the land." The term implies the correct way of life, that is, proper behavior. A famous saying: *"Derech eretz kadma l'Torah /* Proper behavior comes before Torah observance."

din v'cheshbon—A Hebrew term for taking stock of one's spiritual condition, judging oneself and calculating *mitzvos* versus sins. Great rabbis tell us it should be a regular practice of every Jew.

Dovid ha-melech—King David, the archetypal king of Israel, founder of the dynasty from which *Moshiach* (the Messiah) will come, author of *Sefer Tehillim* (the Book of Psalms).

dvar Torah—Hebrew for "word of Torah." Explanation of a Torah passage.

Eden, Garden of—*See* Gan Eden.

El Al—Israel's national airline.

Eliahu ha-Novi—Elijah the Prophet, who will accompany *Moshiach.*

Eretz Yisroel—The Land of Israel, promised by G-d as an eternal inheritance to Abraham, Isaac, Jacob, and their descendants, the Jewish people.

Esav—Esau, brother of Yaakov (Jacob). The archetypal anti-Semite and enemy of the Jew. Esau was not interested in serving G-d.

Ethics of the Fathers—*See* Pirkay Avos.

family purity—*See* taharas ha-mishpocha.

farbissener—Yiddish for "grumpy." Someone in a bad mood.

fermisht—Yiddish for "confused."

fershtay—Yiddish for "understand."

Gan Eden—The Garden of Eden, where G-d intended us to live. Our ancestors were exiled from Paradise as a result of sin. We hope through *teshuva* to merit a return to Gan Eden.

Gemora—Elucidation and explanation of the Mishna. Completed in written form about 432 years after the destruction of the Second Temple, about 1500 years ago. The *Gemora* and the *Mishna* comprise the Talmud.

goy kadosh—"Holy nation" (Exodus 19:6). This refers to the Jewish people.

hachnasas orchim—The *mitzvah* of welcoming guests, learned from our Father Avraham, who welcomed all people into his tent and taught them about G-d.

haftara—Portion from the Prophets read after the Torah reading on Shabbos and holidays.

Hagar—The second wife of Abraham. Mother of Ishmael.

Haggadah—The ancient text for the Pesach *Seder.*

hakoras ha-tov—Expressing gratitude, a crucial principle in Torah life.

halacha—Jewish law.

ha-malach ha-goayl—Hebrew for "the angel who redeems." From our Father Yaakov's blessing to his sons, referring to the angel who protected him throughout his many trials and challenges (Genesis 48:16).

Haman—Descendant of Amalek, the eternal antagonist of Israel. Haman led the plot against the Jews as described in *Megilas Esther*, the Scroll of Esther.

Hashem—Hebrew for "the Name," meaning the name of G-d. G-d's names are holy, and we don't use the actual name unless we are permitted to, as in prayer and making a blessing.

hatzola—Hebrew for "saving," in the sense of rescuing someone.

havdalah—Hebrew for "separation." Ceremony marking the end of Shabbos, in which the difference is stressed between the holy and secular, light and dark, Shabbos and the weekday, Israel and the other nations.

Hineni—Hebrew for "Here I am," the answer given by Abraham and other prophets when G-d called out to them. Rebbetzin Esther Jungreis has chosen this as the name of her international organization for bringing Jews back to Torah.

Kabbolas Shabbos—Hebrew for "welcoming Shabbos," the prayers inserted between the afternoon and evening services on Fridays. Contains *"L'cha Dodi,"* the famous song through which we welcome the Shabbos Queen.

Kaddish—A prayer that G-d's name may be sanctified and exalted in this world. *Kaddish* serves as a divider between sections of the prayer service. Mourners say *Kaddish* in memory of the deceased.

kallah—Hebrew for "bride."

kashrus—Hebrew for the laws of what is permitted ("kosher") and prohibited.

kavana—Hebrew for "intention." Frequently applied to the proper mental and emotional state during prayer or the performance of other *mitzvos*.

kesuba—Hebrew for "marriage contract," given to the *kallah* (bride) by the *chosson* (groom) under the *chupa*.

kever—Hebrew for "burial place."

kibbutz—From the Hebrew word "to gather." A type of communal settlement found in Israel, where many tasks are done collectively.

Kiddush—Blessing over wine made on Shabbos and holidays. Also used to refer to the collation held after a synagogue service.

kiddush Hashem—Hebrew for "sanctification of G-d's Name," an act performed by a Jew that elevates the stature of G-d and His Torah in the eyes of the world.

kinderlach—Yiddish for "children."

Kodesh Kodoshim—The inner sanctum of the Holy Temple, containing the *aron* (ark).

Kohayn (plural, Kohanim)—Hebrew for "Priest," a descendant of Aaron, Moses' brother. *Kohanim* officiated in the Holy Temple. Even today, when there is no Temple, *Kohanim* have certain extra privileges and also restrictions.

kosher—Ritually fit or permitted.

Kotel—Hebrew for "wall." Used specifically to refer to the remaining Western Wall of the Temple in Jerusalem, a place of great sanctity, intense prayer, and emotion.

kugel—A pudding, frequently made with noodles.

kvitel (plural, kvitlach)—A message asking G-d or a holy person for a blessing. There is a tradition to place *kvitlach* in the cracks of the Western Wall.

L'cha Dodi—Song welcoming Shabbos into the world, sung Friday evening.

leibedik—Yiddish for "lively."

loshon ha-ra—Hebrew for "evil talk." It destroys life in this world and the World to Come. Talk does not have to be false to be evil; one can say true things about another person in a way that harms him. Evil talk leads to *sinas chinom* (causeless hatred).

Maimonides—One of the greatest of all rabbis, born in Spain in 1135. Also a famous physician. His full name was Rabbi Moshe ben (son of) Maimon, so he is known also as RaMBaM.

malach (plural, malachim)—Hebrew for "angel." Angels accompany the husband home from *shul* every Friday night and bestow their blessing. A good angel, who protects us, is created every time we do a *mitzvah*.

mamleches Kohanim—Hebrew for "kingdom of Priests," (Exodus 19:6), a reference to the Jewish people.

manna—The bread G-d provided to feed the Jews in the desert. On Friday, a double portion fell, which lasted through Shabbos.

Megillas Esther—Scroll of Esther, read on Purim. The story of how Mordechai and Queen Esther saved the Jewish Nation from Haman's plot.

Melave Malka—Hebrew for "escorting the Queen." The tradition of having a special meal following the departure of Shabbos is associated with King David. A candle is lit and songs are sung beseeching G-d to send Elijah the Prophet and *Moshiach* speedily.

mesiras nefesh—Hebrew for "devoting one's soul," referring to sacrifice for the sake of Torah.

mensch—Yiddish for "man." This word also suggests the qualities of compassion and goodness, a "complete" man.

mezuza—Hebrew for "doorpost." Also, the name given to the parchment on which a scribe has written specified Biblical verses. Torah law requires Jews to affix *mezuzas* to doorposts and gates.

midos tovos—Hebrew for "proper values," which result in good behavior.

Midrash—A commentary on the Torah.

mikveh—Hebrew for "pool," specifically a pool of pure water used for spiritual purification. The wife's monthly immersion in the *mikveh* is central to *taharas ha-mishpocha*, the laws of family purity.

Mincha—The afternoon prayer service. Also refers to a grain offering brought in the Temple.

minyan—A quorum of ten men, required for many important activities, including prayer services.

Mishna—The Oral Law, passed down from G-d to Moses on Mount Sinai and transmitted through each generation to the present. Completed in written form about one hundred fifty years after the destruction of the Second Temple, about 1,800 years ago. With the *Gemora*, the *Mishna* makes up the Talmud.

mishpocha—Hebrew for "family." The immediate family; also the entire Jewish family, from Father Avraham and Mother Sarah to this very generation.

mitzvah (plural, mitzvos)—Hebrew for "commandment." G-d gave 613 *mitzvos* to the Jewish people.

Moav—A nation descended from Lot, the nephew of Avraham. The territory of Moav is east of the Dead Sea.

mohel—A man specially trained to perform a *bris milah*, the covenant of circumcision. The Yiddish pronunciation sounds like "moyl."

Moshe Rabbeinu—Moses, Our Rabbi. The greatest man who ever lived.

Moshiach—Hebrew for "Messiah," King of the Jewish people, who will lead us to a complete Torah life in the Land of Israel at the end of history. "*Moshiach* ben Dovid" refers to the fact that *Moshiach* will be a descendant of King David.

Mount Sinai—The mountain in the Sinai Desert upon which G-d gave the Ten Commandments and the Oral Torah to Moshe Rabbeinu in the presence of all the Children of Israel.

mussar—Ethical correction, the art of refining one's character according to Torah ideals.

nachas—The sense of spiritual satisfaction that a parent derives from seeing his or her children walking in the path of Torah.

nebbach—Yiddish for "a pathetic, unsuccessful person."

neshoma—Hebrew for "soul." The essence of man. The *neshoma* is created by G-d and lives forever. G-d sends it into this world in a body, and after our death it returns to Him, hopefully in a state of great dignity and worthy of honor.

neshoma yesayra—Hebrew for "additional soul," which we receive on Shabbos.

parsha—The weekly portion of the Torah, which serves as a convenient way of dividing and identifying sections of the Five Books of Moses. *Parshas Berayshis*, for example, is the portion found at the very beginning of the Torah.

payos—Hebrew for "corners." In its most widely known usage, this refers to the areas of a man's face where Biblical law prohibits shaving. Chassidic men often have long *payos* ("sidelocks").

Pirkay Avos—The Ethics of the Fathers, a tractate of the *Mishna* containing practical ethical and moral teachings, traditionally studied on Shabbos from Pesach to Rosh ha-Shana.

pogrom—Officially sanctioned attack against the Jews, especially in eastern Europe. A recurring feature of our two-thousand-year exile. The Holocaust was the largest and most efficiently conducted pogrom in history.

Purim—Springtime holiday celebrating our salvation from Haman's plot to "destroy, slay, and exterminate" all the Jews.

rachamim—Hebrew for "compassion." A quality for which the Jewish people are known. Derived from the word *rechem* (womb). We should feel for each other as a mother does for the child who grew in her womb.

rachmonis—The manifestation of *rachamim*. To have *rachmonis* on someone means to act with compassion or to have pity.

Rashi—Acronym for Rabbi Shlomo ben Yitzchok, the great commentator on the Torah and Talmud who lived in France (1040–1105 C.E.)

rebbe—Leader of a chassidic community. Also, a rabbi who teaches at a *yeshiva*. In general, one's spiritual adviser. "He is my *rebbe*."

rebbetzin—A rabbi's wife.

Ribono Shel Olam—Hebrew for "Master of the World." One of the ways we refer to G-d.

Rus—The great-grandmother of King David. Rus was a convert from the land of Moav.

Seder—Hebrew for "order." Specifically refers to the order of the first night of Passover (first two nights in the Diaspora) as we recount the events of the Exodus and try to comprehend the panorama of Jewish history. *See also siddur.*

sefer (plural, seforim)—Jewish holy book, including the Bible itself, the *Talmud*, and the thousands of commentaries written over the centuries.

Sfard (plural, Sefardim)—Refers to those Jews who traveled south and west after the destruction of the Second Temple, settling in Spain and North Africa. *See* Ashkenaz.

Shabbaton—A group Shabbos, frequently at a hotel.

Shabbos—The Sabbath, the seventh day, on which we separate ourselves from weekday activities and immerse ourselves in the joy of closeness to G-d and family.

Shach—Acronym for Rabbi Shabsai Cohen, ancestor of the Jungreis family and famous commentator on the *Shulchan Aruch*. He lived in seventeenth-century Poland.

shadchun—Hebrew for "matchmaker," one who brings about a *shidduch*.

shaliach—Hebrew for "representative." The man who leads prayers is called the *shaliach tzibur*, representative of the congregation.

shaloch manos—Gifts of food distributed on Purim, as described in *Megillas Esther*.

shalom alaychem—Hebrew for "peace to you." A greeting. Also, a song sung after the men return from *shul* on Friday night, through which the family welcomes the Shabbos angels into the home.

shalom bayis—Hebrew for "peace in the home," the basis of Jewish family life, possible only in a home sustained by Torah law and the presence of G-d.

sheifela—"Little lamb." Yiddish term of endearment.

shaytl (plural, shaytlach)—Yiddish for "wig." Jewish law prohibits married women from appearing in public with their hair uncovered.

Shema Yisroel—"Hear, O Israel," a prayer that Jews are Biblically commanded to say twice daily.

Shemoneh Esray—A prayer recited silently. On weekdays, it consists of eighteen blessings (plus one added later), hence the name *Shemoneh Esray*, which means "eighteen."

shidduch—Yiddish form of the Hebrew, meaning "joining," referring to the introduction of one marriage partner to another. Traditionally, the family helps the child find his or her mate. This is still true in the religious community and at certain organizations like Hineni, where singles are introduced to potential marriage partners.

shiva—Hebrew for "seven." Refers to the seven days that mourners sit on the floor or a low stool following the burial of a close relative.

shlepp—Yiddish for "move" or "drag." How many frozen chickens did I *shlepp* for Mama over the years, when she was cooking for the *yeshiva*! I strengthened myself by realizing that each job I did for Mama was a *mitzvah*.

shmattah—Yiddish for "rag." In popular usage, a *shmattah* is something whose intrinsic worth is very little. "She felt like a *shmattah*" means she felt worthless.

shofar—The ram's horn blown on Rosh Ha-Shana and Yom Kippur. The "great shofar" will herald the arrival of *Moshiach*.

shtetl—In prewar Europe, a Jewish village.

shtick—Yiddish for "put-on behavior," pretense.

shuckle—To sway rhythmically during prayer. Man's soul is compared to a flame that moves back and forth as it reaches upward.

shul—Yiddish for "synagogue."

Shulchan Aruch—Hebrew for "set table." The *Code of Jewish Law*, a compilation of Jewish law organized by subject.

siddur—Prayer book. The word *siddur* is related to *seder*, which means "order" and refers to the order of the prayers. The Pesach *Seder* is the order of the service we perform that night.

simcha—Hebrew for "happiness." A *Yiddishe simcha* is an occasion of happiness based on attaining a Torah milestone, like a *bris, bar mitzvah*, wedding, etc.

sofer—Hebrew for "scribe," one who writes Torah scrolls, *tefillin*, and *mezuzos*, an arduous undertaking by skilled craftsmen.

taharas ha-mishpocha—Hebrew for "family purity." The Torah laws relating to physical contact between husband and wife have kept Jewish marriage and lineage pure. *See also* mikveh.

tallis—Four-cornered man's garment with *tzitzis* at each corner. Among most Ashkenazic Jews, a big *tallis* is worn by married men over the clothing during prayers. A small *tallis* (*tallis koton*) is worn all day, usually under the clothing.

talmid chacham—Hebrew for "wise student," a student of the Torah who has achieved wisdom and depth in his learning; a great scholar.

Talmud—*See Gemora*.

tattie—Yiddish for "father."

tefillin—Leather boxes containing Biblical verses written on parchment by a *sofer*, bound on the arm and forehead by men during weekday morning services.

Tehillim—The Book of Psalms.

Temple—*See* "Bays ha-Mikdosh."

teshuva—Hebrew for "repentance." A Jew should "do *teshuva*" (review and correct his thoughts and actions) constantly. This process reaches a culmination during the Ten Days of Teshuva, from Rosh ha-Shana through Yom Kippur

tichl (plural, tichlach)—A woman's head covering. Jewish law prohibits married women from appearing in public with their hair uncovered.

tisch—Yiddish for "table." A chassidic rebbe presides at his *tisch* every Shabbos and Yom Tov.

Tisha b'Av—The ninth day of the Hebrew month Av, during which Jews observe a full-day fast. This is the date on which both Temples were destroyed and many other calamities occurred.

Torah—The Law of G-d, given on Mount Sinai to Moshe Rabbeinu and the Children of Israel, consisting of the Written Torah (Five Books of Moses) and the Oral Torah.

tzaddik (plural, tzaddikim)—Hebrew for "righteous man." Yosef is called *ha-tzaddik* in the Torah. He literally ran away from temptation and sin.

tzadekes—Hebrew for "righteous woman."

tzitzis—Hebrew for "fringes," specifically those attached to a four-cornered man's garment. Each fringe consists of four long strands tied in such a way as to remind the wearer of the obligation to observe all the precepts of the Torah.

tzouris—Yiddish for "trouble."

Western Wall—*See* Kotel.

yahrzeit—Yiddish for "anniversary of death." On the *yahrzeit* we light a candle, visit the grave, and remember our beloved relative in many other ways.

yarmulka—Yiddish term for the headcovering worn by a male. The name derives from the term *yira malchus*, the constant awareness of G-d that is supposed to be engendered by covering one's head.

yaytzer ha-ra—Hebrew for "evil inclination," the force that G-d created in the world to push us away from Him and His Torah. Our lifelong struggle against this force brings us closer to G-d.

Yerushalayim—Hebrew for "Jerusalem."

yeshiva—A school in which Torah is taught.

Yisgadal v'yiskadash . . .—Beginning of the *Kaddish* prayer. *Kaddish* is part of every prayer service. It is also recited by a mourner after the death of a close relative.

Yom Kippur—The Day of Atonement, on which Jews fast and pray for G-d to forgive our sins. It is the anniversary of the day on which Moshe Rabbeinu descended from Mount Sinai with the second set of tablets.

yom tov—Hebrew for "holiday." The Biblical holidays are Pesach, Shavuos, Rosh ha-Shana, Yom Kippur, Sukkos and Shemini Atzeres/Simchas Torah.

zayda—Yiddish for "grandfather."

zmiros—Ancient songs composed by holy sages, sung at the Shabbos table.

zt"l—Acronym (pronounced *zatzal*) for the Hebrew words *zaycher tzaddik livracha,* which means "the mention of a holy person [*tzaddik*] brings blessings." This refers to a great person who has passed away.

About the Author

ROY NEUBERGER was educated at the Ethical Culture Schools, where he met Linda Villency, his future wife. They attended the University of Michigan and were married after Roy's sophomore year. After a year at Oxford University, they returned to America, where Roy became Director of Conservation for the City of New York. Following two years in government, the Neubergers moved to Cornwall-on-Hudson, New York, where Roy became publisher and editor of a weekly newspaper. After a move to Long Island in 1974, Roy worked as a newspaper editor, a *yeshiva* administrator, a hedge fund operator and, most recently, on this book. The Neubergers' children and grandchildren live in Israel and the New York metropolitan area.